UTAH
CAMPING

FOGHORN OUTDOORS

UTAH
CAMPING

The Complete Guide to
More Than 400 Campgrounds

FIRST EDITION

Gayen and Tom Wharton

AVALON
TRAVEL

FOGHORN OUTDOORS: UTAH CAMPING
The Complete Guide to More Than 400 Campgrounds

FIRST EDITION

Gayen and Tom Wharton

Published by
Avalon Travel Publishing
5855 Beaudry Street
Emeryville, CA 94608 USA

Printing History
1st edition—March 2001
5 4 3 2 1

ISBN: 1-56691-286-5
ISSN: 1533-0044

Editor: Angelique S. Clarke
Series Manager: Marisa Solís
Copy Editor: Chris Hayhurst
Index: Lynne Lipkind
Graphics Coordinator: Erika Howsare
Illustrations: Bob Race
Production: Darren Alessi
Map Editor: Mike Ferguson
Cartography: Mike Morgenfeld, Doug Beckner

Front cover photo: © Peter Marbach

Distributed in the United States and
Canada by Publishers Group West
Printed in the U.S.A. by Publishers Press

Please send all comments, corrections, additions,
amendments, and critiques to:
FOGHORN OUTDOORS: UTAH CAMPING
First Edition
AVALON TRAVEL PUBLISHING
5855 BEAUDRY ST.
EMERYVILLE, CA 94608, USA
email: info@travelmatters.com
www.travelmatters.com

We dedicate this book to the adventurous folks who forsake the comforts of home in exchange for getting out into the world and seeing it! We hope all who visit our state will be kind and leave it unspoiled for our children and grandchildren.

—Gayen and Tom Wharton

TABLE OF CONTENTS

MAPS

UTAH STATE

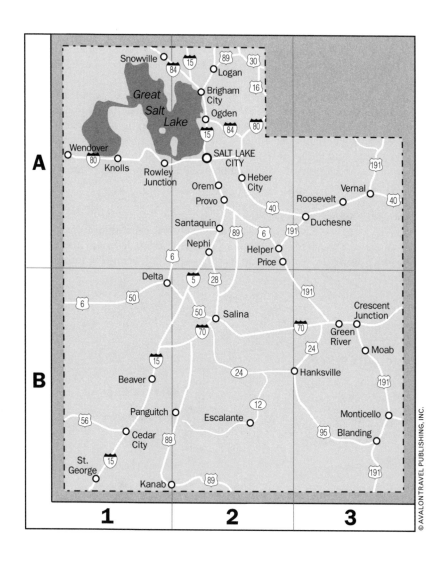

HOW TO USE THIS BOOK

Finding a Campsite

You can search for your ideal campsite in two ways:

1. If you know the name of the campground you'd like to visit or the nearest town or geographical feature (national or state forest, national or state park or recreation area, wildlife area, park, lake, river, mountain), look it up in the index beginning on page 259 and then turn to the corresponding page.

2. If you'd like to camp in a particular part of Utah, turn to the state maps on pages ix or in the back of this book. Find the zone you'd like to visit (such as A2 for the Salt Lake City area), then turn to the corresponding chapter. Each chapter opens with a map that clearly numbers every campground in that area. Locate individual camping destinations on the map and then turn to those numbered sites in the chapter for detailed descriptions.

About the Maps

The maps in this book are designed to show the general location of each campground. Readers are advised to purchase a detailed state map before heading out to any campground, particularly when venturing into remote areas.

ACTIVITY SYMBOLS

🥾	= Hiking	〰	= Hot or cold springs
🚲	= Biking	🐕	= Pets permitted
🏊	= Swimming	🛝	= Playground
🎣	= Fishing	♿	= Wheelchair access
🚣	= Boating	🚐	= RV sites
⛷	= Winter sports	⛺	= Tent sites

RATING

1　2　3　4　5　6　7　8　9　10

poor　　　　**fair**　　　　**great**

What the Symbols Mean

Camp listings in this book feature activity symbols that represent the recreational offerings at or within walking distance of the campground. Other symbols identify whether there are sites for RVs or tents, or any wheelchair-accessible facilities. Wheelchair accessibility has been indicated if it was mentioned by campground managers. Concerned persons should call the contact number to ensure that their specific needs will be met.

What the Ratings Mean

Every camping spot in this book is rated for its scenic beauty on a scale of 1 to 10. Other factors that can influence a trip, such as noise or restroom cleanliness, can change from day to day and do not affect the ratings.

Our Commitment

We are committed to making *Foghorn Outdoors: Utah Camping* the most accurate, thorough, and enjoyable camping guide to the state. With this first edition, you can rest assured that every camping spot in this book has been carefully reviewed and accompanied by the most up-to-date information available. However, with the change of seasons, you can bet that some of the fees listed herein have gone up, and that camping destinations may have opened, closed, or changed hands. If you have a specific need or concern, it's a good idea to call the campground ahead of time.

If you would like to comment on the book, whether it's to suggest a tent or RV spot we overlooked, or to let us know about any noteworthy experience—good or bad—that occurred while using *Foghorn Outdoors: Utah Camping* as your guide, we would appreciate hearing from you. Please address correspondence to:

Foghorn Outdoors: Utah Camping, First Edition
Avalon Travel Publishing
5855 Beaudry Street
Emeryville, CA 94608
U.S.A
email: info@travelmatters.com

ACKNOWLEDGMENTS

Compiling current information on campgrounds in Utah would be impossible without the cooperation of the state and federal agencies that manage most of the state's campgrounds. We thank them for their help. Kathy Jo Pollock of the U.S. Forest Service was especially generous with her time.
—Gayen and Tom Wharton

INTRODUCTION

ISLAND IN THE SKY,
CANYONLANDS NATIONAL PARK

CAMPING TIPS

WHAT TO PACK FOR YOUR CAMPING TRIP

Want to know how much gear to bring on your camping trip? Here's a tip: Keep it simple. Campers often stuff lots of fancy gadgets into their packs and cars, but only a few items are essential: a sleeping bag, tent, stove, cooking utensils, cooler or water bottles, water filter, flashlight or headlamp, and first-aid kit. The hard part is determining how much money to spend on those essentials. Your best bet is to play it safe and buy top-quality gear that will withstand whatever weather conditions you might encounter. Nothing is worse than a tent that leaks in a rainstorm or gets blown away by a strong gust of wind. And if a tent is too poorly made to weather a wicked storm, what good is it anyway? Camping is no fun when the main goal is survival.

Before you invest in some gear, consider how it's going to be transported. If you plan to car camp with a van or a truck, you may have enough room for a large tent, stoves and heaters fueled by propane tanks, and bulky sleeping bags. Campers traveling in small cars, however, will need more compact camping gear. If you're backpacking, purchase the lightest equipment you can find (and afford).

Here's what you should look for when buying the camping basics:

Sleeping Bags and Pads
Selecting the appropriate sleeping bag for the varied terrain and temperatures of Utah can be difficult. The desert's hot summer nights mandate a lightweight bag, whereas the cooler nights of alpine areas demand a model that can keep you warm in lower temperatures. Of course, the best plan of action is to buy two sleeping bags—one for cold weather and another for the hot desert temperatures. If funds are limited, however, invest in the cold-weather bag; you can always sleep on top of it during hot-weather spells, covering yourself with a blanket or sheet. Winter bags should be rated for at least zero-degree-Fahrenheit (i.e., freezing) weather and still be light and small enough to

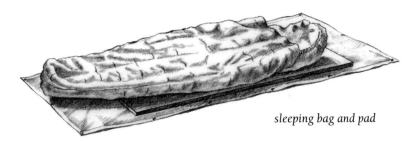

sleeping bag and pad

strap onto a backpack. Bags with a hood are ideal for cold nights because they cover your head. On nights when the temperature dips below 32 degrees Fahrenheit, sleep in a tent and wear a wool hat and at least one layer of clothing.

The most compact bags (and typically the costlier ones) are stuffed with goose down. But even down sleeping bags have their downsides. They can be difficult to clean and, if they get wet on a camping trip, they're useless. More expensive down bags include a waterproof coating on the outside. Bags filled with artificial fibers are easier to clean and hold up better in wet weather. Couples should consider purchasing sleeping bags that can be zipped together—snuggling next to one another under the stars on a cool night is not only romantic, it generates extra heat.

Sleeping pads are recommended for extra comfort and warmth. Self-inflating pads cost more than traditional air mattresses or bulky foam, but they seldom spring a leak and take up little storage space. Cots are another option for those with circus-size tents.

arched tent

Tents

Backpackers and car campers tend to prefer small, lightweight, nylon tents. But if you're taking the entire family car camping and you own a large vehicle, a roomier canvas tent might make the troops happier.

If you plan to buy a tent, find a store that specializes in camping equipment. Many of the best specialty stores have display tents set up for you to examine. Crawl inside several of them to check for roominess and to compare other features. Inspect the tent's stitching; top-quality tents are double or triple stitched at all of the stress points. Be sure to find out if a tent is designed for four-season or three-season use or for summer weather only. Summer-use and three-season tents tend to be lightweight and more breathable than their counterparts. They may

dome tent

not be as weatherproof as a four-season tent, but unless you're planning on mountaineering, three-season and summer-use tents will suffice. Finally, ask a salesperson to demonstrate the ABCs of assembling the tent you're considering. Keep in mind that if a tent is too tricky to erect in the comfort of the store, it'll surely be too difficult to set up in the middle of a howling rainstorm in the dark.

Whether you're shopping for tents or an outer layer of clothing, it's wise to be on the lookout for materials promising some protection against moisture. Don't let the lexicon fool you.

Waterproof: impervious to water. Though rain won't penetrate this material, if you're at all mobile you'll soon find yourself wet from perspiration that can't evaporate.

Water-resistant: resistant but not impervious to water. You'll stay dry using this material only if it isn't pouring.

Stoves

The standard Coleman stove is a staple of most car and RV campers—it's virtually indestructible, works well in most weather conditions, and the fuel is typically less expensive than that of other brands. Several models of the basic two- and three-burner stove are available in different sizes. The only decision a camper may need to make is whether to purchase the model that operates on white gas or the newer version that burns either white or unleaded gas. The white-gas-only model

white gas stove

requires pumping air into the stove before lighting it; if you want an instant flame (i.e., no pumping required), buy a stove that runs on propane. Propane stoves cost more, and although they don't work quite as well in cold weather or burn as hot as gas models, they light quickly and easily and are usually equipped with a barbecue grill. One disadvantage is that the fuel canisters are expensive; car campers with large vehicles may want to purchase a propane tank to save money. If you plan to backpack or car camp with a small car, a tiny, lightweight, single-burner backpacking stove may be the best option. Most operate on white gas, unleaded gas, propane, or butane.

single-burner stove

Cooking Utensils

Selecting the right cooking equipment for a camping trip is primarily a matter of personal taste. Some prefer to keep it simple by packing an old frying pan, plastic utensils, paper plates and bowls, and disposable cups, although gourmands might be happiest toting their favorite wok, a grill, or even a Dutch oven that can be used over an open fire.

One of the simplest and handiest camping-cookware sets consists of a "nesting" package—a medium-size pot that contains a frying pan, one or two other pots, a coffee pot, handles for the pots and frying pan, and cups and plates. These cookware packages tend to last for years and won't set you back more than $50.

To save time when you're packing, keep the cooking basics—a can opener, ladle, large spoons, salt and pepper, spatula, and cleaning gear—together with the cookware in a large plastic storage box. Store standard supplies such as coffee, tea, hot chocolate, spices, a first-aid kit, and flashlights (with spare batteries) inside the box, and make sure you replace any used items after every trip. Consider having everything in a rugged plastic "action packer" box so all you have to do is put the box in the car each time you camp.

Coolers, Water Jugs, and Bottles

The size of the cooler and water jug you'll need often depends on the length of your trip, how much room you have in your vehicle, and how far from civilization you'll be. Since coolers are relatively inexpensive, consider buying a large one for extended trips in isolated places where you need to pack in a lot of food. Get a medium-size cooler for weekend trips and a small one for

---

Campfire Precautions

If you're like most campers, you can't wait to scour your campsite for dry branches, pile them into a mound, and strike a match. For some, camping isn't complete without the smell and sounds of a blazing fire, provider of warmth and hot meals.

Everyone has his or her trick for building and maintaining the perfect fire, but not everyone considers their personal and environmental safety when lighting up— or putting out. So, before you even gather a single twig, please remember the following:

- Where fires are permitted, use existing fire rings away from large rocks or overhangs. If a fire ring is not available, use a lightweight stove for cooking.
- Don't char rocks by building new rings.
- Gather sticks from the ground that are no larger than the diameter of your wrist.
- Don't snap branches of live, dead, or downed trees, which can cause personal injury and also scar the natural setting.
- Put the fire "dead out" and make sure it's cold before departing. Remove all trash from the fire ring and sprinkle dirt over the site.
- Remember that some forest fires can be started by a campfire that appears to be out. Hot embers burning deep in the pit can cause tree roots to catch fire and burn underground. If you ever see smoke rising from the ground, seemingly from nowhere, dig down and put the fire out.

day trips and overnighters. Consider paying a little more for a heavy-duty insulated model with a better seal. These keep ice longer. Some campers prefer packaged "blue" ice, which can be reused, but it won't last longer than a couple of days. For extended trips, dry ice is preferable because it often lasts longer than cubed ice. Block ice also lasts longer than cubes.

Lights

A light for cooking, reading, or even to help you find your way to a campground restroom late at night is an essential part of any camping package. This light could be as simple as a miniature flashlight (the kind you might stash in your glove compartment) or as fancy as a propane-powered lantern.

Most car and RV campers tote along a Coleman gas lamp, which burns white gas or, in newer models, unleaded gas. They come in a variety of sizes: The large models emit more light, often burning two mantels at once, while the small lanterns fit better in compact cars. Some of these lanterns also use propane, which, although slightly more expensive, ignites more quickly than white or unleaded gas and doesn't require pumping air into a tank.

Some campers prefer a battery-operated fluorescent light. Although they're not quite as bright as the gas and propane models, they're easier to use—just flip the switch. They are also space savers because they can double as flashlights. Batteries can be expensive, however, especially if you plan to use the light on several camping trips. A reliable, no-frills flashlight will also do the job. A flashlight that snaps onto a headband, or a headlamp, like those used by miners, works great as a reading lamp and as a light source for getting chores done in the dark, such as washing the dishes.

Extra Gear

If you have room for additional car-camping gear, consider packing a propane-powered heater. Your chances of finding wood for a campfire are scarce in many parts of Utah, and in several desert regions wood gathering is prohibited. Extra blankets might be handy, too.

In regions with a lot of biting insects, a mosquito-net tent that fits over a picnic table can make eating a meal in the outdoors much more pleasant. Such shelters also provide shade in the summer months (a godsend in the desert) and a windbreak on blustery days.

CAMPGROUND ETHICS

As America's cities and towns become increasingly crowded, a growing number of people are turning to the outdoors for serenity, simplicity, and solitude. That's the good news. The bad news is that as urban centers become maxed out, more people are bringing their bad habits—primarily thoughtlessness toward fellow campers and a disrespect for the land—into the backcountry. Even folks who

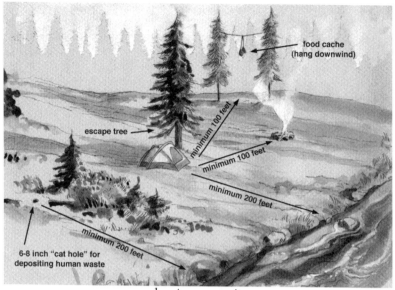

choosing a campsite

have the best intentions sometimes unwittingly go awry, taking the "great" out of the Great Outdoors for others.

You may wonder what is meant by "campground ethics." It's simply another way of saying use common sense and consideration while camping. Common sense in a campground means keeping quiet; noise is the most common breach of campground ethics. It arrives in a variety of amplitudes, from the laughter of children sitting at a campfire roasting marshmallows at midnight to an all-out brawl between drinking buddies. A gas-powered electrical generator that can't be heard inside a well-insulated motor home is torture for tent campers up to six sites away. A group that breaks up camp at first light—rattling dishes, shouting orders, and running the car (or, worse, motorcycle) engine—can wake up an entire campground.

Other ways in which disrespect is manifested in the Great Outdoors include carelessness with litter, spur-of-the-moment vandalism, and destruction of the natural environment. Litter—from trash left on a picnic table or strewn around a campsite to beer cans, aluminum foil, and glass tossed into a campfire pit—can be unsightly and annoying. It can also be a health hazard—have you ever been greeted by sewage left by an RVer who was too lazy to dispose of it at a dump station?

Vandalism and malicious destruction are increasing in the backcountry, too. Vandalism is immediately identifiable: graffiti; picnic tables and tree trunks carved with knives; and signs, garbage cans, and outhouses shot up for target practice. Considering recent and looming cuts in the budgets of the state and federal government agencies that oversee public lands, vandalized facilities may never be repaired or replaced. Worse, if picnic tables are smashed or cut up for firewood, toilets are removed from privies, and water pumps are knocked over by vehicles, the campground itself may be in danger of being closed permanently.

What can be done? Here are some suggestions:

- **Take personal responsibility for backcountry ethics.** When entering a campground, even if only for a night, read the posted rules and observe them closely. Be sure to register and pay your camping fees promptly. This enables campground hosts and park rangers to spend their time maintaining the facilities instead of informing you of campground rules and regulations or making sure you've paid your fees.
- **Observe quiet hours.** Most campgrounds have established quiet hours, usually between 10 P.M. and 7 A.M. During this time, campers should speak softly, use headphones for music, refrain from running generators, and keep children under complete control—in other words, be courteous to other campers. When setting up or breaking down camp, make as little noise as possible and, if it's dark, try to avoid shining bright flashlights or headlights everywhere.
- **Dispose of your litter.** Litter is pollution. Whenever you're tempted to leave garbage behind, think of how you feel when you find other people's plastic bags, tin cans, or aluminum foil in your yard. Properly dispose of your trash in frequently emptied public dumpsters. Even organic refuse, such as apple cores, orange peels, and eggshells (which take months to decompose), is trash. Always leave your campsite in better condition than when you found it, even if it means picking up the litter of those who came before you.
- **Keep restroom facilities clean.** Tidy up messes you make when brushing your teeth, shaving, or using toiletries. Do not put any kind of garbage in vault toilets; trash, such as plastic bags, sanitary napkins, and diapers, cannot be pumped and must be picked out, piece by piece, by some poor soul. If there is running water, use biodegradable soap for washing dishes and cleaning up. If showers are available, bathe quickly so others can also use the facilities.
- **Respect the land.** Leave the foliage and natural setting around the campground intact. Do not cut down limbs or branches or remove leaves from trees. If you want to build a fire, bring your own wood or buy some from a store or concessionaire. Before leaving a campsite, always make sure the fire is completely out.
- **Respect the animals that inhabit the area.** Don't feed or harass animals that visit your campground. Animals need to stick to their natural diets or else they might become ill. Keep your camp area clean, especially if you're in or near bear country, so you don't tempt any animals to visit your site. Keep food out of your tent and try to place your garbage away from your sleeping quarters at night. Backpackers often tie their garbage to a tree branch for the night, making it harder for small animals to indulge.

- **Camp and hike in established areas.** Camp only in designated campsites, which are usually selected because they are durable under constant use. Stay on the trails when walking to and from restrooms, visitor centers, or stores, or when venturing into the backcountry. This is especially important in desert areas, where the cryptobiotic soil—a black crust that prevents erosion and takes years to form—is easily destroyed.
- **Avoid conflict and respect fellow campers.** If a situation arises with inconsiderate or uncooperative neighbors, try to avoid confrontations, which can easily escalate and turn ugly, especially when alcohol is involved. Talk to a campground host, park ranger, or someone in authority and let him or her address the problem. Meanwhile, make sure nobody has cause to complain about you. Show your camping neighbors the same respect that you expect from them and everyone will camp happily ever after.

HELPFUL HINTS FOR HIKERS

Few spots on the planet have terrain as diverse as Utah. In one weekend, hikers can trek up mountain peaks with elevations of more than 12,000 feet, then wander through a vast desert basin that's barely above sea level. Between these two extremes is a wide range of landscapes—from ponderosa-pine forests and grassland prairies to slickrock canyons and lush river bottoms.

Not surprisingly, the climates in these distinct environments vary dramatically. The higher elevations of most mountain ranges are great for summer and fall hikes, but snow usually covers the trails and access roads from winter to early spring. The desert is an ideal setting in the winter, but the heat and sun are potentially deadly in the summer. If you want to avoid places that are too hot or too cold, here's a good rule to live by: Hike in areas above 5,000 feet in the summer and fall, and seek out locations below 5,000 feet in the winter and spring.

Drink Up!

Water is one of the most important supplies to take into the backcountry—especially in desert terrain. Day hikers and backpackers should carry at least one gallon of water per person per day. You'll probably need more than a gallon a day if you're visiting a desert area where the temperature is pushing 100°F, or if you'll be engaging in aerobic activity, such as climbing steep hills.

It's critical to carry all the water you need because, in most places in Utah, finding water is a rarity. And even if you encounter a flowing creek or stream, you shouldn't drink the water unless you treat or filter it. As with most backcountry locations in the lower 48 states, the bacteria *Giardia lamblia* abounds in water—even in seemingly pristine locations—due to animal waste.

Hiking-Gear Basics

Do you know how much a gallon of water weighs? Try eight pounds. Fortunately, in recent years equipment manufacturers have made it much easier for hikers to carry their own water. You may want to consider buying a hydration system, which straps on like a day pack and holds about two quarts. Various makers of fanny packs have also designed products with a liter-size water-bottle holder that fits on either side of the hip bag.

In addition to water, other critical supplies include sunblock, sunglasses (with 100 percent UV protection), and a hat to guard against heat exhaustion. A light-colored, brimmed hat made of cotton or straw is ideal, or try one of those specially designed "desert rat" hats (which are white and have a duckbill brim and neck flap) available at many outdoor outfitters.

Traversing the rugged terrain, whether you're in the mountains or the desert, requires a sturdy pair of hiking boots with lug soles. Heavy mountaineering-type boots aren't necessary, but you should have at least medium-weight, ankle-high boots. A rugged nylon and/or leather construction will stand up against sharp objects, such as cactus spines and rocks. If you hike through shallow snow or water during the cooler months, wear boots with a waterproof liner to keep your feet warm and dry. In hot weather, a fabric/leather boot offers the most ventilation—an important factor for minimizing sweaty feet and, ultimately, painful blisters. Boots made of synthetic materials will also dry quicker should they become wet. Be sure to break in a new pair of boots before your first trip by wearing them around town for *at least* a week. All-leather boots require more break-in time than the fabric/leather variety; a general rule is to put 50 street miles on new boots before showing up at the trailhead.

DAYHIKER'S BASICS

Before trekking into the backcountry, load a large fanny pack or day pack with the following essential items, which should help prepare you for an outdoor emergency:

- binoculars
- compass
- extra clothing for cool or wet conditions
- first-aid kit
- flashlight
- food such as Gorp or an energy bar
- map
- matches
- moleskin
- sunblock
- Swiss army knife
- water

A good pair of boots won't do much to prevent blisters or keep your feet warm if you aren't wearing quality hiking socks. Cheap cotton tube socks won't do the job. Wool socks work well, but socks made of a wool/synthetic blend are preferable. These high-tech materials wick away moisture, dry quickly, and provide extra padding.

A hiking staff can be a useful tool when traversing difficult desert or mountain terrain. It can help you hike down steep cliffs, climb up rocky hills, keep your footing steady when crossing streams, and, perhaps most importantly, divert angry rattlesnakes.

Keep on Track

Never go hiking in the backcountry without a map, and study your route prior to setting out. Most hiking trails in Utah are charted on either National Forest Service or National Park Service maps, which can be purchased at their respective ranger district and park offices. However, these maps provide little detail and often aren't sufficient for long hikes in remote areas.

Since there is so much public land in Utah and the federal land management agencies have limited recreational budgets, many excellent hiking trails are not maintained or marked. As long as you have the right U.S. Geological Survey topographical map, this shouldn't be a problem because these maps show the landscape in great detail, including exact elevations and the location of springs, washes, and even abandoned roads and buildings. The 7.5-minute map series is preferable, because it shows the most detail; in many desert regions, however, only the less detailed 15-minute maps are available. U.S.G.S. maps are sold for a few dollars at many outdoor stores or may be

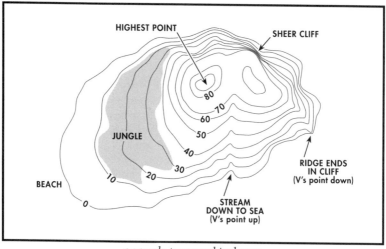

a sample topographical map

ordered by writing to: U.S. Geological Survey, Distribution Section, Denver Federal Center, Building 41, Denver, CO 80225.

If you're an avid hiker or plan to spend a lot of time exploring the backcountry, consider learning how to use a map and compass. Many books offer advice on orienteering skills. One particularly useful manual is *The Essential Wilderness Navigator: How to Find Your Way in the Great Outdoors*, by David Seidman (Ragged Mountain Press).

To ensure your hike is an enjoyable and safe adventure, contact the appropriate land-management office before heading out. A ranger or park official can usually tell you about the current trail conditions and offer other up-to-date information on the area.

SAFETY AND FIRST-AID TIPS

The Utah region is a land of beautiful extremes, but one that requires visitors to come prepared for its equally extreme climate. The warm sunshine that so many people come to enjoy can cause serious sunburn and sunstroke, and getting caught in a summer thunderstorm at higher elevations can result in hypothermia, even if the temperature stays above 50°F. Also bear in mind that there are few sources of water that don't require treatment before drinking, and when it comes to poisonous plants, animals, and insects, the region has its fair share. So before you set up camp familiarize yourself with the region's hazards and take steps to ensure a safe and healthy trip.

Sunburn

It's commonly known that extended exposure to the sun's ultraviolet rays can cause skin cancer. For that reason, you'll see many savvy folks in the desert wearing long-sleeved clothing and hats for protection, as well as religiously applying sunscreen throughout the day.

Sunscreen is assigned a numerical "sun protection factor" (SPF) rating. Use a sunscreen with a minimum SPF rating of 15; anything lower won't provide enough protection. An SPF 15 rating means a user can stay in the sun without getting burned 15 times longer than without protection. The FDA recently put a cap of 30 on SPF ratings, stating that higher ratings, such as SPF 45, are no more effective than SPF 30. Most sunscreens work against UV-B rays. Look for sunscreens containing benzophenones, titanium dioxide, zinc oxide, or Parsol 1789 to make sure you also receive UV-A protection.

No matter what time of year you venture here, always apply sunscreen before heading outdoors and reapply it periodically throughout the day. Some of the worst sunburns are incurred during winter skiing and ice-fishing trips, because the bright sun is reflected off the snow and ice. If you forget to lather up with sunscreen or miss a hard-to-reach spot, treat the burned area by washing it with cold water (if available, add one teaspoon of boric acid per quart of water). Aloe vera gels help restore moisture to the skin, but prevention, of course, is the best medicine.

Heat Illnesses

Dehydration is a major cause of heat-related illnesses, such as heatstroke, which is a result of reduced blood flow to the brain. Symptoms range from hot, dry skin to light-headedness and fainting. To prevent a heat illness, force yourself to drink lots of water during hikes or any other activity in hot weather. Each person should carry at least one gallon of water per day. Replace electrolytes (salt, potassium, and bicarbonate) by drinking fruit juice, an energy drink such as Gatorade, or an occasional soft drink. Although physicians once recommended that hikers take salt pills, they now believe that regular diets, including dehydrated foods that backpackers often bring on trips, provide enough salts without supplements.

Heat exhaustion usually occurs from prolonged activity in hot weather. Symptoms include weakness, cool and clammy skin, headaches, and a body temperature at or below normal. Symptoms of heatstroke, on the other hand, include a fever and skin that is red, dry, and hot. It's not uncommon for victims of heatstroke to become unconscious. If you or someone in your group becomes ill due to heat exposure, stop physical activity immediately and look for a shady place to lie down. Cover the person's skin with wet towels or clothing to cool the body. A massage can help move blood to the extremities. Give him or her some water to slowly replenish bodily fluids. If the person has lost consciousness, seek medical attention immediately. Even mild heat illness can become serious if not treated properly, so don't take any chances.

Because of the extreme heat of Utah in the summer, when you're most likely to be camping, a few simple traveling precautions might spell the difference between a routine and a life-threatening experience. First, make certain your car has had the best care. Fuel and fluids should be full. Carry at least a gallon of extra water for the car (some anti-freeze is also good to have along). Spare belts and hoses, spare tire and jack, tool kit, flares, and a shovel are also essential items for desert car camping.

If your car gets hot or overheats, stop until it cools off. Never open the radiator if the engine is steaming. After a while, squeeze the top radiator hose to check the pressure; if it's squeezable, it's safe to remove the radiator cap. Never pour water into a hot radiator. If you start to smell rubber, your tires are overheating, which makes them highly susceptible to blowouts. Stop, in the shade if possible, to let them cool.

If your vehicle gets stuck in the sand, don't panic. Let some air out of the tires for traction. If you can't get on the road again, stay with the vehicle until after the sun has gone down, then try to dig it out. If outside help is required, send the strongest member of the party to the main road, but not until after sunset. Most desert deaths occur from dehydration brought on by walking too long in the sun.

Hypothermia

When your core body temperature falls dangerously low, you are suffering from hypothermia. Symptoms include impaired judgment, disorientation, and involuntary shaking, which is the body's way of trying to generate warmth. In advanced stages of hypothermia, a person might appear to have stopped breathing.

Treatment for mild hypothermia can be as simple as putting on warm, dry clothes and doing exercises to stimulate blood flow. Get out of the elements and seek any shelter that will reduce exposure to wind and cold temperatures. Remove wet, cold clothing and drink warm liquids to help raise the body temperature. Curl up in a dry sleeping bag inside of a tent. If you are assisting someone in an advanced stage of hypothermia, soak towels or clothing in hot water and wrap them in plastic bags. Place the bags on the person's skin, especially around the lungs and heart, but be careful not to scorch the skin; rewarming too fast can be dangerous. In extreme cases, CPR may be necessary.

Frostbite

If a person is exposed to extreme cold long enough, skin tissue may freeze. This usually occurs in a person's extremities. If hands and feet are not properly protected from the elements, frostbite could lead to amputation. At first, the skin will become red and painful. Later, it can become white and numb as feeling in that area is lost. If untreated, the skin will die and turn black. Preventing frostbite is as easy as dressing properly and preparing for cold weather. Bring gloves, hat, and extra socks. If a body part suffers mild frostbite, slowly rewarm it against another part of your body. Do not rub the area or use direct heat (campfire, lamp, etc.) to rewarm. The key is to rewarm slowly. As the person's tissue heats up, there may be some pain. Administer aspirin if this happens.

Water Treatment

No matter where campers venture in the outdoors, they face the challenge of making the water they find safe for drinking. The safest way to purify water is by boiling it for at least five minutes to eliminate bacteria and parasitic cysts (unfortunately, this may require using a fair amount of your cooking-fuel supply).

The only sure way to beat *Giardia* and other water-borne diseases is to filter or boil your water before drinking, eating, or brushing your teeth. And the best way to prevent the spread of *Giardia* is to bury your waste products at least eight inches deep and 100 feet away from natural waters.

Many campers use water filters to remove bacteria and parasitic cysts such as *Giardia lamblia* and *Cryptosporidium*. Not all purifiers are the same, however, and there continues to be debate about how effective filters are against viruses that cause diarrhea or hepatitis. The popular Katadyn ceramic filters are dependable but expensive; the First Need filter is a less-expensive option that also performs well. Pur filters work well in the backcountry. All filters are fairly easy to use, but they can be bulky. Filters can also become clogged if the water source is extremely dirty.

For increased safety, consider adding a chemical treatment to the filtered water. Chlorine or iodine products are readily available and capable of purifying water if the correct amount is left in the water for a sufficient period of time. Most packaged iodine solutions come with instructions for the length of time the water must be treated (which varies depending on the water's temperature and its organic content). Follow instructions on the iodine treatment kit and have a thermometer handy to measure water temperature.

Cuts

Your knife, hatchet, or ax can be your best friend—or your worst enemy—when camping. It only takes one bad swing with an ax or a careless slice with a knife to turn an enjoyable camping trip into a disaster, especially if you're 50 miles from a hospital. Always proceed cautiously before chopping wood or peeling the bark off a marshmallow stick.

FIRST-AID KITS

If you ask some campers about the contents of their first-aid kits, many will tell you they carry the usual things needed for headaches, blisters, and minor cuts, such as aspirin, Band-Aids, and moleskin. But that's not enough. Don't wait for a major accident to happen in the outdoors to convince you that you need a fully equipped kit. Here's what every camper should bring along:

1. Acetaminophen, ibuprofen, or aspirin, for pain relief
2. Activated charcoal, the miracle cure for food poisoning
3. Adhesive tape
4. Aloe vera–based burn ointment
5. Antibiotic ointment, for minor cuts and scrapes
6. Band-Aids, for minor cuts and scrapes
7. Betadine solution, for disinfection
8. Elastic bandages, to wrap sprains
9. Extractor, for snake venom and nasty insect bites
10. Gauze pads (extra thick and four inches square) or sanitary napkins, to reduce the flow of blood from major wounds
11. Insect repellent
12. Moleskin, to treat blisters
13. Notebook and pencil, to record the details of any accident or injury that might be needed by a physician
14. Plastic gloves for sanitary protection when treating wounds involving blood
15. Sunscreen (at least SPF 15), to prevent sunburn
16. Syringe (10–50cc), to flush wounds
17. Thermometer, also handy in measuring water temperature for proper water treatment
18. Tweezers, to extract splinters and ticks
19. Water filter, plus chlorine or iodine treatment

If a cut occurs, apply direct pressure to the wound. This will help collapse the blood vessel and allow clots to form. Use a sterile pad to stop the blood flow; anything from a gauze pad to a sanitary napkin will suffice. After the flow of blood has been slowed or stopped, carefully clean the wound. Physicians specializing in wilderness medicine encourage campers to carry a 10cc to 50cc syringe to flush out wounds with clean water.

Use butterfly bandages, wound-closure strips, or adhesive tape to close larger wounds instead of using sutures. Sewing up a wound in the wilderness may only slow the healing process and trap infectious dirt or bacteria. After closing the wound, cover it with a gauze dressing treated with an antibiotic ointment, then secure it with an elastic bandage or tape. If the cut is serious, consult a doctor as soon as possible.

Blisters

The best way to prevent blisters is to spend a lot of time breaking in new boots or other footwear before you use them on a camping or hiking trip. Make sure your socks are clean and fit your feet, and avoid wrinkles in your socks, which can cause blisters. Wear a thin polypropylene sock inside a thick wool sock—some campers even wear three pairs of socks when backpacking. It's also wise to change your socks periodically and to expose your feet to the air and give them time to dry off. Some campers apply antiseptic liquid bandages such as New Skin or even just a strip of duct tape to their feet before hiking or backpacking.

To treat blisters and "hot spots" (areas on the foot where it feels like blisters are forming), cut a square of moleskin large enough to surround and protect the blister, then cut out a hole in the center of the square so the moleskin doesn't actually touch the blistered skin. After the moleskin is in place, tape it down snugly with adhesive tape. If necessary, drain the fluid from the blister with a sterile needle; however, the chance of getting an infection is reduced if the surface skin remains intact.

Snakebites

Rattlesnakes are the most common venomous snakes in the Southwest. Some are extremely poisonous, but your chances of getting bitten by a snake are very slim. Most people who die from snakebites are bitten while handling snakes. The rule of thumb here is quite clear: Don't mess with them and they won't mess with you.

On those rare occasions when a snake does strike, in most cases it will not inject venom into the victim. If venom is injected, you will probably experience immediate swelling and pain. For most bites, if you are within an hour or two of a hospital, you only need to remove rings, watches, bracelets, and other constrictions near the bite and get medical help as soon as possible. Keep the injured limb at the same level as the heart; this helps keep the venom from pooling if the wound is below the heart, or spreading if it is above the heart.

If you're more than a two-hour trip from a hospital, suction is recommended. Do not cut the fang marks, even with a sterilized blade. Use a venom extractor, available at sporting goods and mountaineering stores such as REI, to remove the venom; follow the explicit directions included in the kit. Extraction should be attempted within 30 minutes of being bitten. Always seek professional medical attention promptly.

Scorpions
These arachnids can be deadly. To avoid scorpions, check your clothing carefully before dressing in the morning (especially your shoes or boots, which are favorite hiding spots), and use caution when moving sticks and rocks where they may be hiding. Scorpion stings can cause convulsions, especially in children. Applying ice to the wound can ease the pain, but administering the antivenin— available at most hospitals—is essential.

Ticks and Other Insects
Although tick bites are not a major problem in Utah, they occur occasionally and can cause Lyme disease. Sometimes a pair of tweezers can be used to successfully extract a tick from your body, but it depends on how deeply the tick is embedded in your skin. To avoid the risk of breaking the tick in half (leaving a portion of the critter burrowed inside you), get medical help. Always save the tick in a plastic bag—your doctor might be able to identify the species if the bite becomes infected. Mosquitoes are a more prevalent problem, particularly near ponds and rivers. Your best defense is to carry insect repellent. If you get a nasty bite that's itching like crazy, you might want to use an extractor—the same kind used to remove snake venom—to treat the bite. Extractor kits are available at mountaineering shops.

Mosquito repellent
Vitamin B1 and garlic are reputed to act as natural insect repellents, but we've met a lot of mosquitoes that are not convinced. A better bet is to examine the contents of the repellent in question for non-diethyl-metatoluamide. That is the poison, and the percentage of it in the container must be listed and will indicate that brand's effectiveness. Inert ingredients are just excess fluids used to fill the bottles.

Plague
Parts of Southern Utah have several types of plague, which are transmitted through flea bites or contact with a sick animal. The disease is predominantly carried by prairie dogs, rock squirrels, field rats, and chipmunks. Campers should not handle any animal—especially an animal that appears to be ill. The symptoms of plague include acute fever, malaise, and swelling of the lymph nodes, usually in the neck or groin. Typically, plague victims contract the disease from their own pets, often dogs or cats. If symptoms appear, seek immediate medical attention; antibiotics must be administered as soon as possible.

Hantavirus Pulmonary Syndrome
In 1993, a mysterious illness began killing people who lived in or visited rural areas of southern Utah and central Nevada. Eventually the culprit was

identified and named hantavirus pulmonary syndrome, a disease that's transmitted via the bodily waste of deer mice and causes fever, muscle aches, coughing, and respiratory distress. The disease progresses rapidly, necessitating hospitalization and often ventilation within 24 hours. At the present time, there is no specific treatment or "cure" for hantavirus. If the infection is recognized early and the victim is taken to an intensive care unit, there's a chance of survival. In intensive care, patients are incubated and given oxygen therapy. The earlier the patient is brought in to intensive care, the better. If a patient is experiencing full distress, it is less likely the treatment will be effective. Any home, building, or woodpile infested with rodents could be a source of the disease. Keep away from rodents when camping or hiking, and clean up if you do find evidence of their presence. Though the disease is known to exist in Utah, it is very unlikely you will contract hantavirus. For more information, call the Centers for Disease Control and Prevention's Hantavirus Hot Line at 800\532-9929.

EIGHT GREAT TIPS FOR CAMPING WITH CHILDREN

Camping is a terrific way to introduce a child to the world of nature. Everything—playing, eating, sleeping, learning—is done under the sun and the clouds and the moon and the stars. More than a fun vacation (although it should be that, too), it's a chance to learn lifelong skills and experience nature outside of the everyday routine.

In addition, camping is one of the more affordable trips families can take. Sleeping in campgrounds is much less expensive than staying at a motel or hotel, and activities such as hiking, fishing, and exploring nature are not as pricey as amusement-park admission fees. And since you're cooking your meals at the campsite, the high cost of eating in restaurants is avoided.

When planning a camping trip with the kids, remember a few simple rules: Tailor the trip to their capabilities; focus on their interests; and adjust to their limitations, which are generally defined by their age and development level.

Babies can be great campers, as long as you're prepared to limit your outdoor activities and can address their special requirements (crib, stroller, formula, diapers, etc.). Toddlers especially appreciate exploring a new environment. They love to get dirty and wet, collect leaves and rocks, and watch wildlife and insects.

Elementary school–age children are typically enthusiastic campers, anxious to learn about the outdoors, help with the chores, and participate in all the camping activities. They like to swim, hike, build fires, and roast hot dogs and marshmallows. And they can't resist hearing a good ghost story or tall tale about falling stars or wild animals.

Teenagers? Well, you're on your own there. Some teens like to camp, especially if it's an annual family vacation routine. Others consider it a drag and will take every opportunity to remind you of it. Try to involve teens in every aspect of the trip: deciding where to go, what to take, what to eat, what to do. Let them bring a friend and give them a little more freedom than they get at home. They'll be much better company during group activities and meals if they know they'll be able to go off and hike, fish, swim, or whatever on their own later.

Here are some tips on how to ensure that a fun, rewarding vacation is had by all:

- **Expect short attention spans.** By staying a step or two ahead of the kids in the planned-activities department, you can keep them from getting bored or into trouble. Unlike adults, kids need action on a vacation. Plan activities and games to keep them occupied. That means staying prepared by knowing what the next fun event will be—an activity that will inspire or distract a restless child.
- **Bring the right gear and games.** What you pack partly depends on where you'll be camping and what your children like to do. Are you camping at a sandy lake with toddlers? Then buckets, shovels, sieves, toy trucks, and plastic molds are in order. Will you be sleeping on top of old Smoky? Then binoculars, a telescope and star chart, a magnifying glass, and an altimeter are ideal. Will there be a river nearby? Then bring along a fishing rod. No matter where you go, pack along a ball, a Frisbee, a pack of cards, pens and paper, or crayons and coloring pads for younger kids.
- **Have a camera ready to capture the moment.** A still or video camera is a great thing to tote along. Photographs or videos of your family in the outdoors—hiking up a mountain, catching a fish, taking down the tent—will go a long way toward helping your kids hang on to memories of the last trip and build up a head of steam for the next.
- **Let your kids help with the practical stuff.** When you're camping, there are essential campground tasks that must be done—such as setting up camp, building a fire, cooking dinner—and kids would rather be involved than just watch you do everything. Show them how to help put up the tent, collect sticks for the campfire, add water and stir the pancake mix, and read a compass.
- **Help your children learn, but also let them play.** Spending time outdoors provides the opportunity to teach them outdoor skills and safety, campground ethics, even some lessons about life. While teaching them to pick up after themselves (and others) and to respect the outdoors is very important, remember that taking your children to the woods, mountains, or desert doesn't have to be strictly an educational experience. This is first and foremost a vacation—and kids need to relax, too.
- **Let them have a say in the agenda.** It's everybody's trip. Listen to what the kids want to do and don't want to do. If a hike is planned and they want to spend the day swimming or tossing a Frisbee instead, let the majority rule. Follow their lead sometimes, go with their flow, let the adventure happen.
- **Set rules for acceptable behavior.** Giving the youngsters a say in the

agenda doesn't mean letting them run wild. Rules and limits are essential to ensure kids' safety and their consideration for other campers. Let them know what behavior is acceptable around a campfire, how close they can come to a cliff or wildlife, and why it's important to stay within sight.

- **Prepare kids for the ups and the downs.** Enthusiasm is a key ingredient for a successful camping trip, but letting children become excessively excited can backfire when things don't go their way. If it rains or is unseasonably cold, if the fish aren't biting, or if one of them twists an ankle or catches a cold, it could ruin the whole experience for them. Tell them about the possible negative as well as the positive aspects of the trip. That way they'll be better prepared for whatever little disasters or disappointments come their way.

CAMPING GEAR CHECKLIST

There's nothing like driving for hours to get to that prime campsite in the woods, only to discover that you forgot to pack your sleeping bag. Your best bet for avoiding such disasters is to make a list and check it twice. Create your own camping checklist and check off each item as it is packed—it's one way to guarantee nothing gets left behind. Here's a list to get you started:

SLEEPING GEAR
- Blankets, extra
- Ground cloth/tarp
- Pillow
- Sleeping bag
- Sleeping pad
- Tent

COOKING UTENSILS
- Aluminum foil
- Can opener
- Charcoal
- Coffee, tea, and hot chocolate
- Cooking kit
- Cooler
- Cups
- Forks, knives, and spoons
- Fuel
- Grill or cooking stove
- Matches
- Plates
- Salt and pepper
- Spatula
- Stove
- Tablecloth
- Water jugs or bottles

PACKING AND CLEANING SUPPLIES
- Biodegradable dish soap
- Cloth towels
- Plastic bags (large and small)
- Sponge

RECREATIONAL GEAR
- Binoculars
- Books and magazines
- Camera and film
- Car games for kids
- Deck of cards
- Field guides
- Fishing rod, reel, and tackle box
- Journal
- Portable stereo and tapes or CDs

FIRST-AID KIT
- See First-Aid Kit chart.

MISCELLANEOUS GEAR
- Camp chairs
- Compass
- Day pack
- Firewood
- Flashlight/headlamp and extra batteries
- Hat
- Insect repellent
- Lantern
- Maps
- Mosquito-net tent
- Portable table
- Propane heater
- Sunscreen
- Water filter

VIEW FROM DESERET PEAK

MAP A1

One inch equals approximately 11 miles.

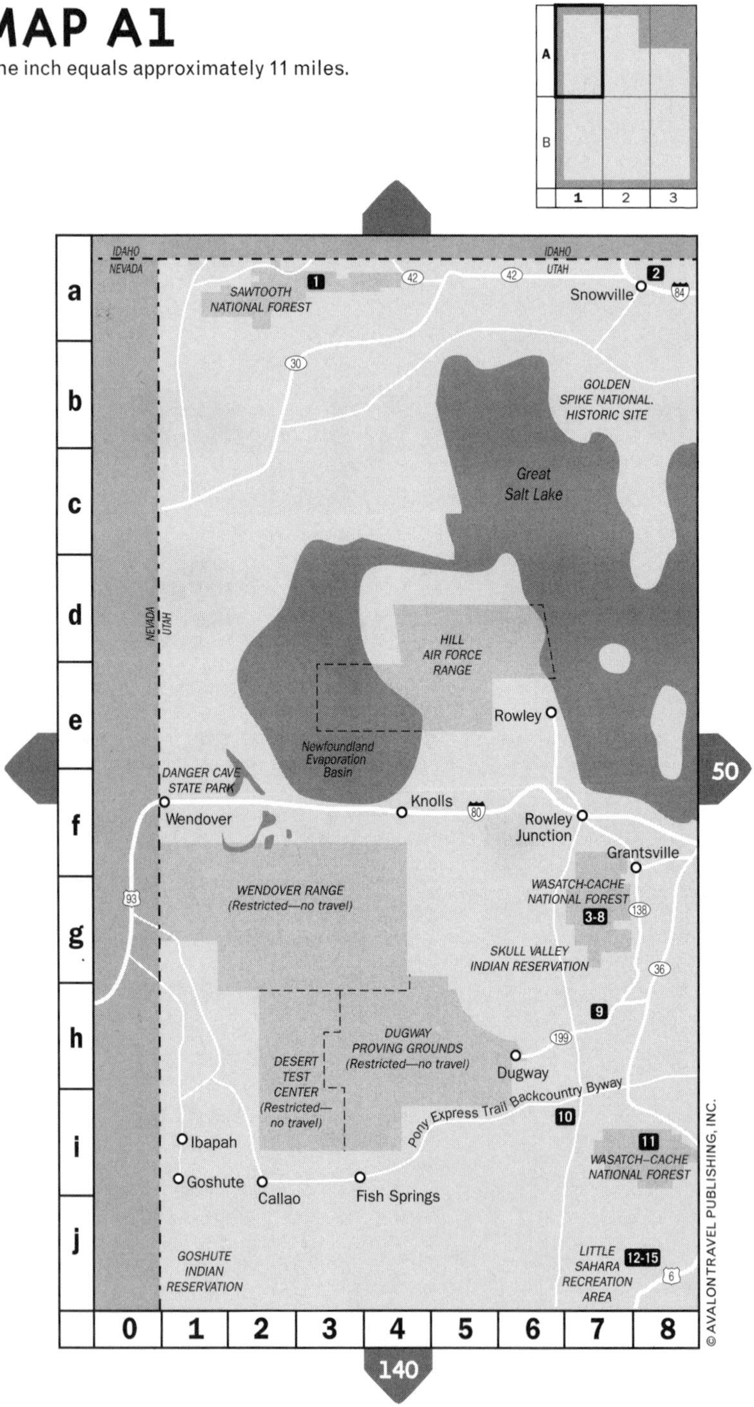

CHAPTER A1

The northwest corner of Utah could be called a no-man's-land. The Great Salt Lake and its salty barrens dominate the landscape. Early travelers including the ill-fated Donner-Reed wagon train fought thirst and mud in their struggle to reach California. None willingly stayed for long. Even today, few tourists venture here.

There are those, however, who cherish the solitude and stark beauty they find in Utah's Great Basin. The Great Basin is made up of a series of basins, or valleys, and mountain ranges. Highways and dirt roads allow drivers of air-conditioned automobiles to experience the desert in a new way. Explorers willing to forgo shopping opportunities and gas stations will find a world of contrast between the rugged mountains and dry valleys and the lush wildlife refuges that spring from the middle of nowhere. This is a land of primitive beauty surrounding a space-age Air Force testing range and chemical-weapons disposal facility.

Three-Day Itinerary: South Willow ⚑ Simpson Springs ⚑ Little Sahara Recreation Area

In three days, a visitor can sample the Great Basin by hiking to the top of an 11,030-foot peak, viewing waterfowl at a federal bird refuge before camping at a historic Pony Express stop, and rolling in sand dunes left over from ancient Lake Bonneville.

Day One
From Salt Lake City, take I-80 west to the Grantsville exit. In Grantsville, take the road signed to the Wasatch National Forest Recreation Areas of South and North Willow Canyons (see directions to Cottonwood on page 42). Take your choice of six campgrounds along South Willow Creek. Wade in the stream, fish, or just relax. Or, take the six-mile (round-trip) hike to Tooele County's highest mountain,

Deseret Peak (11,030 feet). The trailhead is at the end of the canyon. The moderately strenuous trail takes hikers through aspen and Douglas fir forests and wildflower meadows and ends in stands of ancient bristlecone pine. At the top, the civilized world is gone and one sees only the Great Salt Lake, its salty flats, and hazy mountain ranges marching off into the distance.

Day Two

After a cool night on the mountain, leave South Willow Canyon and head south toward State Route 36 (see directions to Simpson Springs, page 45). Follow the dirt road (passable when dry for sedans) that is also the old Pony Express and Stage route to Simpson Springs. Simpson Springs is the site of an old Pony Express station. Set up camp if you wish, and then continue on the Pony Express trail to Fish Springs National Wildlife area. Check in at the refuge headquarters to see what birds to look for, then drive around the refuge. Fresh water arriving underground from hundreds of miles away has created an oasis for countless waterfowl. If you feel like driving some more, head further into the Great Basin and see the Deep Creek Mountains and the ghost town of Gold Hill.

Day Three

Return to State Route 36 and go south to Vernon. During January and February, bald eagles perch in the trees here, looking for rabbit dinners. State Route 36 meets U.S. 6 at the old mining town of Tintic. If you like old ghost towns like Tintic, you should take the short detour to Mammoth and Eureka. Read from George Thompson's *Some Dreams Die* to get the colorful history of these towns. The Tintic Mining Museum in Eureka's City Hall is a funky collection of mining artifacts, historic newspapers, and a mineral display. It also offers a self-guided 35-mile driving tour (passable when dry) of the mining district including the Mammoth, Dividend, Diamond, and Silver City ghost towns. Call ahead (435/433-6842) to arrange to have a volunteer meet you at the museum. From Eureka, double back and go south on U.S. Highway 6 to Little Sahara Recreation Area. The 60,000 acres of white sand dunes in this area are administered by the Bureau of Land Management for recreational use by off-highway vehicles, hikers, four-wheelers, dune-buggy drivers, dirt bikers, and ATV owners. There are four campgrounds. Jericho is the best for non-motorized recreationists. A large area of the dunes has been fenced off so those on foot can romp without fear of collisions with motorized vehicles.

Seven-Day Itinerary: Little Sahara Recreation Area 🏕️ Wheeler Peak 🏕️ Simpson Springs 🏕️ South Willow 🏕️ Salt Flats 🏕️ Golden Spike National Historic Site

Day One

From Salt Lake City, the fastest way to Little Sahara Recreation Area is via I-15 south to Santaquin. From Santaquin, take U.S. Highway 6 to Little Sahara Recreation Area (see Three-Day Itinerary, Day Three) and spend the night. Get up early the next day to take advantage of the early-morning light and cool dunes.

Day Two
Retrace your route north on U.S. Highway 6 to Tintic. Visit the Eureka Mining Museum and take the self-guided driving tour (see Three-Day Itinerary, Day Three). Continue down memory lane and the old Pony Express trail to Simpson Springs (see Three-Day Itinerary, Day Two).

Days Three and Four
From Simpson Springs, head north again to South Willow Canyon (see Three-Day Itinerary, Day One). Spend the day relaxing and enjoying the cool canyon. Get up early the next morning to climb Deseret Peak.

Days Five and Six
Return to State Route 138 north to Grantsville and then I-80. Go west on I-80 toward Wendover. Look for an 87-foot-tall "Tree of Life" cement-and-tile sculpture sprouting from the side of the freeway. The artist was obviously uncomfortable with the uncluttered view of miles and miles of salt flats and got the money to clutter it with his "work of art". Make sure to stop at the Salt Flats rest stop. The Bonneville Salt Flats is the site of many automobile speed and endurance records. During the spring, saline water covers the flats. As the water evaporates, a perfectly level crystalline surface remains. Independence Day and other movies have taken advantage of the extraterrestrial scenery.

The city of Wendover sprawls from Utah into Nevada. Visitors to the Nevada side can visit a casino, take in a buffet, and fill up the gas tank before heading out into the desert again. Travel on I-80 for 32 miles and take the exit to Nevada State Road 233. This road becomes State Road 30 in Utah. Go another 109 miles to the junction with State Route 42. Follow the directions to the Clear Creek campground (page 42) in the Sawtooth National Forest. Plan to stay a couple of nights here. Spend one day exploring the mountain. Adventurous souls can take the moderate hike to the top of Box Elder County's highest peak, Bull Mountain. Locate the trail to the 9,920-foot summit at the end of the campground. Spend the next day exploring Locomotive Springs Waterfowl Management Area.

Day Seven
About 30 miles from the Clear Creek campground, on State Route 30, get on I-84 and head for Salt Lake City. Take exit 24 to Golden Spike National Historic Site. Plan to spend the day touring the museum and hiking the Big Fill Trail. Few places in the United States capture critical points in the nation's history as well as this. During the summer, a reenactment takes place where replicas of the two engines, the Jupiter and the #119, steam down the tracks and meet head to head, symbolizing the linking of the continent by rail.

◼ Clear Creek

      8

Despite its remote location, this campground set in somewhat open country can fill up quickly on weekends. A small, fishable stream is nearby, and hikers and bicyclists will discover plenty of pines and wildflower-covered fields. Also close by is the Bull Flat Trailhead, accessible to hikers, horses, mountain bikes, and all-terrain vehicles. On the Bull Flat Trail, hikers can either take the turnoff to Bull Flat or continue on the main path to the Lake Fork Trail; this leads to Bull Lake, located beneath sheer, glacier-formed quartzite cliffs.

Location: In Sawtooth National Forest; map A1, grid a3.

Campsites, facilities: There are 10 sites with picnic tables and fire grills. Vault toilets and drinking water are available.

Reservations, fees: Sites are free and are first come, first served.

Open: June–Sept.

Directions: From Snowville, head west on State Route 30. In about 18 miles, look for the junction with State Route 42. Take State Route 42 about 8.5 miles, keeping an eye out for the Strevell Road 3600 South sign. (Note: It's a small street sign that can be difficult to see at night.) Turn left onto Strevell Road, go about 3.2 miles to Clear Creek Campground Road, turn left, and continue for another six miles.

Contact: Burley Ranger District, Sawtooth National Forest, 303/202-0430.

◼ Lottie Dell

 2

This campground is located within the boundaries of Snowville, a small and quiet town. Not far away is the Golden Spike National Historic Site, where the tracks of the Transcontinental Railroad were joined in 1869. Here, during the summer, one of two steam engines periodically chugs out of the train-house, providing a touch of living history; exhibits also tell the story of the momentous event.

Location: In Snowville; map A1, grid a8.

Campsites, facilities: There are 34 sites with hookups, 14 camping cabins, and a large, grassy area for tents. Laundry facilities, restrooms, showers, picnic tables, and a public phone are available. Pets are allowed.

Reservations, fees: Reservations are accepted. Sites with hookups are $15, tent sites are $11, and cabins are $20.

Open: Year-round.

Directions: Follow I-84 to Snowville, then take either exit 5 or 7 and drive into town, where the campground is located.

Contact: Lottie Dell Campground, 435/872-8273.

◼ Cottonwood

  5

Named for its tall and sheltering cottonwood trees, this campground basically consists of a small parking area to the left of the road; like most of the campgrounds nearby, it's sandwiched between the road and the steep walls of South Willow Canyon. Hikers come here to tackle 11,031-foot Deseret Peak, set in the heart of a beautiful designated wilderness area not far away. Those who make the summit enjoy spectacular views of the Wasatch Mountains, the Great Salt Lake, Great Basin, and the Bonneville Salt Flats. A small stream flows through the campground and is occasionally stocked with rainbow trout. Campers must haul their gear down to the sites closest to the stream. The alpine canyon provides a cool and shady counterpoint to the stark, arid surroundings.

Location: In Wasatch-Cache National Forest; map A1, grid g7.

Campsites, facilities: There are two sites with picnic tables and vault toilets, but there is no drinking water. Eight people and one vehicle are allowed at each site. Check in time is 2 P.M., check out is 1 P.M. No access permitted 10 P.M.–6 A.M. Maximum stay is 10 days. Dogs on leash only.

Reservations, fees: Sites are $5 and are first come, first served.

Open: May–Oct.

Directions: From Salt Lake City, drive west on I-80. Take exit 99 and go left on State Route 36, following the signs to Grantsville and Tooele. After about 10 miles, turn right on State Route 138 to Grantsville. Drive most of the way through town, and look for the brown sign with directions to the Wasatch National Forest Recreation Areas of South Willow and North Willow. Turn left on 400 West and, after about five miles, take the right turnoff to South Willow. Follow the paved road to the Forest Service boundary, then continue on the gravel (passable by two-wheel-drive vehicle) for another 9.2 miles to the campground.

Contact: Salt Lake Ranger District, 801/943-1794, www.fs.fed.us.wcnf/slrd.

◢ Intake

  4

The road to Intake campground is a sharp jag to the left down a dirt road; as with most campgrounds in South Willow Canyon, there's sometimes a fine cover of road dust. Still, the campsites here, set along a small stream, are a little more secluded from the road and spaced farther apart than at other campgrounds nearby, and they're shaded by box elder and Rocky Mountain big-tooth maple trees. There's good fishing at nearby Grantsville Reservoir for planted rainbow trout, especially in the spring. Hikers can explore the designated wilderness area of nearby 11,031-foot Deseret Peak or attempt the summit itself.

Location: In Wasatch-Cache National Forest; map A1, grid g7.

Campsites, facilities: There are four sites with picnic tables and fire grills. Vault toilets are available, but there is no water. Check-in time is 2 P.M. Check out is 1 P.M. No access allowed 10 P.M.–6 A.M. Maximum stay is 10 days. Dogs on leash only.

Reservations, fees: Sites are $5 and are first come, first served.

Open: May–Oct.

Directions: From Salt Lake City, take I-80 west to exit 99, then turn left on State Route 36 and follow the directions to Grantsville (see Cottonwood, page 42). Continue past Cottonwood a short distance up the canyon. The campground is 9.9 miles from Grantsville.

Contact: Salt Lake Ranger District, Wasatch National Forest, 801/943-1794, www.fs.fed.us.wcnf/slrd.

◢ Boy Scout

  5

Boy Scout is an excellent little spot in which to beat the heat and avoid all the crowds in the campgrounds located closer to the Wasatch Front. Since it is equipped with long tables, it's also well suited to larger groups, as the name "Boy Scout" suggests. The campground is separated from the road by a stream and shaded by cottonwood trees. Hikers not up for climbing nearby Deseret Peak can opt for shorter walks from the trailhead instead.

Location: In Wasatch-Cache National Forest; map A1, grid g7.

Campsites, facilities: There are five sites with picnic tables and fire grills. Vault toilets are available, but there is no water. Check-in time is 2 P.M. Check out is 1 P.M. No access allowed 10 P.M.–6 A.M. Maximum stay is 10 days. Dogs on leash only.

Reservations, fees: Sites are $5 and are first come, first served.

Open: May–Oct.

Directions: From Salt Lake City, follow the directions to

South Willow Canyon in the Cottonwood campground (see page 42), continuing on past Cottonwood for about another quarter of a mile. The Boy Scout campground is 10.2 miles southwest of Grantsville.

Contact: Salt Lake Ranger District, Wasatch National Forest, 801/943-1794, www.fs.fed .us.wcnf/slrd.

Lower Narrows

 5

Campers must haul their gear across a bridge to this campground, since parking is only along the road and the sites are across the stream. Many campers come to Lower Narrows to explore the nearby Deseret Peak Wilderness Area or to fish for rainbow trout in the small creek that runs through South Willow Canyon.

Location: In Wasatch-Cache National Forest; map A1, grid g7.

Campsites, facilities: There are five sites with picnic tables and fire grills. Vault toilets are available, but there is no water. Check in time is 2 P.M. Check out is 1 P.M. No access allowed 10 P.M.–6 A.M. Maximum stay is 10 days. Dogs on leash only.

Reservations, fees: Sites are $5 and are first come, first served.

Open: May–Oct.

Directions: From Salt Lake City, follow the directions for South Willow Canyon in the Cottonwood campground (see page 42) and continue on to Lower Narrows. The campground is half a mile up the canyon, 10.7 miles southwest of Grantsville.

Contact: Salt Lake Ranger District, Wasatch National Forest, 801/943-1794, www.fs.fed .us.wcnf/slrd.

7 Upper Narrows

5

Tooele County residents know this small campground is a great place to escape the pounding summer heat. Campers can spend a day at the Great Salt Lake State Park beaches northwest of Grantsville, then head back into the forest. Anglers can fish for rainbow trout in the nearby small stream or down the road at Grantsville Reservoir. All parking is along the road; campers must walk to their sites along the stream, just before the narrowest part of the canyon.

Location: In Wasatch-Cache National Forest; map A1, grid g7.

Campsites, facilities: There are eight sites with picnic tables and fire grills. Vault toilets are available, but there is no water. Check in time is 2 P.M. Check out is 1 P.M. No access allowed between 10 P.M. and 6 A.M. Maximum stay is 10 days. Dogs on leash only.

Reservations, fees: Sites are $5 and are first come, first served. The entire campground can be reserved, however, as a group tent single site. The fee as a groupsite is $21.75.

Open: May–Oct.

Directions: From Salt Lake City, follow the directions to South Willow Canyon in the Cottonwood Campground (see page 42). This campground is eight-tenths of a mile farther up the canyon, 11.5 miles southwest of Grantsville.

Contact: Salt Lake Ranger District, Wasatch National Forest, 801/943-1794, www.fs.fed.us .wcnf/slrd. For group sites, 877/444-6777, www.ReserveUSA.com.

8 Loop

 5

This campground serves as the trailhead for 11,031-foot Deseret Peak, a popular place for hikers who love a breathtaking view (see Cottonwood campground, page 42). It's also a great base for anglers looking to find rainbow trout at Grantsville Reservoir or the nearby small stream. The well-spaced campsites at 6,320 feet are located along the road under a grove of tall aspens, which in mid-September are brilliantly ablaze with the colors of fall.

Location: In Wasatch-Cache National Forest; map A1, grid g7.

Campsites, facilities: There are nine sites with picnic tables and fire grills. Eight of the sites are singles, which hold eight people and one vehicle. One site, a double, holds 16 people and up to four vehicles. Vault toilets are available, but there is no water. Check in time is 2 P.M. Check out is 1 P.M. No access allowed 10 P.M.–6 A.M. Maximum stay is 10 days. Dogs on leash only.

Reservations, fees: Sites are $5 and are first come, first served.

Open: May–Oct.

Contact: Salt Lake Ranger District, Wasatch National Forest, 801/943-1794, www.fs.fed. us.wcnf/slrd.

Directions: From Salt Lake City, follow the directions to South Willow Canyon in the Cottonwood campground (see page 42) and continue for almost four miles. Loop campground is at the end of the canyon, 13 miles southwest of Grantsville.

9 Clover Springs

  5

This campground is in a popular horseback-riding area in one of the more remote parts of Utah. Across the road there are established horse and hiking trails, but the wide-open country beckons adventurers to ramble off the beaten path. Try not to yield to temptation as RVs are discouraged. The camping itself is in a riparian canyon at an elevation of 6,000 feet, so temperatures can be on the cool side. Campers looking for a quiet spot should enjoy this one.

Location: In the Onaqui Mountains; map A1, grid h7.

Campsites, facilities: There are 11 camping spaces with no hookups, plus group facilities and vault toilets. Equestrian facilities include horse tie-ups, unloading docks, and feeding troughs.

Reservations, fees: Camping is $4 a night and is first come, first served.

Open: Apr.–Nov.

Directions: Driving south from Tooele, take State Route 36 south to Highway 199; head west eight miles to the campground.

Contact: Salt Lake Bureau of Land Management, 801/977-4300.

10 Simpson Springs

    7

The stark desert scenery of the Great Basin takes some getting used to if you're accustomed to greener terrain, but the desolate beauty has an appeal all its own. History buffs will enjoy touring the remains of the Pony Express Trail Station on the dirt road near the entrance, where interpretive signs tell the story of the historic route. This is literally wide-open territory for horseback riders and hikers, with few developed trails; mountain bikers often use the dirt road. Bird-watchers can spot many different types of migrating shorebirds, waterfowl, and raptors at the nearby Fish Springs National Wildlife Refuge. Keep in mind the Simpson Springs campground is quite popular with off-road-vehicle enthusiasts and can be crowded in spring and fall.

Location: On the Pony Express Trail; map A1, grid i6.

Campsites, facilities: There are 14 sites (plus a large overflow area) with no hookups. Picnic tables, fire grills, and vault toilets are available, but there is no water.

Reservations, fees: Campsites are $4 and are first come, first served.

Open: Year-round.

Directions: This extremely remote campground is about 120 miles from the cities of Provo (via Lehi) and Salt Lake City (via Tooele), off State Route 36.

Turn off State Route 36 at Vernon, and head west for 31 miles on the graveled Pony Express Trail Back-country Byway. Look for the signs directing visitors to the Pony Express Trail and Fish Springs National Wildlife Refuge.
Contact: Salt Lake Bureau of Land Management, 801/977-4300.

Vernon Reservoir

   5

Here's a truly out-of-the-way spot that's perfect if you're trying to avoid the crowds. Fishing for stocked trout at nearby Vernon Reservoir can be good, especially in the spring. Though the launching facilities are somewhat primitive, small boats, canoes, and rafts are allowed on the reservoir. The campground is in Wasatch-Cache National Forest, but is managed by Uinta National Forest.
Location: In Wasatch-Cache National Forest; map A1, grid i8.
Campsites, facilities: There are 10 sites with picnic tables and fire grills. Tent sites, vault toilets, and water are available.
Reservations, fees: All sites are free and first come, first served.
Open: Apr.–Nov.
Directions: This remote campground, off State Route 36 and south of Vernon, is 120 miles from both Provo (via Lehi) and Salt Lake City (via Tooele). Take State Route 36 to Vernon, turn onto Forest Road 005, and head south for 11 miles to the campground.
Contact: Spanish Fork Ranger District, 801/798-3571.

White Sands

 8

The surrounding Little Sahara Recreation Area is a huge complex of dunes, so this campground is popular with off-road-vehicle owners. The fenced-in play area protects kids and adults from the dune buggies and dirt bikes. Hiking the shifting dunes is more like a freewheeling romp in the sand. The campsites are set against the sandy hills near juniper trees.
Location: In Little Sahara Recreation Area; map A1, grid j7.
Campsites, facilities: There are 50 sites with picnic tables, fire grills, restrooms with flush toilets, drinking water, and a fenced recreation area in the dunes.
Reservations, fees: Sites are $6 and are first come, first served.
Open: Year-round, though the water may be turned off in the winter.
Directions: Drive 24 miles north of Delta or 18 miles south of Eureka on U.S. Highway 6 to Jericho Junction. Just past the visitors center, take the first road north and drive 4.5 miles to the campground.
Contact: Bureau of Land Management, Fillmore, 435/743-3100.

Oasis

 8

This campground is the number-one favorite with folks who like to take their dune buggies, dirt bikes, or other all-terrain vehicles onto the extensive dune system at Little Sahara. That means hikers need to be careful on the dunes. Like other campgrounds nearby, this one is in a hilly, sandy area in the midst of some juniper trees.
Location: In Little Sahara Recreation Area; map A1, grid j7.
Campsites, facilities: There are 84 sites with no hookups (this is a popular place to bring self-contained RVs). Picnic tables, fire grills, flush toilets, and drinking water are available.
Reservations, fees: Sites are $6 and are first come, first served.
Open: Year-round, though the water may be turned off in the winter.
Directions: Take U.S. Highway 6 to Jericho Junction, located 24 miles north of Delta and

18 miles south of Eureka. Then follow the signs to the campground, heading south and west for about seven miles.

Contact: Bureau of Land Management, Fillmore, 435/743-3100.

Jericho
 8

Set in the dunes, this might be the best camping spot in the area for families with young children. Here, in the big fenced play area, kids and adults can build sand castles, roll down the sandy slopes, or gaze at the dramatic scenery without worrying about collisions with all-terrain vehicles. The campground terrain is largely open; covered picnic tables provide the only shade.

Location: In Little Sahara Recreation Area; map A1, grid j7.

Campsites, facilities: There are 41 sites with no hookups. Picnic tables, fire grills, flush toilets, and drinking water are available, along with a fenced sandy play area that's off-limits to all-terrain vehicles.

Reservations, fees: Sites are $6 and are first come, first served.

Open: Year-round, though the water may be turned off in the winter.

Directions: Travel 24 miles north of Delta or 18 miles south of Eureka on U.S. Highway 6 to Jericho Junction. Then follow the signs to the campground, heading southwest for just over seven miles.

Contact: Bureau of Land Management, Fillmore, 435/743-3100.

Sand Mountain
 7

Four-wheel-drive-vehicle owners love the wide-open spaces of Sand Mountain. All hiking is on the dunes, with no marked trails. Though facilities are limited, the area can accommodate large numbers overnight. Campers park their RVs at the base of Sand Mountain, one of the largest dunes in the 60,000-acre area.

Location: In Little Sahara Recreation Area; map A1, grid j7.

Campsites, facilities: There are no designated campsites although tent sites are available. This is a popular spot for self-contained RVs. Flush toilets are available, but there is no water.

Reservations, fees: Campsites are $6 and are first come, first served.

Open: Year-round.

Directions: On U.S. Highway 6, drive 24 miles north from Delta or 18 miles south from Eureka to Jericho Junction. Then follow the signs, heading southwest for just over 12 miles to the end of the road near Sand Mountain.

Contact: Bureau of Land Management, Fillmore, 435/743-3100.

MARSHY SHORELINE, GREAT SALT LAKE

MAP A2

One inch equals approximately 11 miles.

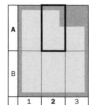

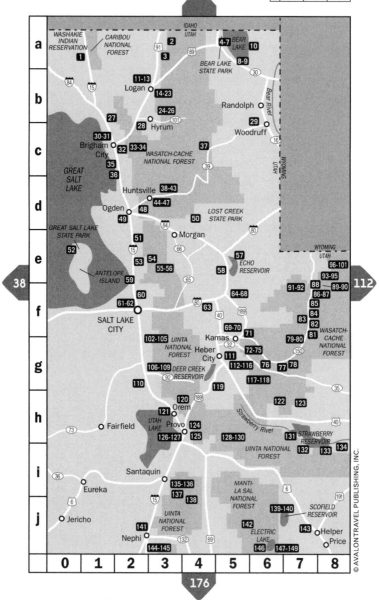

CHAPTER A2

(CONTINUED ON NEXT PAGE)

The Wasatch and Uinta Mountains dominate this part of the state. From Olympic winter-sports venues to fishing lakes, from wildflower-filled meadows to craggy mountain peaks, there is something for every taste in this area. Except for skiing and snowmobile trips, travel to this part of the state is possible only after the snow melts, which is usually late-June to Labor Day.

One of the nation's only mountain ranges extending east to west, the High Uintas bustle every summer with campers, hikers, bikers, horseback riders, ATV users, and anglers. Nearly half a million acres of the Uintas have been set aside as wilderness. The Wasatch-Cache National Forest along the Wasatch Front, with more than one million inhabitants, is one of the heaviest-used forests in the nation, yet it contains six wilderness areas. Hikers can ascend from city to wilderness in anywhere from just a few minutes to several hours in areas such as the Lone Peak and Mount Olympus Wilderness Areas.

(CONTINUED ON NEXT PAGE)

Three-Day Itinerary: Mirror Lake Highway 🏕 Bear Lake 🏕 Logan Canyon

Day One

Head north from Salt Lake City on I-80. Travel east past Park City and take the Highway 40 exit to Heber City. There, look for the turnoff to Kamas and State Road 150. Stop in at the Forest Service office in Kamas on your way to the scenic Mirror Lake Highway. Inquire about camping and recreational activities. During the summer months, wise campers call ahead to reserve a campground (U.S. Forest Service National Reservation System, 800/280-2267). Spend a lazy day fishing or canoeing in one of the many small lakes along the highway, or hike some of the hundreds of miles of trails interlacing the forest.

Day Two

Visitors could spend weeks exploring the High Uintas. Those who prefer to cover more territory, however, can head farther north to Bear Lake. Take State Road 150 north another 50 miles to Evanston, Wyoming, then Wyoming State Road 89 to Woodruff, Utah. The road in Utah is State Road 16. From Woodruff, go to Sage Creek Junction and turn west on State Road 30 to Laketown. Bear Lake is large and brilliant-blue, and is home to two endemic fish, the Bonneville cutthroat trout and the Bonneville cisco. It is a freshwater Pleistocene relic left from Lake Bonneville. The Great Salt Lake is its saltwater remnant. The west and south shores of Bear Lake are covered with public and private campgrounds, cabins, and condominiums. Bear Lake Rendezvous Beach State Park is a popular campground. Sites can be reserved (800/322-3770). It is definitely a group experience, however, with sites jammed right next to one another. Bear Lake South Eden is more remote and primitive, but there is no sandy beach. Bear Lake visitors can spend the day playing on the beach, touring the lake in a personal watercraft or other boat, or fishing.

Day Three

During July, visit Garden City and order a famous Bear Lake raspberry malt. Then leave Bear Lake and climb back into the Wasatch National Forest on Highway 89 south toward Logan. There are 10 campgrounds along this scenic highway. Most of them sit beside the Logan River. Reservations can be made at a few of them (800/280-3620). Don't miss Tony Grove, however. Tony Grove Lake sits in a glacial cirque with a rugged peak and rich forest surrounding the campground. Take the guided nature walk around the lake or canoe its peaceful surface. Alternatively, take one of several hikes and explore the mountains in the area.

Seven-Day Itinerary: Nebo Scenic Loop 🏕 Strawberry Reservoir 🏕 Mirror Lake Highway 🏕 Bear Lake 🏕 Logan Canyon 🏕 Willard Bay

Day One
Keep in mind that a week would be well spent in any of Utah's national forests. This itinerary is a sampling of the forests near the Wasatch Front that can be accessed within a few hours drive of Salt Lake City. A scenic trip anytime, but especially beautiful in autumn, is the Nebo Scenic Loop Drive. Take I-15 south of Salt Lake City to Nephi. At exit 222, go east on State Road 132 to Fountain Green. Look for the turnoff for the Nebo Scenic Byway. The paved road is narrow in spots. It traverses the top of a high plateau with lakes and an occasional glimpse through the aspen groves of the valleys on either side. Stay the night at one of the campgrounds on the loop (see page 57). The Payson Lakes campground can be reserved (800/280-2267). A paved trail lines the lake which, anglers will be happy to learn, is generously stocked with trout.

The Great Salt Lake Wildlife Refuges

The Great Salt Lake has been designated as a site of Hemispheric Importance to Shorebirds. Birds one would expect to find along the Pacific Ocean actually stop to feed in the salty waters and mud flats of the Great Salt Lake as part of their migration from their northern breeding grounds in Canada to the wintering grounds of the coasts and wetlands of South America. At various parts of the year, visitors can spot huge flocks of Wilson's phalarope and large numbers of avocet, black-necked stilts and long-billed curlew. Gunnison Island, in the lake, is home to 10,000 white pelicans. They nest in safety on the island and fly to nearby wetlands or distant Utah Lake to find food. The state bird of Utah, the California gull, is ubiquitous around the lake and the Salt Lake Valley.

Farmington Bay Waterfowl Management Area is a good place to see the birds. A raised viewing area has been constructed and visitors can walk along the dikes. The Layton Waterfowl Management Area is managed by the Nature Conservancy. Bear River Bird Refuge is managed as a freshwater wetlands and was the first in the federal system.

Check with Antelope Island State Park for the date of the annual Migratory Bird Festival week of festivities, during which educational activities and tours of the wildlife areas are given.

For more information contact Utah Department of Wildlife Resources, 801/538-4776, 1594 W. North Temple, Suite 2110, Box 146301, Salt Lake City, Utah 84114-6301.

Day Two

Join up with I-15 at Payson. Travel north to the exit for Highway 189 and Mount Timpanogos Scenic Byway. Take the 1.5-mile (one-way, straight up) hike to Timpanogos Cave at Timpanogos Cave National Monument. Tickets for the cave tour must be picked up ahead of time in the busy summer months. Timpanogos Cave has a large number of impressive formations, including flowstone, stalactites and stalagmites, and soda straws. It is perhaps most famous for a large hanging formation in the shape of a human heart.

If the hike to the cave seems daunting, continue up canyon and take the Cascade Springs Scenic Highway, a 7.5-mile paved road off the Alpine Scenic Loop. Stop at Cascade Springs for a picnic and a stroll along a boardwalk over a series of flowing springs and limestone pools. Fish can be seen in the crystal-clear water. This drive affords impressive views of the eastern slopes of Mount Timpanogos.

From the springs, continue on the scenic drive to Heber City. Take the Highway 40 exit to Strawberry Reservoir, perhaps 30 miles to the east. There are four large campgrounds on Strawberry Reservoir. The reservoir is also one of the top cutthroat-trout fisheries in the world. Boats and motors can be rented at the marina. Fly fishers can try their hand in the Strawberry River, the blue-ribbon trout stream below the dam. If you visit in fall, be sure to stop in at the visitors center to watch spawning Kokanee salmon.

Day Three

Go north on Highway 40 to Heber City. Continue north. Take the Kamas/Mirror Lake Highway exit. Spend a day camping along the highway in one of the 10 campgrounds (see Three-Day Itinerary, Day One). Backpackers should consider one of scores of trails into the High Uintas Wilderness Area. The state's highest summit, King's Peak (13,528 feet), is but one of a number of impressive destinations above tree line. Another possibility is to stay at Jordanelle State Park along Highway 40, a new and modern facility that features a variety of camping, boating, and fishing opportunities. Kids might like a stop at the Rock Cliff Nature Center where the Provo River dumps into the reservoir.

Day Four

Come down a little in altitude and try out the cold waters of Bear Lake (see Three-Day Itinerary, Day Two).

Day Five

Head back up to the mountains again, and camp in Logan Canyon (see Three-Day Itinerary, Day Three).

Day Six

Drive down Logan Canyon to Logan. Visit the Jensen Historical Farm. This museum offers living-history displays of Utah farm life in the early 1900s. Pick up Highway 91 (it turns into Highway 89) and follow it to Brigham City. Stay off the freeway. Instead, continue on along Highway 89, known to locals at this point as Fruit Way. In the summer, visit fruit stands brimming with apricots, peaches, apples, and garden produce. Spend the night at Willard Bay State Park, on the beach of a diked-in, freshwater arm of the Great Salt Lake.

Day Seven

Spend a night on Antelope Island in the Great Salt Lake. From Willard Bay, take I-15 to the Syracuse and Antelope Island exit. Stop at the visitors center after driving across a causeway to the island. Acquaint yourself with the unusual and, to some, intimidating world of the Great Salt Lake. Visit the Fielding Garr ranch house, the oldest inhabited house in Utah. It was home to Mormon pioneers in the late 1800s when they took care of a large cattle herd on the island. Drive, hike, or bike the island. Look for the resident bison, pronghorn antelope, Rocky Mountain bighorn sheep, coyotes, and chukars (upland game birds). There is nothing like a dip in the Great Salt Lake. The salinity level varies, but it's usually high enough to allow easy floating with the feathery pink brine shrimp. Showers are available on the beach. Reservations are recommended for this small campground (801/773-2941). Come nightfall, either camp here or head for civilization in Davis County or Salt Lake.

1 Belmont Hot Springs

 1

Overnight amenities are somewhat limited at this resort, so it's really better for daytime visits, unless you have a self-contained RV. Tent sites are exposed, picnic tables are scarce, and the showers and restrooms are confined to the swimming-pool area, so it's port-a-potties only at night. The RV sites, more pleasantly situated on a hill above the resort, are cooler and command a tranquil valley view.

Location: In Plymouth; map A2, grid a1.

Campsites, facilities: There are 70 sites with full hookups and a grassy area for tents. Restrooms, showers, picnic tables, a video-game room, a snack shop, a nine-hole golf course, and a mineral hot pool are available.

Reservations, fees: Reservations are recommended. Sites are $15 for full hookups, $8 for RV parking without hookups and for tent camping.

Open: Apr.–mid-Oct.

Directions: From Brigham City, drive north on I-15 about 30 miles. Take exit 394, turn right after the exit, and drive past the truck stop. At the stop sign, turn right on State Route 13, go three miles, turn right at the sign for Belmont Hot Springs, and proceed another half mile to the resort.

Contact: Belmont Hot Springs, P. O. Box 36, Fielding, UT 84311; 435/458-3200.

2 High Creek

 6

High Creek (elevation 5,000 ft.) is a favorite with hikers, who like to take the trail that leads from here to another local campground called Tony Grove. It's also small enough to offer an escape from the weekend crowds—if you come early enough to get a site.

Location: Northeast of Richmond; map A2, grid a3.

Campsites, facilities: There are six sites for tents or RVs (but no hookups) with picnic tables, fire grills, and vault toilets, but no water.

Reservations, fees: Sites are free and are first come, first served.

Open: June–Sept.

Directions: From Logan, drive 14 miles north on Highway 91, past Richmond. Then head east on High Creek Road approximately four miles (the road eventually becomes Forest Road 48) to the campground, which is about 2.5 miles east of the forest boundary.

Contact: Logan Ranger District, 435/755-3620.

3 Smithfield Canyon

 6

Located in a shaded area by the river, this campground is largely paved, and the road is also paved all the way to the National Forest Service boundary. There's a communal area for group activities.

Location: In Smithfield Canyon; map A2, grid a3.

Campsites, facilities: There are six sites with picnic tables and fire pits. Vault toilets and drinking water are available.

Reservations, fees: Sites are $10 and are first come, first served.

Open: May 15–Sept. 15.

Directions: From Logan, drive north on Highway 91 to Smithfield, head northeast five miles on Smithfield Canyon Road, and take Forest Road 49 to the campground.

Contact: Logan Ranger District, 435/755-3620.

4 Bear Lake State Recreation Area

 6

This marina campground is right at the edge of turquoise-blue, 71,000-acre Bear Lake. Though the water can be on the chilly side, it's a popular place for boating, fishing, sailing, rafting and waterskiing, and two privately operated golf courses are not far away. Nearby Logan Canyon has hiking trails for short nature walks as well as all-day treks. In summer, when the raspberries are ripe, visitors pick their own or enjoy berry shakes and sundaes at one of the drive-in snack bars. All campsites are in the marina area, with a corresponding row of parking spaces in a lot by the beach. A grassy area separates the parking lot from the beach, where campers can also pitch their tents.

Location: On Bear Lake; map A2, grid a5.

Campsites, facilities: There are 15 lakeside campsites adjacent to a marina located in a sheltered harbor, with 176 boat slips and an 80-foot-wide concrete launching ramp. Handicapped-accessible restrooms and hot showers are also available. A park visitors center and marina sanitary disposal station are nearby.

Reservations, fees: Reservations are available up to three days in advance for a nonrefundable $6.25 fee per site; call 800/322-3770 Mon.–Fri. 8 A.M.–5 P.M. Sites are $13. Utah residents age 62 or older with a Special Fun Tag get a $2 discount Sun.–Thurs., excluding holidays.

Open: May 1–Oct. 1.

Directions: From Garden City on Highway 89, drive two miles north and look for the turnoff to Bear Lake. The marina and campground are next to the lake.

Contact: Bear Lake State Park Headquarters (open year-round), 435/946-3343.

⏚ Bear Lake KOA

 5

Located across the highway from Bear Lake, this grassy campground is in mostly open terrain, affording a good view of the sagebrush-covered mountains and the lake. The sites are rather close together, but amenities abound, including a gas station and a car wash, tennis and horseshoe facilities, and even miniature golf (for an extra charge).

Location: In Garden City; map A2, grid a5.

Campsites, facilities: There are 100 RV sites and 50 tent sites. Amenities include restrooms, showers, a video-game room, and a swimming pool.

Reservations, fees: Reservations, available year-round, are highly recommended in July and August. Sites with full RV hookups are $23.50 (subject to increase); smaller sites with water are $21.50.

Open: Open year-round, but call to be sure as bad weather or no business will close the KOA for a week or more at a time.

Directions: From Salt Lake City, take I-15 to Brigham City; then follow Highway 89 to Logan and continue on to Garden City and Bear Lake. Take Highway 89 north for one mile, toward the Bear Lake Marina. The KOA is on the north side of the road.

Contact: Bear Lake KOA, U.S. Hwy. 89, Garden City, UT 84028; 435/946-3454.

⏛ Sunrise

 5

The sites here are mostly out in the open on a hill overlooking Bear Lake, one of the state's most popular water-recreation areas, where anglers can fish for lake and cutthroat trout. Golf enthusiasts will find several golf courses nearby.

Location: In Garden City near Bear Lake; map A2, grid a5.

Campsites, facilities: There are 40 sites with water and electricity, picnic tables, and fire grills; restrooms and showers are available.

Reservations, fees: Reservations are accepted. Fees are $15–20, depending on the size of the site.

Open: Memorial Day–Labor Day.

Directions: From Salt Lake City, take I-15 to Brigham City; then take Highway 89 to Logan and continue on to Garden City and Bear Lake. Follow the highway north to the Bear Lake Marina. The campground is located just north of the marina on the west side of the road.

Contact: Sunrise Campground, 435/946-8620.

7 Bluewater Beach

     5

Like the other campgrounds on Bear Lake, this one isn't really much to look at: It's basically a gravel and grass parking lot surrounded by trees, with the sites themselves clumped very close together. The big draw here is the lake, with its scenic appeal and various water sports. The beach, where personal watercraft and boat rentals are available, is a short walk away, depending on the water level. There's also a basketball and a volleyball court on the premises, with a golf course across the street.

Location: In Garden City; map A2, grid a5.

Campsites, facilities: There are 140 sites; 50 have full RV hookups and 90 have water and electricity (for tents or RVs). Also available are restrooms, showers, laundry facilities, an RV disposal site, picnic tables, a lounge, barbecue grills, a swimming pool, a public phone, and volleyball and basketball courts. Some facilities are handicapped accessible.

Reservations, fees: Reservations are recommended in the summer. This is a private member campground with limited space for non-members, especially on busy weekends. Sites with full hookups are $29; all others are $25.

Open: May 29–Sept. 30.

Directions: From Salt Lake City, take I-15 north to Brigham City; then take Highway 89 to Logan and continue on to Garden City and Bear Lake. From there, take State Route 30 south for four miles to the campground.

Contact: Bluewater Beach Campground, 2126 S. Bear Lake Blvd., Garden City, UT 84028; 435/946-3333.

8 Sweetwater RV Park and Marina

    5

During summer, especially holiday weekends, this place is packed, notably with water buffs lured by the personal watercraft and boat rentals at the Ideal Beach Resort a quarter mile away. The campsites, too, are packed close together on what's basically a big patch of gravel and grass, and there's no beach.

Location: In Garden City on Bear Lake; map A2, grid a5.

Campsites, facilities: There are 24 sites for self-contained RVs only. No water or restrooms are available.

Reservations, fees: Reservations are recommended. Sites are $12.

Open: May–Sept.

Directions: From Salt Lake City, drive north on I-15 to Brigham City; then take Highway 89 to Logan and continue another 40 miles to Garden City, located on Bear Lake. Take the turnoff for State Route 30 south, drive past the Bluewater Beach Campground, and look left (east) for a large campground sign after a bend in the road.

Contact: Ideal Beach Resort, 435/946-2711.

9 Bear Lake Rendezvous Beach State Park

     6

Set in the midst of towering cottonwoods, this campground is the nicest on Bear Lake and tends to fill up fast, especially on summer weekends. Beach lovers come here to swim, build sand castles, and play sand volleyball or Frisbee. The Cottonwood section is set along a car-and-RV parking strip, with a grassy area separating the asphalt from the beach. Big Creek is bordered by a stream to the south and by Bear Lake to the north, and the vehicle back-ins and pull-throughs are on a paved loop that runs partly by the lake and partly under the trees.

Location: On Bear Lake; map A2, grid a5.

Campsites, facilities: There are 138 sites spread out among three different areas— Big Creek, Cottonwood, and

Willow—with handicapped-accessible restrooms, hot showers, and sewer and electrical hookups. Camping is adjacent to a 1.25-mile sandy beach, one of the longest stretches of public shorefront on Bear Lake. A concessionaire rents small boats.

Reservations, fees: Reservations are available 120 days in advance for a nonrefundable $6.25 per site; call 800/322-3770. The 46 full-hookup sites in the Big Creek campground are $19; at Cottonwood (60 sites) and Willow (32 sites), fees are $15. Utah residents 62 years and older with a Special Fun Tag get a $2 discount Sun.–Thurs., excluding holidays.

Open: May 1–Oct. 1, except Big Creek, which is open all year.

Directions: From Salt Lake City, follow the directions to the Bear Lake area (see Bear Lake State Recreation Area, page 57). Then, on State Route 30, drive just west of Laketown to the park entrance.

Contact: Bear Lake Rendezvous Beach State Park, 435/946-3343.

🔟 Bear Lake South Eden

    5

Located on Bear Lake's eastern, more primitive side, this place is a favorite with scuba divers as well as anglers looking for whitefish or cutthroat and lake trout. In January, fishing buffs also come with dip nets to catch the six-inch-long cisco, a sardinelike fish found only in Bear Lake (prompting locals to nickname these parts Cisco Beach). There's a 28-foot-wide concrete launch ramp for small fishing boats. Golfing, water-skiing, and rafting are allowed although concession facilities may not be available.

Location: On Bear Lake; map A2, grid a5.

Campsites, facilities: There are tent sites and 20 primitive campsites with handicapped-accessible vault toilets. There is no water.

Reservations, fees: Reservations are available 120 days in advance for a nonrefundable

$5 fee per site; call 800/322-3770 Mon.–Fri. 8 A.M.–5 P.M. Sites are $7. Utah residents 62 years and older with a Special Fun Tag get a $2 discount Sun.–Thurs., excluding holidays.

Open: Open year-round.

Directions: From Salt Lake City, follow the directions to the Bear Lake area (see Bear Lake State Recreation Area, page 57). Then, from State Highway 30, drive 10 miles north of Laketown on the narrow, unlabeled road that heads west along the east side of the lake.

Contact: Call the state park at 435/946-3343.

11 Western Park

 1

This campground, part of a suburban mobile-home park, consists of a few open spaces for overnighters on the gravel. In other words, if you're desperate for a place to spend the night, it's an option.

Location: In Logan; map A2, grid b2.

Campsites, facilities: There are 13 RV sites with water and electricity.

Reservations, fees: Reservations are available. Sites with water and electricity are $17.

Open: Open year-round.

Directions: In Logan, turn west off Main Street at 800 South. Go three blocks west, turn left at 300 West, and continue to 350 West and the campground.

Contact: Western Park Campground, 435/752-6424.

12 River Side RV Park and Campground

  2

This is yet another strangely located Logan RV park—basically a parking lot in an industrial part of the city. Small and out in the open, the sites consist of cement pads with grass in between. Again, it's only a good choice if you can't find a camping spot in the

nearby national forest or need to stay in town.

Location: In Logan; map A2, grid b2.

Campsites, facilities: There are 15 sites with full hookups, four sites with water and electricity only, and a grassy area for tents. The campground has handicapped-accessible restrooms, showers, laundry facilities, a couple of picnic tables, and a few barbecue grills in the tent area. No dogs weighing over 20 pounds are allowed.

Reservations, fees: Reservations are recommended on holidays. RV sites are $18.50 for full hookups or water and electricity; tent sites are $10.

Open: Open year-round.

Directions: Take Highway 89 to Logan, then follow Main Street to the south side of town. Just north of a warehouse on 1700 South, look for the sign and turn right. The campground is just past the railroad tracks on the left.

Contact: River Side RV Park and Campground, 435/245-4469.

13 Country Cuzzins RV Park

  1

Although stuck way at the back of a gas station, this RV park is also at the edge of town, so at least it's somewhat in the open with views of the mountains. The sites are strips of gravel surrounded by grass. The showers and restroom are next to the gas station's car wash. Again, it's a decent choice if you need to be in town.

Location: In Logan, map A2, grid b2.

Campsites, facilities: There are 26 sites with full hookups. Tent sites are on a grassy area. The park has a restroom, showers, laundry facilities, an RV disposal site, picnic tables, public phones, and a convenience/gift store.

Reservations, fees: Reservations are accepted. Campsites are $14.

Open: Open year-round.

Directions: In Logan, take Main Street to the north part of town. The park is at the junction of Highway 89 and Highway 91, behind the Phillips 66 gas station.

Contact: Country Cuzzins RV Park, 1936 N. Main St., Logan, UT 84341; 435/753-1025.

14 Wood Camp

   5

As with all campgrounds in narrow Logan Canyon, this one is close to the highway. Still, the place is situated amid tall deciduous trees, with a view of the river and the mountains. Sites are set along a row of pull-throughs, one right after the other, and there's a horse-unloading ramp for riding fans. This is basically an RV campground; site 6, however, is a good place for a tent. Anglers can fish for brown trout and planted rainbow trout nearby in the Logan River. West of the property, the Jardine Juniper Trail offers a short nature walk for hikers.

Location: In Wasatch-Cache National Forest; map A2, grid b3.

Campsites, facilities: There are seven sites with picnic tables and fire pits. Vault toilets are available, but there's no water.

Reservations, fees: Sites are $10 and are first come, first served.

Open: Apr.–Oct.

Directions: From Logan, drive 10.3 miles up Logan Canyon on Highway 89. The campground is on the left side of the road.

Contact: Logan Ranger District, 435/755-3620.

15 Lodge

 7

Located near the Logan River, this campground is a good place for anglers hoping to find trout in either the river or the impoundments adjacent to the property. It's also one of the smaller campgrounds in this scenic alpine setting (elevation 5,600 ft.).

Location: In Wasatch-Cache National Forest; map A2, grid b3.

Campsites, facilities: There are 10 sites, plus drinking water, vault toilets, picnic tables, and fire grills.

Reservations, fees: All sites are $10 and are first come, first served.

Open: Late May–mid-Sept.

Directions: From Logan, drive 12.7 miles east on Highway 89 in Logan Canyon to the campground.

Contact: Logan Ranger District, 435/755-3620.

16 Lewis M. Turner

    8

This forested campground is located near prime hiking country: the Mount Naomi Wilderness. There's also good canoeing on nearby Tony Grove Lake, and fishing fans can choose from either the lake or the nearby Logan River.

Location: In Wasatch-Cache National Forest; map A2, grid b3.

Campsites, facilities: There are 10 sites, plus picnic tables and fire pits. Flush toilets and water are available.

Reservations, fees: All sites are $10 and are first come, first served.

Open: July–Oct.

Directions: From Logan, follow Highway 89 about 19 miles up Logan Canyon. Take the turnoff to the Tony Grove Lake area.

Contact: Logan Ranger District, 435/755-3620.

17 Red Banks

   6

Named for the deep red-orange exposed earth of the mountain behind it, this campground is situated in an open area amid aspen trees. To the south, a rail fence affords views of a meadow and the mountains. The Logan River is a favorite with fly-fishing buffs. The pull-through sites are located near the river.

Location: In Wasatch-Cache National Forest; map A2, grid b3.

Campsites, facilities: There are 12 sites with picnic tables and fire pits. Water and vault toilets are available.

Reservations, fees: Sites are $10 and are first come, first served.

Open: May–Oct.

Directions: From Logan, take Highway 89 and go 20.2 miles up Logan Canyon. Look for the campground on the left side of the highway.

Contact: Logan Ranger District, 435/755-3620.

18 Tony Grove

   10

Reached by a seven-mile paved, winding, uphill road, Tony Grove Campground is surrounded by the high cliffs of a glacial cirque, near a picturesque forest and lake. There's a horse ramp on the premises for riders; for hikers, a parking lot serves as a trailhead for paths leading in several directions. A nature trail goes around the lake, which is popular for rafting and canoeing.

Location: In Wasatch-Cache National Forest; map A2, grid b3.

Campsites, facilities: There are 39 sites with picnic tables and fire pits. Tent camping is permitted. Drinking water and both flush and vault toilets are available.

Reservations, fees: Reservations are strongly recommended during summer; call the U.S. Forest Service National Reservation System at 800/280-2267. Sites are $12 for a single, $24 for a double.

Open: July–Oct.

Directions: From Logan, take Highway 89 19.2 miles up Logan Canyon. Take the turnoff to the Tony Grove Lake Area and continue for another seven miles to the campground.

Contact: Logan Ranger District, 435/755-3620.

Bridger

 9

Nicely located across the river and away from the highway, sites at this campground are set farther apart than most others in the Logan Canyon area. They're also well sheltered by the streamside vegetation and tall deciduous trees. Fishing in the Logan River is a favorite activity here. The road is paved and the campsites are on gravel.

Location: In Wasatch-Cache National Forest; map A2, grid b3.

Campsites, facilities: There are 10 sites with picnic tables and fire pits. Tent camping and RVs are permitted. Water and flush toilets are available.

Reservations, fees: All sites are $10 and are first come, first served.

Open: May–Oct.

Directions: From Logan, take Highway 89 3.3 miles up Logan Canyon. The campground is on the right side of the highway.

Contact: Logan Ranger District, 435/755-3620.

Spring Hollow

Spring Hollow is right on the highly fishable Logan River. Set at a lower elevation than other campgrounds along the river, this one sometimes gets a little wetter in rainy years, but its sites are also a bit farther apart. Some sites are better suited to RVs; others can accommodate tents.

Location: In Wasatch-Cache National Forest; map A2, grid b3.

Campsites, facilities: There are 12 sites with picnic tables and fire pits. Drinking water and both flush and vault toilets are available.

Reservations, fees: For reservations, call the U.S. Forest Service National Reservation System at 800/280-2267. Sites are $12.

Open: May–Oct.

Directions: From Logan, take Highway 89 4.3

miles up Logan Canyon. The campground is on the right side of the highway, just up the canyon from a broad, flat spot in the Logan River.

Contact: Logan Ranger District, 435/755-3620.

Guinavah-Malibu

This place is really two campgrounds: Guinavah is to the right as you turn off the highway, Malibu is to the left. Both have paved roads and gravel sites that are well spaced. In Guinavah, the sites are under tall cottonwood trees, and there's a bridge over the river; Malibu is in a more open, grassy area with broad, flat sites. In each facility, one loop is designated for tents and one for RVs, though some sites can accommodate either.

Location: In Wasatch-Cache National Forest; map A2, grid b3.

Campsites, facilities: There are 40 sites with picnic tables and fire pits. Water and flush toilets are available.

Reservations, fees: Reservations are strongly recommended for weekends during the summer; call the U.S. Forest Service National Reservation System at 800/280-2267. Sites are $12 for a single, $24 for a double.

Open: May 15–September.

Directions: From Logan, take Highway 89 5.3 miles up Logan Canyon. The campground is on the right side of the highway.

Contact: Logan Ranger District, 435/755-3620.

Sunrise

Nestled in a stand of aspen and pine trees, this is the last campground at the end of Logan Canyon, and the last U.S. Forest Service campground before you come to Bear Lake. Some Bear Lake fans stay here to enjoy the trees and high terrain, commuting to the lake for the fishing and water sports. Other campers like the proximity to the Limber Pine Trailhead, a popular hiking spot. The campground road and sites are paved, with relatively level pull-throughs and back-ins; the best tent sites are well spaced and set back from the road among the trees.

Location: In Wasatch-Cache National Forest; map A2, grid b3.

Campsites, facilities: There are 27 sites with picnic tables and fire pits. Water and vault toilets are available.

Reservations, fees: Reservations are strongly recommended during the summer; call the U.S. Forest Service National Reservation System at 800/280-2267. Sites are $12.

Open: June–Oct.

Directions: From Logan, take Highway 89 31 miles up Logan Canyon. The campground is on the right side of the highway.

Contact: Logan Ranger District, 435/755-3620.

23 Preston Valley

 7

Though the sites here are gravel and close together, they're nicely separated from each other by a screen of vegetation and conveniently located near the river and the paved road. The fishing is excellent. Hikers can pick up information about local trails in the Logan Ranger District office at the mouth of the canyon.

Location: In Wasatch-Cache National Forest; map A2, grid b3.

Campsites, facilities: There are nine sites with picnic tables and fire pits. Tent and RV sites, water, and flush toilets are available.

Reservations, fees: Sites are $10 and are first come, first served.

Open: May 15–Sept.

Directions: From Logan, drive 7.8 miles up

Logan Canyon on Highway 89. The campground is on the right side of the highway.

Contact: Logan Ranger District, 435/755-3620.

24 Friendship

 9

Friendship Campground is set on a gravel road in a canopy of maple trees, near the excellent fishing on the Left Fork of the Blacksmith Fork River. The gravel road is primitive but is usually passable in a two-wheel-drive vehicle.

Location: In Wasatch-Cache National Forest; map A2, grid b3.

Campsites, facilities: There are six sites with picnic tables, fire pits, and pit toilets, but no drinking water.

Reservations, fees: Sites are $6 and are first come, first served.

Open: May 15–Sept. 15.

Directions: From Hyrum, drive east on State Highway 101. Look for Forest Road 245, a gravel road heading north and east, and take it three miles to the campground.

Contact: Logan Ranger District, 435/755-3620.

25 Spring

 9

This out-of-the-way campground is surrounded by maple trees and located in a beautiful canyon near the Left Fork of the Blacksmith Fork River. Drive up the canyon to see the creatures and interpretive displays at the Utah Division of Wildlife's Hardware Ranch, where as many as 800 elk spend the winter.

Location: In Wasatch-Cache National Forest; map A2, grid b3.

Campsites, facilities: There are three sites with picnic tables, fire pits, and pit toilets, but no drinking water.

Reservations, fees: All sites are $6 and are first come, first served.

Open: May 15–Oct. 31.

Directions: From Hyrum, drive east on State Highway 101. Look for Forest Road 245, a gravel road heading north and east, and take it three miles to the campground.

Contact: Logan Ranger District, 435/755-3620.

26 Pioneer

   7

This campground has large, secluded sites under tall trees, on the eminently fishable Blacksmith Fork River. The road through the campground is unpaved and is not always RV-friendly. Sites 16 through 18 are not on a loop, and the road is too narrow to allow a large vehicle to turn around; the very private sites 3, 4, and 5, set on spurs, don't have much turnaround room either. Best bets for RVs are sites 6–15, set along a loop road.

Location: In Wasatch-Cache National Forest; map A2, grid b3.

Campsites, facilities: There are 18 sites with picnic tables and fire pits. Water and vault toilets are available.

Reservations, fees: Sites are $10 and are first come, first served.

Open: May–Oct.

Directions: In Hyrum, take State Route 101 to Hyrum State Park. Follow the signs to Hardware Ranch and turn off the highway at the sign to Pioneer Campground. The campground is nine miles from Hyrum.

Contact: Logan Ranger District, 435/755-3620.

27 Crystal Springs Resort

     5

Honeyville is a rural community, so campers here have a full view of the valley and the mountains to the east. The sites are in the open, with the camping area bordered by tall cottonwood trees; tents are in an area separate from the RVs. Restrooms are a short walk from the campground, and showers are part of the swimming complex. This resort's big attraction, the mineral pools, vary in temperature from cool to warm.

Location: In Honeyville; map A2, grid b1.

Campsites, facilities: The resort has 83 full hookups and a grassy area for tents, plus handicapped-accessible restrooms, showers, laundry facilities, picnic tables, a game room, a playground, and several mineral pools.

Reservations, fees: Reservations are recommended in the summer. Sites for full hookups are $18; tents are $9.

Open: Year-round.

Directions: From Brigham City, drive north on I-15 about 10 miles. Take exit 375 to Honeyville. Go east one mile to Highway 69 North. Take it north one mile to Crystal Hot Springs and continue for about three miles to the campground.

Contact: Crystal Springs Resort, 8215 N. Hwy. 38, Honeyville, UT 84314; 435/279-8104.

28 Hyrum State Park

    8

This campground is set partly in the open. In one section, sites overlook Hyrum Reservoir in a broad, high-mountain valley, and flush toilets are available. Another section has sites along a parking area near a grassy picnic spot, with vault toilets and stairs leading to the water. No matter where you sleep, the fishing for yellow perch and rainbow trout can be good here (even through the ice in the winter). The 470-acre reservoir is also a good spot for water skiing and power boating. Parents will appreciate the roped-off swimming beach near the day-use area. As a side trip, try driving 16 miles up Blacksmith Fork Canyon for more fishing and a look at the wildlife at Hardware Ranch. Kids should also enjoy the nearby Ronald Jensen Historical Farm on Highway 89/91.

Location: On Hyrum Reservoir; map A2, grid c2.

Campsites, facilities: There are 40 sites (most of them near the reservoir) and a group camping area where tents are permitted, plus a swimming beach, a boat-launching ramp, and modern restrooms, but no showers.

Reservations, fees: Reservations are available 120 days in advance for a nonrefundable $6 fee; call 800/322-3770 Mon.–Fri. 8 A.M.–5 P.M. Sites are $10. Utah residents age 62 and older with a Special Fun Tag get a $2 discount Sun.–Thurs., excluding holidays.

Open: Apr.–Oct.

Directions: Take Highway 89/91 between Logan and Brigham City. Turn east on State Route 101, and go about 19 miles toward the town of Hyrum. Follow the signs to the park, located on the city's southern limits.

Contact: Hyrum State Park, 435/245-6866.

29 Birch Creek

   5

The main attraction here is the fishing at Upper Birch Creek Reservoir, stocked with catchable rainbows by the Utah Division of Wildlife Resources. Canoeing on the flat reservoir is a peaceful pursuit. The campsites themselves are primitive and in an open, arid, sparsely vegetated setting.

Location: On Bureau of Land Management property near Upper Birch Creek Reservoir; map A2, grid c5.

Campsites, facilities: There are four sites plus overflow space for self-contained RVs. Pit toilets and seven picnic tables are available, but there is no water.

Reservations, fees: Sites are free and are first come, first served.

Open: Open year-round.

Directions: From Woodruff, take State Route 16 to State Route 39 and drive nine miles west. Look for the sign for the reservoirs on the north side of the highway.

Contact: Salt Lake City office of the Bureau of Land Management, 801/977-4300.

30 Golden Spike RV Park

 7

This campground has a grassy farmland setting, with open views and a few young, tall trees. Though right off the highway, it's protected by a barrier of vegetation. The restroom building is newer than most.

Location: In Brigham City; map A2, grid c1.

Campsites, facilities: There are 60 sites, 38 with full hookups, plus 20 for tents and two cabins. Also available are restrooms, showers, laundry facilities, an RV waste-disposal site, picnic tables, a hot tub, cable TV, a small convenience store, a putting green, and a swing set.

Reservations, fees: Reservations are accepted but not usually necessary. RV sites are $18–19, tent sites are $13–14, and cabins are $14–15.

Open: Open year-round.

Directions: From Ogden, take I-15 to the Brigham City turnoff, exit 364, and go east over the viaduct. Drive one mile east on Highway 89 to the campground, which is on the north side of the road.

Contact: Golden Spike RV Park, 905 W. 1075 South, Brigham City, UT 84302; 801/723-8858.

31 Brigham City KOA

    7

This campground is in an orchard and farmland setting, with some tall, venerable trees. There's a nice grassy area for tents, plus some pull-through sites in the middle. All sites are fairly close together.

Location: In Brigham City; map A2, grid c1.

Campsites, facilities: There are 55 sites, including 25 with full hookups and 25 with water and electricity only, plus a grassy area on the perimeter for tents. Most sites have barbecue grills. Also available are restrooms, showers, laundry facilities, an RV waste-disposal site, picnic tables, a game room, a convenience and gift store, and a playground. Wheelchair access is limited.

Reservations, fees: Reservations are recommended June through August. Sites with full hookups are $24.25, sites with water and electricity are $22.25, and tent sites are $18.
Open: Year-round.
Directions: From Salt Lake City, take I-15 north to Brigham City and get off at exit 364. Go east over the viaduct and east on Highway 89 to the light. Turn right and drive south for four miles. A KOA sign marks the turnoff to the campground, located a little farther down the road past the cherry orchards.
Contact: Brigham City KOA, P. O. Box 579, Brigham City, UT 84302; 435/723-5503.

32 Mountain Haven

    6

True to its name, this reservoir campground is in a high-mountain valley, in mostly unforested sagebrush country. Yet the property itself, surrounded by farmland, is grassy and shady. A trail leads from the campground up the hill to the water. To the north is a boat ramp campers can use for canoeing, fishing, and water skiing. Kids will especially like the selection of penny and nickel candy in the small store.
Location: On Mantua Reservoir; map A2, grid c2.
Campsites, facilities: There are 52 sites with full hookups, and a grassy area for tents. The campground has restrooms, showers, an RV waste-disposal site, picnic tables, barbecue grills, a public phone, a convenience and gift store, cable TV hookups, and a playground. Leashed pets are permitted.
Reservations, fees: Reservations are rec-

ommended, especially on summer weekends. All sites are $16.
Open: Apr.–Oct.
Directions: From Salt Lake City, take I-15 north and get off at the Brigham City exit; then take Highway 89 (which turns into Hwy. 91) and go four miles to Mantua Reservoir. The campground is on the west side of the reservoir.
Contact: Mountain Haven Campground, 830 N. Main St., Mantua, UT 84324; 435/723-1292.

33 Box Elder

  7

This is a little out-of-the-way campground on a stream, smack in the middle of tall cottonwoods and other stream-loving trees. Boating is popular on nearby Mantua Reservoir, and a side trip to the Mantua fish hatchery is a good bet with kids.
Location: In Wasatch National Forest; map A2, grid c3.
Campsites, facilities: There are 26 sites with picnic tables and fire pits. Vault toilets and water are available.
Reservations, fees: For reservations, call the U.S. Forest Service National Reservation System at 800/280-2267. Sites are $10.
Open: May 15–Sept. 30.
Directions: From Brigham City, take Highway 89 northeast to Mantua, get off at the Mantua exit, and turn right. Where the road comes to a T before entering the town, turn left and follow signs to the campground.
Contact: Ogden Ranger District, 801/625-5112.

34 Willard Basin

 8

This small, remote campground (elevation 9,000 ft.) is a favorite overnight stop for hikers planning to tackle the summit of 9,764-foot-high Willard

Peak, with its fantastic views of the Great Salt Lake.

Location: In Wasatch National Forest; map A2, grid c2.

Campsites, facilities: There are four tent sites with pit toilets, picnic tables, and fire grills, but no water.

Reservations, fees: Sites are free and are first come, first served.

Open: June–Oct.

Directions: From the town of Mantua, drive eight miles south on Forest Road 084 to the campground.

Contact: Ogden Ranger District, 801/625-5112.

35 Willard Bay North

      4

Boating is the number-one draw at this 9,900-acre freshwater reservoir, but the relatively low elevation (4,200 ft.) and proximity to Wasatch Front also make it a summer favorite with water-skiers and watercraft owners. And don't forget the fishing rods: Anglers can catch crappie and walleye, and ice-fishing fans will find the state park and some of its facilities open in winter. The campground itself is pleasantly shaded by trees, with paved road loops, covered picnic areas, and sandy beaches within walking distance.

Location: On the Great Salt Lake's Willard Bay; map A2, grid c2.

Campsites, facilities: There are 62 sites with no hookups. Facilities include picnic tables, fire grills, handicapped-accessible restrooms, hot showers, some covered areas, a dump station, fish-cleaning stations, beaches, a boat ramp, and boat-slip rentals during the season.

Reservations, fees: Reservations are available for a nonrefundable $6.25 per site; call 800/322-3770 Mon.–Fri. 8 A.M.–5 P.M. Sites are $12. Utah residents 62 years and older with a Special FunTag get a $2 discount Sun.–Thurs., excluding holidays.

Open: Early May–early Oct.

Directions: From Ogden, drive 15 miles north on I-15, looking for the Willard exit. Signs on the Interstate direct you to the campground, which is visible to the west.

Contact: Willard Bay State Park, 801/734-9494.

36 Willard Bay South

     4

This campground is located east of the tall dike that created 9,900-acre Willard Bay as a freshwater arm of the Great Salt Lake. Though there are some shade trees, Willard Bay South is more in the open than its neighbor to the north (see Willard Bay North). The bay is popular with water skiers, jet-skiers, and fishermen. The marina offers excellent boating close to the Wasatch Front. Those who enjoy picking through army surplus might want to stop at the nearby Smith & Edwards store.

Location: On the Great Salt Lake's Willard Bay; map A2, grid c2.

Campsites, facilities: There are 30 sites with no hookups. Facilities include picnic tables and fire pits, handicapped-accessible restrooms with flush toilets (but no showers), a boat ramp, and a small commercial marina.

Reservations, fees: Campsites are $12 and are first come, first served.

Open: Apr.–Oct.

Directions: From Ogden, drive eight miles north on I-15, then follow the signs to Willard Bay South, heading north and west on a paved road to the marina.

Contact: Willard Bay State Park, 801/734-9494.

37 Monte Cristo

  10

This is a magnificent setting high in the mountains—a haven of lush grass, wildflowers, and tall trees. The paved road has pull-throughs and back-ins; the sites (also paved) include some great places for tents and are spaced far apart. The privacy, together with the distance from the highway, makes this a quiet, reflective place to spend the night.

Location: In Wasatch National Forest near Ogden; map A2, grid c4.

Campsites, facilities: There are 45 sites with picnic tables and fire pits. Flush and vault toilets and water are available.

Reservations, fees: Sites are $9 and are first come, first served.

Open: July–Sept.

Directions: From Woodruff, drive 22 miles southwest on State Route 39.

Contact: Ogden Ranger District, 801/625-5112.

38 Botts

  4

Botts is your basic Forest Service campground, set along the banks of the South Fork of the Ogden River, but it makes a nice, quiet alternative to the more hectic campgrounds on nearby Pineview Reservoir. The graveled sites are shaded by cottonwood and box elder trees, and there's decent fishing in the river and at the reservoir.

Location: In Wasatch National Forest near Ogden; map A2, grid d3.

Campsites, facilities: There are six individual sites and one double with no hookups. Picnic tables, fire grills, drinking water, and vault toilets are available.

Reservations, fees: Sites are $10 and are first come, first served.

Open: May 15–Oct. 31.

Directions: From Ogden, drive east on State Highway 39 past Pineview Reservoir. The campground is on the south side of the road, 6.5 miles east of Huntsville.

Contact: Ogden Ranger District, 801/625-5112.

39 South Fork

  4

This is the largest of the campgrounds on the South Fork of the Ogden River, and as such is a popular summer spot for anglers and kids who like riding their inner tubes downstream. At an elevation of 5,200 feet, this is also a good place to see the changing fall colors of the oaks, maples, and aspens of the nearby canyon.

Location: In Wasatch National Forest near Ogden; map A2, grid c3.

Campsites, facilities: There are 35 single sites and eight double sites with picnic tables and fire pits. Vault toilets and drinking water are available.

Reservations, fees: Sites are $10 and are first come, first served.

Open: May 15–Oct. 31.

Directions: From Ogden, drive east on State Route 39 past Pineview Reservoir. The campground is on the south side of the road, seven miles east of Huntsville.

Contact: Ogden Ranger District, 801/625-5112.

40 Perception Park

   5

This might be Utah's best Forest Service campground for people with disabilities. The paved, wheelchair-accessible nature trail has signs in Braille; several fishing piers are wheelchair accessible as well. With its shady setting, high elevation (5,200 ft.), and proximity to the fishable South Fork of the Ogden River, this campground also has much to recommend it to families.

Location: In Wasatch National Forest near Ogden; map A2, grid c3.

Campsites, facilities: There are 24 individual sites and three group sites with picnic tables, fire grills, vault toilets, and a paved, wheelchair-accessible interpretive trail along the river. There is no water.

Reservations, fees: Reservations are available for some sites by calling the U.S. Forest Service National

Reservation System at 800/280-2267. Individual sites are $11. Group sites vary.
Open: May 15–Sept. 20.
Directions: From Ogden, drive east on State Highway 39. The campground is on the south side of the road, 7.5 miles east of Huntsville.
Contact: Ogden Ranger District, 801/625-5112.

Lower Meadows

 5

This small retreat is located by the highway next to the fishable South Fork of the Ogden River, under some towering cottonwood trees. At an elevation of 5,300 feet, Lower Meadows is popular with valley people hoping to escape the summer heat. It's also a fine place to spot elk, mule deer, and the occasional moose.
Location: In Wasatch National Forest near Ogden; map A2, grid c3.
Campsites, facilities: There are 19 individual sites and two double sites with picnic tables and fire grills. Drinking water and vault toilets are available.
Reservations, fees: Campsites are $10 and are first come, first served.
Open: May 15–Sept. 30.
Directions: From Ogden, drive east for about 16 miles on State Highway 39. The campground is eight miles east of Huntsville.
Contact: Ogden Ranger District, 801/625-5112.

42 Upper Meadows

  5

In the fall, this can be a spectacular place to camp; the maple, aspen, and oak trees typically begin to turn in mid-September. The 5,300-foot elevation also keeps things comfortable in summer yet relatively warm in spring and fall as well. Anglers can find whitefish and rainbow trout in the South Fork of the Ogden River.
Location: In Wasatch National Forest near Ogden; map A2, grid c3.

Campsites, facilities: There are eight sites with picnic tables and fire grills. Vault toilets and drinking water are available.
Reservations, fees: Sites are $8 and are first come, first served.
Open: May 15–Sept. 30.
Directions: From Ogden, drive east for about 16 miles on State Highway 39. The campground is eight miles east of Huntsville.
Contact: Ogden Ranger District, 801/625-5112.

43 Willows

  5

Of the cluster of Forest Service campgrounds in the area, this one, on the banks of the South Fork of the Ogden River, is the farthest from the city. That means it's slightly more remote than the others, though still popular on weekends. Wildlife watchers should keep an eye out for deer, elk, and even an occasional moose.
Location: In Wasatch National Forest near Ogden; map A2, grid c3.
Campsites, facilities: There are 12 sites with picnic tables and fire pits. Drinking water and vault toilets are available.
Reservations, fees: Sites are $10 and are first come, first served.
Open: May 15–Sept. 30.
Directions: From Ogden, drive east for about 16 miles on State Highway 39. The campground is eight miles east of Huntsville.
Contact: Ogden Ranger District, 801/625-5112.

44 Anderson Cove

      5

This campground, located close to the reservoir near the Wasatch Front, fills quickly on summer weekends, so be sure to make reservations. The main appeal is the warm water of 110,000-acre Pineview Reservoir, one of Utah's most popular boating and water-skiing lakes. And anglers will find that the crappie, bluegill, bullhead catfish, and yellow perch often bite fast, making this an ideal place to teach children how to fish. The reservoir has two boat ramps, two swimming areas, and nature trails, with golf nearby. Shade trees shelter many of the campsites.

Location: In Wasatch National Forest near Ogden; map A2, grid d3.

Campsites, facilities: There are 58 individual sites and two group sites with picnic tables and fire grills. Tents are permitted. Drinking water, vault toilets, and a dump station are available.

Reservations, fees: Reservations are recommended for summer weekends; call the U.S. Forest Service National Reservation System at 800/280-2267. Sites are $12.

Open: May 15–Sept. 30.

Directions: The campground is just off State Highway 39 on Pineview Reservoir, 2.5 miles southwest of Huntsville and about eight miles east of Ogden.

Contact: Ogden Ranger District, 801/625-5112.

45 Jefferson Hunt

 5

Located on the southeast corner of popular Pineview Reservoir, Jefferson Hunt fills fast, especially on weekends, so plan to arrive early. In addition to all the boating and fishing available in the area, campers can visit the nearby Trappist Monastery in Huntsville, where vespers and some other services are open to the public. The monks also sell flavored honey and fresh whole-wheat bread at a small visitors center.

Location: In Wasatch National Forest near Ogden; map A2, grid d3.

Campsites, facilities: There are 29 individual sites that are also suitable for families, with picnic tables and fire grills. Tents are permitted. Wheelchair-accessible vault toilets and drinking water are available.

Reservations, fees: Sites are $9 and are first come, first served.

Open: June–Sept.

Directions: The campground is north of State Highway 39, approximately nine miles east of Ogden and two miles southwest of Huntsville.

Contact: Ogden Ranger District, 801/625-5112.

46 Magpie

 5

Contrary to its name, this is a truly soothing place to camp, set in a riparian area along the South Fork of the Ogden River, amid the sound of flowing water and the shade of tall trees. The river is great for summer innertube trips and for fishing (especially in spring and fall, when the tubing traffic abates).

Location: In Wasatch National Forest near Ogden; map A2, grid d3.

Campsites, facilities: There are 27 individual sites and two double sites with picnic tables and fire grills. Vault toilets and drinking water are available.

Reservations, fees: Sites are $10 and are first come, first served.

Open: May 15–Oct. 31.

Directions: From Ogden, drive east for about 16 miles through Ogden Canyon on State Route 39. The campground is six miles east of Huntsville on the south side of the road.

Contact: Ogden Ranger District, 801/625-5112.

47 Hobble

 4

Campers will find only the basics at this small spot on the South Fork of the Ogden River (elevation 5,200 ft.), but it's just the ticket for anyone on a budget. Box elder and cottonwood trees shade the rather primitive sites, and drinking water can be obtained by visiting nearby Forest Service campgrounds. Look for deer and elk on the sides of the nearby canyons.

Location: In Wasatch National Forest near Ogden; map A2, grid d3.

Campsites, facilities: There are four sites with picnic tables, fire grills, and one vault toilet, but no drinking water.

Reservations, fees: Sites are $5 and are first come, first served.

Open: May 15–Oct. 31.

Directions: From Ogden, drive east on State Highway 39, through Ogden Canyon and past Pineview Reservoir. The campground is on the north side of the highway, six miles east of Huntsville.

Contact: Ogden Ranger District, 801/625-5112.

48 The Maples

  5

This campground is unpaved, on a loop just off the highway, with sites set close together under cottonwood trees. Some sites are pull-throughs, some are back-ins. Nearby is a fishable river. Water sports are available at Pineview Reservoir, about eight miles away.

Location: In Wasatch National Forest near Ogden; map A2, grid d3.

Campsites, facilities: There are 26 sites with picnic tables and fire grills. Vault toilets are available, but there's no drinking water.

Reservations, fees: Sites are free and are first come, first served.

Open: June–Oct.

Directions: From Ogden, drive east on State Route 39 through Ogden Canyon. Look for the turnoff to the Snowbasin Ski Area, and travel on the paved road approximately three miles to the campground.

Contact: Ogden Ranger District, 801/625-5112.

49 Century RV Park

   2

This campground is in a residential mobile-home park, with the permanent structures located near the back. But its outside-of-town location makes for a fairly rural setting.

Location: In Ogden; map A2, grid d2.

Campsites, facilities: There are 180 RV spaces, with a grassy area for tents, plus restrooms, showers, laundry facilities, an RV waste-disposal site, picnic tables, a game room, a swimming pool, two public phones, cable TV, a store with light groceries, and a playground.

Reservations, fees: Reservations are recommended in the summer. Sites are $25 with full hookups and $22 with water and cable. Tent sites are $17.

Open: Year-round.

Directions: In Ogden, take exit 346 off I-15, and go east on 2100 South. The campground is on the left side of the road at 1399 West 2100 South.

Contact: Century RV Park, 1399 W. 2100 S., Ogden, UT 84401; 801/731-3800.

50 Lost Creek State Park

   5

There's not much to this state park, located near the banks of the Lost Creek Reservoir in open terrain, other than the most basic facilities. But there is much to recommend if you like trout fishing. Because of the 6,000-foot elevation, the water stays cool well into the summer, keeping the fish active and hungry for bait.

Location: On Lost Creek Reservoir; map A2, grid d4.

Campsites, facilities: This is an undeveloped campground with a few scattered picnic tables, pit toilets, and a boat-launching ramp.

Reservations, fees: Campsites are free and are first-come, first served.

Open: Year-round.

Directions: From Morgan, travel north on I-84 to the Croyden exit. Follow the signs for about 10 miles to Lost Creek Reservoir, heading northeast on a county road that turns from pavement to dirt. The campground and boat ramp are located on the southeast part of the reservoir.

Contact: East Canyon State Park headquarters, 801/829-6866.

51 Circle L. Mobile Home Park

   1

This place definitely has the feel of a mobile-home park stuck in the middle of Main Street—and indeed, most of the RVs, parked on the blacktop at the end of the park, are permanent. The setting is well shaded. Still, campers can do better in the mountains nearby.

Location: In Layton; map A2, grid e2.

Campsites, facilities: There are four sites with full hookups and a grassy area for tents. The park has a restroom, showers, laundry facilities, an RV waste-disposal site, picnic tables, barbecue grills, and a playground.

Reservations, fees: Reservations are accepted. Campsites are $15.

Open: Year-round.

Directions: Traveling south from Ogden or north from Salt Lake City on I-15, get off at exit 332 in Layton. Turn north on Main Street and go over the viaduct and through the first light. The park is on the left at 229 Main Street.

Contact: Circle L. Mobile Home Park, 78 Layton Circle, Layton, UT 84041; 801/544-8945.

52 Antelope Island State Park

    9

This is the place for a wonderful experience on the Great Salt Lake. Swimmers off the white-sand beaches can float like a cork in the salty water. On the hiking, mountain-biking, and horseback-riding trails, campers can try to spot birds, or perhaps a member of the 800-strong herd of buffalo who call the park home. (For close-ups, check out the park's buffalo roundup in early November.) Another attraction is the Fielding Garr ranch house on the southwest corner of the island; open weekends during spring, summer, and fall, it's the oldest home still standing on its original foundation in the entire state. The park itself is an interesting place to visit in any season.

Location: On Antelope Island in the Great Salt Lake; map A2, grid e0.

Campsites, facilities: There are 26 individual sites and five large group camping areas, all with picnic tables, fire grills, and vault toilets, near a white-sand beach. There's also beach parking near covered picnic pavilions for self-contained trailers and RVs, plus a visitors center and restrooms with running water and showers.

Reservations, fees: For single sites, call 800/322-3770. For group sites, call the park directly at 801/773-2941. Sites are $10 per vehicle per night, including a $7 park-entrance fee.

Open: Year-round.

Directions: Traveling south from Ogden or north from Salt Lake City on I-15, take the Syracuse exit, then turn onto Gentile Drive. Drive west for nine miles and cross to the island on a paved 7.5-mile causeway.

Contact: Antelope Island State Park, 801/773-2941.

53 Cherry Hill

 4

The Cherry Hill campground is more like a bona fide resort. Though the grassy sites are close together, there's a full-scale water park, facilities for miniature golf and arrowball (a trampoline game with elements of volleyball and basketball), batting cages, a children's play area called Hamster Haven, two snack bars, a restaurant, and a group pavilion. And if that's not enough, it's all located just north of Lagoon, Utah's largest amusement park, with myriad roller coasters, assorted rides, a huge water park, and historical Pioneer Village.

Location: In Kaysville; map A2, grid e2.

Campsites, facilities: There are 240 sites, including 119 with full hookups, 40 with water and electricity, 17 with electricity only, and 59 without hookups. Also available are restrooms, showers, laundry facilities, an RV disposal site, picnic tables, two game rooms, a public phone, a pool, a convenience and gift store, a playground, a group picnic pavilion, and rentable barbecue grills. The restrooms are wheelchair accessible; the showers are not.

Reservations, fees: Reservations are recommended, especially on weekends and holidays. Sites with full hookups are $24, sites with water and electricity are $22, and tent sites are $19. Groups of more than two pay an additional $1.50 per person.

Open: Apr.–Oct.

Directions: From Salt Lake City, drive north on I-15 to Kaysville. Get off at exit 326 and take Highway 89 two miles north. The campground is on the left side of the highway.

Contact: Cherry Hill Campground, 1325 S. Main St., Kaysville, UT 84037; 801/451-5379.

54 Sunset

  9

Set in a narrow, forested canyon along a popular scenic drive, this campground (elevation 6,400 ft.) is a pretty place to watch the changing fall colors and escape the hype and the hordes at the huge Lagoon amusement park west of Farmington.

Location: In Wasatch National Forest near Farmington; map A2, grid e3.

Campsites, facilities: There are 10 sites with picnic tables, fire grills, and vault toilets, but no water.

Reservations, fees: Sites are $6. Addition-

al vehicles are $3. Sites are first come, first served.

Open: June–Sept.

Directions: Take the Farmington exit off I-15 between Ogden and Salt Lake City. Drive through Farmington and head four miles northeast of town on Forest Road 007 to the campground.

Contact: Wasatch-Cache National Forest Supervisor's Office, 801/524-5030.

55 Bountiful Peak

  9

This campground is located at an elevation of 7,500 feet in a beautiful, wooded area near the top of Bountiful Peak, which overlooks Davis County north of Salt Lake City. The chief draw here is the spectacular drive, which takes travelers from the valley bottom to the top of the mountains, offering fantastic views of the Great Salt Lake to the west. This is an especially scenic place to view the changing foliage of fall.

Location: In Wasatch National Forest near Farmington; map A2, grid e3.

Campsites, facilities: There are 26 individual sites and one group site with picnic tables and fire grills, a trailhead for motorized recreation, vault toilets, and drinking water.

Reservations, fees: Individual sites are $8. Additional vehicles are $3. Everything is first come, first served. For group-site information, call 801/524-5030.

Open: June 15–Sept. 7.

Directions: From Bountiful, go east on Forest Road 279 to Forest Road 008 (or, from Farmington, go northeast on Forest Road 007 until it becomes Forest Road 008) and continue to the campground. The campground is located about 9.3 miles northeast of Farmington.

Contact: Wasatch-Cache National Forest Supervisor's Office, 801/524-5030.

56 East Canyon State Park

 8

This is a popular summer destination for Salt Lake City folks wanting to get out on the reservoir with their water skis, powerboats, or personal watercraft. Fishing can also be good, especially in spring or fall when there aren't as many boats. Though camping shuts down in the fall, the park itself is open year-round and is popular with ice fishers.

Location: On East Canyon Reservoir; map A2, grid e3.

Campsites, facilities: There are 31 sites with no hookups near a 680-acre reservoir. Picnic tables, fire grills, and modern restrooms with running water and showers are available, along with covered group picnic areas, a fish-cleaning station, a concrete boat-launching ramp, a concessionaire, boat and personal watercraft rentals, groceries, and a small snack bar.

Reservations, fees: Reservations are available 120 days in advance for a nonrefundable $6.50 fee; call 800/322-3770 Mon.–Fri. 8 A.M.–5 P.M. Sites are $12. Utah residents 62 years and older with a Special Fun Tag get a $2 discount Sun.–Thurs., excluding holidays.

Open: Year-round, with camping available Apr. 1–Oct. 15.

Directions: From Salt Lake City, take I-80 east to State Route 65 and follow it to the campground. From Morgan, travel 12 miles south on State Route 65.

Contact: East Canyon State Park, 801/829-6866.

57 Echo Resort on Echo Reservoir

 2

Fishing and water-skiing are the prime attractions here. The camping quarters are rather close. Trailers are packed together as tightly as possible, though in late summer campers can pitch tents on the beach whenever the water retreats. The picnic area is pleasantly shaded. The South Beach, located south of the main area, has pit toilets, no tables, and generally limited facilities; it's basically a place to park an RV or pitch a tent. This spot is the end of the historic Union Pacific Rail Trail, a 27-mile-long former rail bed originating in Park City that's now popular with mountain bikers, hikers, and horseback riders.

Location: On the Echo Reservoir; map A2, grid e5.

Campsites, facilities: This is essentially a trailer park with some dispersed camping. Facilities include eight sites with full hookups, restrooms with showers, a grassy picnic area, a snack bar, and a boat-launching ramp.

Reservations, fees: Reservations are accepted. Sites are $9 per person.

Open: Memorial Day–Labor Day.

Directions: From Salt Lake City, take I-80 east and look for the turnoff to Echo Reservoir, before the junction with I-84. Then take the small road east to the east side of the reservoir.

Contact: Echo Resort, 435/336-9894.

58 Holiday Hills

 6

Except for the campground at Echo Reservoir (see above), this is the only private campground in the area that isn't for members only. As with many private campgrounds, the sites are close together. On the plus side, the setting is a broad, high-mountain valley that's pleasantly scenic and usually cool. While the property is not especially woodsy, some tall cottonwood and birch trees do provide shade. And for anglers, there's ready access to the Weber River.

Location: In Coalville; map A2, grid e5.

Campsites, facilities: There are about 40 sites for RVs and tents, with full hookups, restrooms, showers, laundry facilities, a swimming pool, a public phone, a communal covered picnic area, and a gas station/grocery store.

Reservations, fees: Reservations are recommended. Sites with full hookups are $19; tent sites are $12.

Open: Year-round.

Directions: From Salt Lake City on I-80, take the Coalville turnoff (exit 164). The campground is just west of the interstate.

Contact: Holiday Hills Campground, 500 W. 100 S., Coalville, UT 84017; 435/336-4421.

59 Great Salt Lake State Park

  7

This campground offers the closest access to the Great Salt Lake from Salt Lake City, so it's heavily used. The large beach leads to a shallow portion of the lake, where the gradual drop-off forces swimmers to walk several hundred yards before reaching waist-deep water. Sailing is popular, as are concerts and dances at Saltair. Traffic noise from I-80 can be a distraction to campers.

Location: On the Great Salt Lake; map A2, grid f2.

Campsites, facilities: There are 25 sites near a sandy beach, with outdoor showers, modern restrooms, and picnic tables, and a 240-slip marina and boat ramp nearby. Nearby Saltair Resort features a county-operated visitors center, souvenir shops, and camel rides.

Reservations, fees: Sites are $10 and are first come, first served. Utah residents 62 and older with a Special Fun Tag get a $2 discount Sun.–Thurs., excluding holidays.

Open: Apr.–Oct.

Directions: Drive 16 miles west of Salt Lake City on I-80 and take the exit to the park.

Contact: Great Salt Lake State Park, 801/250-1898.

60 Lagoon Pioneer Village

   4

The main attraction here is Lagoon—the second-oldest family-owned amusement park in the United States. It has kept up with the times and adds something new almost every year. Along with its several roller coasters, midway, assorted rides, and special ride area for kids, the place offers musical entertainment, a large water-slide park, and historical Pioneer Village, a collection of pioneer-era buildings and artifacts from around the state. The campground itself, grassy and well shaded with closely spaced sites, is smackdab between a horse corral and an old and rather noisy wooden roller coaster.

Location: In Farmington; map A2, grid f2.

Campsites, facilities: There are 209 sites; 44 have full hookups, 49 have water and electricity, 69 are for tents; 46 are pull-throughs with full hookups. The campground has restrooms, showers, laundry facilities, an RV waste-disposal site, picnic tables, a public phone, and a convenience and grocery store.

Reservations, fees: Reservations are recommended June–Sept. Sites with full hookups are $23.50, sites with pull-throughs are $22, sites with water and electricity are $17, and tent sites are $14. Groups of more than two pay an additional $1 for each extra person over age four, and another $1.50 for each additional vehicle per site.

Open: Apr.–Oct.

Directions: From Salt Lake City, go north on I-15 and take exit 325. Follow the signs to Lagoon and turn right through the stone pillars to the campground.

Contact: Lagoon Pioneer Village Campground, P. O. Box 269, Farmington, UT 84025; 801/451-8100 or 800/748-5296 ext. 3100.

picnic tables and fire pits. Tent sites, drinking water, and vault toilets are available. A boat ramp and dump station are nearby.

Reservations, fees: Reservations are available 120 days in advance for a nonrefundable $6 per site; call 800/322-3770 Mon.–Fri. 8 A.M. –5 P.M. Sites are $8.

Open: May 10–Sept. 15.

Directions: From Salt Lake City, drive 45 miles east on I-80, past the Park City and Heber City exits. Take the Wanship exit and drive four miles south on State Route 189. Enter the state park on the south end of Rockport Reservoir, crossing the Weber River. The campground is located on the northeast part of the reservoir, on a paved road.

Contact: Rockport State Park, 435/336-2241.

67 Pinery

 5

The wide-open spaces at this campground near Wanship Reservoir should appeal to folks who don't like regimented, commercialized camping. When it's uncrowded, the grassy turf is an ideal place to toss Frisbees; when other campgrounds are crowded, this one makes a good overflow spot.

Location: In Rockport State Park; map A2, grid f5.

Campsites, facilities: This campground permits tent camping and consists of an open field with no designated sites. Vault toilets, fire pits, and a few scattered picnic tables are available.

Reservations, fees: Campsites are $8 and are first come, first served.

Open: May 10–Sept. 15.

Directions: From Salt Lake City, drive 45 miles east on I-80, past the Park City and Heber City exits. Take the Wanship exit and drive four miles south on State Route 189. Enter the state park on the south end of Rockport Reservoir, crossing the Weber

River. The campground is located on the northeast part of the reservoir, on a paved road.

Contact: Rockport State Park, 435/336-2241.

68 Crandall's

 5

Most state park campgrounds next to reservoirs are large, but this one in Rockport State Park is a nice small-scale alternative. Still, the size and first-come, first-served policy means it fills up with campers early in the day, especially on weekends. There's excellent boating and fishing at the reservoir nearby, as well as on the Weber River, which is stocked regularly with rainbow trout.

Location: In Rockport State Park; map A2, grid f5.

Campsites, facilities: There are five sites with picnic tables, fire pits, and a pit toilet. There is no water.

Reservations, fees: Sites are $8 and are first come, first served.

Open: May 10–Sept. 15.

Directions: From Salt Lake City, drive 45 miles east on I-80, past the Park City and Heber City exits. Take the Wanship exit and drive four miles south on State Route 189. Enter the state park on the south end of Rockport Reservoir, crossing the Weber River. The campground is located on the northeast part of the reservoir, on a paved road.

Contact: Rockport State Park, 435/336-2241.

69 Hailstone

 8

This might be the best campground of its kind in the state-park system, and it's also one of the largest. It offers walk-in sites for tent campers, hookups for large

RVs, and everything in between. The sites are in somewhat open terrain with good views of the reservoir. Because Hailstone is so close to Park City and Salt Lake City, however, it can get pretty crowded. Rangers limit the boats on the water to 300 at a time. There's an excellent day-use area and beach, and rainbow-trout fishing is one of the most popular activities. The park isn't far from the historic Union Pacific Rail Trail State Park, a 28-mile mountain-biking, horseback-riding, and walking trail.

Location: On Jordanelle Reservoir; map A2, grid f5.

Campsites, facilities: There are 230 sites with water and electricity, plus modern restrooms, showers, laundry facilities, a dump station, a park visitors center, sandy beaches, group-use picnic areas, sun shelters, an 80-slip boat marina with utility hookups, a boat fuel dock, a general store, a restaurant, and three play areas for children.

Reservations, fees: Reservations are available 120 days in advance for a nonrefundable $6 per site; call 800/322-3770 Mon.–Fri. 8 A.M.–5 P.M. Sites are $17. Utah residents 62 and older with a Special Fun Tag get a $2 discount Sun.–Thurs., excluding holidays.

Open: Apr.–Oct.

Directions: From Heber City, drive six miles north on Highway 40. The campground is just east of the highway on the west shore of Jordanelle Reservoir.

Contact: Jordanelle State Park, 435/649-9540.

70 Rock Cliff
8

This is a nice, quiet, shady spot for tent campers hoping to get away from RVs. Fishing and water skiing are big on the Provo River or on nearby Jordanelle Reservoir, and hikers like the 17-mile trail around the reservoir. Check with park headquarters for special events associated with the nature cen-

ter, one of the newest in Utah. All campsites are walk-in; many have covered picnic tables.

Location: On the Provo River in Jordanelle State Park; map A2, grid f5.

Campsites, facilities: This is primarily a tent-camping area with 50 walk-in sites. Other facilities include modern restrooms with showers, a nature center, boardwalk nature trails, and a small-boat access ramp.

Reservations, fees: Reservations are available 120 days in advance for a nonrefundable $6 per site; call 800/322-3770 Mon.–Fri. 8 A.M.–5 P.M. Sites are $13. Utah residents 62 and older with a Special Fun Tag get a $2 discount Sun.–Thurs., excluding holidays.

Open: May 15–Oct. 15.

Directions: From Francis, drive two miles west on State Route 32. A sign points the way to the campground, which is located in a clump of trees down the hill next to the Provo River.

Contact: Jordanelle State Park, 435/783-3030.

71 Yellow Pine RV
  5

Yellow Pine is the first and lowest-elevation campground (7,200 ft.) on what is called the Mirror Lake Scenic Byway. That means it's less crowded than other campgrounds in this area and has a longer season, particularly since higher elevations can have snow on the ground until July. A dirt road services the facility. Tall conifers grace the upper part of the campground. Beaver Creek, which is located across the highway, is a decent stream-fishing spot. Horseback riders and all-terrain-vehicle enthusiasts will find a trailhead less than a mile to the west.

Location: In Wasatch National Forest near Kamas; map A2, grid f5.

Campsites, facilities: There are 33 sites; 10 of these are pull-throughs. Vault toilets, picnic tables, and fire pits are available. There is no water.

Reservations, fees: Sites are $6, $3 for each additional vehicle, and are first come, first served.

Open: June–Oct.

Directions: From Kamas, take State Route 150 east for 6.8 miles. The campground is on the north side of the highway.

Contact: Kamas Ranger District, 435/783-4338.

72 Beaver Creek

    6

At this campground on the Mirror Lake Scenic Byway, sites are set along Beaver Creek in an open meadow with tall grass, wildflowers, willows, and a few trees. The creek, traversed by a small bridge, offers plenty of good fishing. Hikers can stroll by the creek or in the mountains nearby. The road and sites are unpaved.

Location: In Wasatch National Forest near Kamas; map A2, grid g5.

Campsites, facilities: There are 14 sites; five of these are pull-throughs. There is no water, but vault toilets, picnic tables, and fire pits are available.

Reservations, fees: Sites are $6, plus $3 for each additional vehicle, and are first come, first served.

Open: June–Oct.

Directions: From Kamas, take State Route 150 east. Beaver Creek is 8.4 miles from town on the south side of the highway.

Contact: Kamas Ranger District, 435/783-4338.

73 Taylor Fork

   6

This campground off the Mirror Lake Scenic Byway is a staging area for all-terrain vehicles: The ATV trail here is the best in northern Utah, and the west end is a parking lot with special ramps for loading and unloading ATVs from trailers or trucks. The roads are dirt. The unpaved, well-shaded, generously

spaced campsites are dispersed along Beaver Creek and have views of the meadow and creek. Fishing is excellent on the creek and in the old beaver pond at the campground's east end.

Location: In Wasatch National Forest near Kamas; map A2, grid f6.

Campsites, facilities: There are 11 sites with picnic tables and fire pits. Water and vault toilets are available.

Reservations, fees: Sites are $10, plus $5 for each additional vehicle, and are first come, first served.

Open: June–Oct.

Directions: From Kamas, drive 9.1 miles east on State Route 150. The campground is on the south side of the highway.

Contact: Kamas Ranger District, 435/783-4338.

74 Shingle Creek

   6

This campground contains the trailhead to Shingle Creek Lake, which, along with nearby Shingle Creek to the north, is a popular fishing spot. An ATV trail takes off from the western end of the campground. The main road and sites are dirt, and half of the loop faces Beaver Creek. The sites themselves are not very level, but in the plus department, the vault toilets are newer than most in the area, and the picnic tables in the upper loop are set back from the road. As with most campgrounds on the Mirror Lake Scenic Byway, this one fills almost every summer weekend.

Location: In Wasatch National Forest near Kamas; map A2, grid f6.

Campsites, facilities: There are 21 sites, nine of them pull-throughs, plus picnic tables and fire pits. Water and vault toilets are available.

Reservations, fees: Sites are $11, plus $6 for each additional vehicle, and are first come, first served.

Open: June–Oct.

Directions: From Kamas, drive 9.5 miles east on State Route 150. The campground is on the south side of the highway.

Contact: Kamas Ranger District, 435/783-4338.

Lower Provo

 7

The best thing about this campground is that it's off the well-traveled Mirror Lake Scenic Byway. Also, the sites here are larger and flatter than their local counterparts, so they're especially hospitable to tents, and tall conifers provide pleasant shade. Hikers can enjoy the nearby High Uintas Wilderness Area, and fishing is decent in the Lower Provo River, which is usually well stocked with rainbow trout.

Location: In Wasatch National Forest near Kamas; map A2, grid g6.

Campsites, facilities: There are 10 sites with picnic tables and fire pits. Water and vault toilets are available.

Reservations, fees: For reservations, call the U.S. Forest Service National Reservation System at 800/280-2267. Sites are $10, plus $5 for each additional vehicle.

Open: June–Oct.

Directions: From Kamas, drive 10.7 miles east on State Route 150, and look for the sign on the right side of the highway. The campground is three-quarters of a mile down a dirt road south of the highway.

Contact: Kamas Ranger District, 435/783-4338.

Soapstone

 8

This is the first paved campground you come to when heading east on the Mirror Lake Scenic Byway. Located here are trailheads for four-wheel-drive roads to Wolf Creek Road, Soapstone Basin, and the Soapstone summer-home area about a mile to the west.

The relatively level campsites, shaded by conifers, face the Provo River, a good hiking and fishing spot. Other nice touches: several large picnic tables and ample parking space at each site.

Location: In Wasatch National Forest near Kamas; map A2, grid g6.

Campsites, facilities: There are 34 sites with picnic tables and fire pits. Water and vault toilets are available.

Reservations, fees: Some reservations are available; call the U.S. Forest Service National Reservation System at 800/280-2267. Sites are $12, plus $6 for each additional vehicle.

Open: June 15–Sept. 15.

Directions: From Kamas, drive 15.8 miles east on State Route 150. The campground is on the south side of the highway.

Contact: Kamas Ranger District, 435/783-4338.

Shady Dell

 7

This campground on the Mirror Lake Scenic Byway has great views of the Uinta Mountains and highly fishable Provo River. Sites next to the river are in open country and surrounded by pine and aspen trees. Roads and sites are paved, with some pull-throughs and room for extra vehicles.

Location: In Wasatch National Forest near Kamas; map A2, grid g7.

Campsites, facilities: There are 20 sites with picnic tables and fire pits. Water and vault toilets are available.

Reservations, fees: Sites are $12, plus $6 for additional vehicles, and are first come, first served.

Open: June 8–Sept. 15.

Directions: From Kamas, drive 17.3 miles east on State Route 150. The campground is on the south side of the highway.

Contact: Kamas Ranger District, 435/783-4338.

78 Cobblerest

   6

Sites are paved and relatively level, but they're also tightly spaced at this wooded campground on the Mirror Lake Scenic Byway. Many sites can accommodate long RVs. Each loop of the paved road offers visitors a number of pull-through sites. The campground's Provo River location makes for decent hiking and fishing.

Location: In Wasatch National Forest near Kamas; map A2, grid g7.

Campsites, facilities: There are 18 sites with picnic tables and fire pits. Water and vault toilets are available.

Reservations, fees: Sites are $11, plus $6 per extra vehicle, and are first come, first served.

Open: June 15–Sept. 15.

Directions: From Kamas, drive 19.1 miles east on State Route 150. The campground is on the south side of the highway.

Contact: Kamas Ranger District, 435/783-4338.

79 Trial Lake

 8

The postcard setting—less than a stone's throw from Trial Lake on the Mirror Lake Scenic Byway—makes this a real find. High above the tree line, gray, majestic Bald Mountain overlooks the conifer-rimmed lake behind Trial Lake Dam. The main through-road is paved, and some of the camping is so close to the water that campers can fish from their site. Anglers can also use a lakeside parking lot near the campground entrance. The water is heavily stocked with rainbow trout (though it's also heavily fished), and the trail leading from here to other lakes is a favorite with hikers. Nonmotorized boats and rafting are allowed. Visitors like to use inflatable rafts or canoes to fish or just enjoy the scenery. Due to the 10,000-foot elevation, this place opens late in the summer.

Location: In Wasatch National Forest near Kamas; map A2, grid g7.

Campsites, facilities: There are 60 sites, with four pull-throughs, plus picnic tables and fire pits. Facilities include water and handicapped-accessible vault toilets.

Reservations, fees: For reservations, call the U.S. Forest Service National Reservation System at 800/280-2267. Sites are $12, plus $6 for each extra vehicle.

Open: June 26–Sept. 10.

Directions: From Kamas, drive 25.7 miles east on State Route 150. The campground is a quarter mile off the highway on the north side of the road.

Contact: Kamas Ranger District, 435/783-4338.

80 Lilly Lake

   8

Located between small Lilly Lake and Teapot Lake, this loop campground on the Mirror Lake Scenic Byway has some sites overlooking the water, but most are up on higher ground. The campground, with a paved road and pads, is at 9,800 feet—almost tree line—so lake visitors have picture-perfect views of the surrounding tall conifers and the bare mountains looming dramatically to the east. Inflatable rafts and canoes are popular here; so is fishing the well-stocked waters from the shore.

Location: In Wasatch National Forest near Kamas; map A2, grid g7.

Campsites, facilities: There are 14 sites with tent site, picnic tables, and fire pits. Water and vault toilets are available.

Reservations, fees: Sites are $11, plus $6 for extra vehicles, and are first come, first served.

Open: June 26–Sept. 10.

Directions: From Kamas, drive 26.7 miles east on State Route 150. The campground is on the north side of the highway.

Contact: Kamas Ranger District, 435/783-4338.

81 Lost Creek

   8

At 10,000 feet up, this campground on the Mirror Lake Scenic Byway is late to open, but you can't beat the scenery. Lost Creek flows past on the east, Lost Lake is to the west, and the sites are set amid tall conifer trees. The road is paved and the loops are separated by pretty meadows. Local lake fishing is excellent, and use a canoe or raft on this small lake. There's plenty of hiking in the nearby High Uintas Wilderness Area.

Location: In Wasatch National Forest near Kamas; map A2, grid f7.

Campsites, facilities: There are 34 sites with tent sites, picnic tables, and fire pits. Water and vault toilets are available.

Reservations, fees: For reservations, call the U.S. Forest Service National Reservation System at 800/280-2267. Sites are $11, plus $6 for extra vehicles.

Open: June 26–Sept. 10.

Directions: From Kamas, drive 26.9 miles east on State Route 150. The campground is on the east side of the highway.

Contact: Kamas Ranger District, 435/783-4338.

82 Mirror Lake

    10

This cool, woodsy, high-country campground (elevation 10,200 ft.) is the largest on the Mirror Lake Scenic Byway and is designed in a series of several loops not far from the lake itself. Surrounding the place are the high Uintas peaks, Bald Mountain, and Hayden Peak. Rafts, canoes, and nonmotorized boats are popular with anglers and nature-watchers, and a trail around the lake offers decent hiking. A small amphitheater occasionally hosts interpretive programs on weekends. Facilities for the disabled are the best in the area.

Location: In Wasatch National Forest near Kamas; map A2, grid f7.

Campsites, facilities: This handicapped-accessible campground has 85 sites with tent sites, picnic tables, and fire pits, plus vault toilets, water, and a boat ramp.

Reservations, fees: For reservations, call the U.S. Forest Service National Reservation System at 800/280-2267. Sites are $12, plus $6 for each extra vehicle.

Open: July–Nov.

Directions: From Kamas, drive east for 31.5 miles on State Route 150. The campground is on the east side of the lake, a quarter mile from the highway.

Contact: Kamas Ranger District, 435/783-4338.

83 Moosehorn

   8

The view from here is superb: at a timberline elevation of 10,400 feet, it's right at the base of majestic Bald Mountain, next to glacier-carved Moosehorn Lake. Both the road and sites are unpaved. This is one of the last campgrounds to open on the Mirror Lake Scenic Byway, and one of the coolest in summer.

Location: In Wasatch National Forest near Kamas; map A2, grid f7.

Campsites, facilities: There are 33 sites with picnic tables and fire pits. Water and vault toilets are available.

Reservations, fees: For reservations, call the U.S. Forest Service National Reservation System at 800/280-2267. Sites are $10, plus $5 for extra vehicles.

Open: July 1–Sept. 7.

Directions: From Kamas, drive east for 30.8 miles on State Route 150. The campground is on the west side of the highway.

Contact: Kamas Ranger District, 435/783-4338.

84 Butterfly

   9

Some sites at this Mirror Lake Scenic Byway

campground (elevation 10,300 ft.) overlook a pretty little lake; all are unpaved and nestled amid tall conifers. Many picnic tables are set far back from the road for more privacy; from that vantage point, campers can gaze up along Hayden Peak and the range leading north—an experience akin to looking down a row of giant pyramids. The Highline Trail, a major hiking artery of the High Uintas, takes off to the east just across the highway. Anglers can use a parking lot near the entrance. Rafts, canoes, and nonmotorized boats are allowed for fishing or recreation. Butterfly opens late because of the high elevation, but it's worth the wait.

Location: In Wasatch National Forest near Kamas; map A2, grid f7.

Campsites, facilities: There are 20 sites with tent sites, picnic tables, and fire pits. Vault toilets and water are available.

Reservations, fees: Sites are $10, plus $5 for each additional vehicle, and are first come, first served.

Open: July–Nov.

Directions: From Kamas, drive 34.2 miles east on State Route 150. The campground is on the west side of the highway.

Contact: Kamas Ranger District, 435/783-4338.

85 Sulphur

 9

Since not very many campers venture past Mirror Lake, this remote campground on the Mirror Lake Scenic Byway is sometimes less crowded than the others. The sites are also farther apart here—a definite plus—with many flat areas for tents and some room for small groups. The setting has the feel of a high-mountain meadow; the trees are not so dense and the sites look out over grassy expanses and the Hayden Fork of the Bear River. Some campers come here to hike and fish, others just to take in the fantastic views of the high Uinta Mountains.

Location: In Wasatch National Forest near Kamas; map A2, grid f7.

Campsites, facilities: There are 26 sites with picnic tables and fire pits. Water and vault toilets are available.

Reservations, fees: Sites are $10 and are first come, first served.

Open: June–Oct.

Directions: From Kamas, drive 38.9 miles east on State Route 150. The campground is on the west side of the highway.

Contact: Evanston Ranger District, 307/789-3194.

86 Beaver View

 8

Beaver View is another secluded campground along the Mirror Lake Scenic Byway, with fairly well-spaced sites, a nice mix of forest and meadow scenery, and great views of the Hayden Fork of the Bear River. The river is a favored fishing and hiking spot, as is the campground's namesake Beaver Pond, located nearby. The road and sites are unpaved, with some gravel pull-throughs for RVs.

Location: In Wasatch National Forest near Kamas; map A2, grid f7.

Campsites, facilities: There are 18 sites (including one group site) with picnic tables and fire pits. Water and vault toilets are available.

Reservations, fees: Sites are $9 and are first come, first served.

Open: June–Oct.

Directions: From Kamas, drive east for 41.9 miles on State Route 150. The campground is on the east side of the highway.

Contact: Evanston Ranger District, 307/789-3194.

87 Hayden Fork

 8

While not recommended for RVs due to the steep and

winding dirt access road, this campground on the Mirror Lake Scenic Byway is a nice place to bring a tent. Some sites are on the Hayden Fork of the Bear River, a favorite with anglers and hikers alike. The fire pits are above-ground stone stoves.

Location: In Wasatch National Forest near Kamas; map A2, grid f7.

Campsites, facilities: There are nine sites with picnic tables and fire pits. Water and vault toilets are available.

Reservations, fees: Sites are $9 and are first come, first served.

Open: June–Oct.

Directions: From Kamas, drive east for 42.3 miles on State Route 150. The campground is on the east side of the highway.

Contact: Evanston Ranger District, 307/789-3194.

88 Wolverine ATV Trailhead

  7

This is primarily a staging area for all-terrain vehicles, with ramps for loading and unloading, numerous dirt roads, and more than nine miles of developed ATV trails. The setting is mainly open terrain with a few young trees, but a tall forest surrounds it all.

Location: In Wasatch National Forest near Kamas; map A2, grid f7.

Campsites, facilities: There are six sites with picnic tables, fire pits, and vault toilets, but no water.

Reservations, fees: Sites are free and are first come, first served.

Open: June–Oct.

Directions: From Kamas, drive east for 49.1 miles on State Route 150. Look for the marked turnoff to Forest Service Road 057. The campground is 1.5 miles up the mountain on the rough dirt road.

Contact: Evanston Ranger District, 307/789-3194.

89 Christmas Meadows

  9

True to its name, small Christmas Meadows campground is set in a beautiful high-alpine meadow, with a few trees and spectacular views of the surrounding mountains. Anglers like to pass the time fishing the Stillwater Fork of the Bear River.

Location: In Wasatch National Forest near Kamas; map A2, grid f8.

Campsites, facilities: There are 11 sites with picnic tables and fire pits. Water and vault toilets are available.

Reservations, fees: Sites are $10 and are first come, first served.

Open: June 15–Sept. 15.

Directions: From Kamas, drive east on State Route 150. Just past the Stillwater campground (see below), look for Forest Service Road 057, the turnoff to Christmas Meadows and Wolverine ATV Trailhead. The campground is four miles down this relatively rough dirt road, which runs parallel to a summer-home development.

Contact: Evanston Ranger District, 307/789-3194.

90 Stillwater

    9

Stillwater, on the deep and wide Bear River, is farther off the highway and has bigger sites than most other campgrounds along the Mirror Lake Scenic Byway. The road and sites are unpaved. Some of the sites are large enough for groups; most are relatively level and right by the water. Fishing and hiking are big attractions here.

Location: In Wasatch National Forest near Kamas; map A2, grid f8.

Campsites, facilities: There are 21 sites with picnic tables and fire pits. Water and vault toilets are available.

Reservations, fees: Sites are $10 and are first come, first served.

Open: June–Oct.

Directions: From Kamas, drive east 45.6 miles on State Route 150. The campground is on the east side of the highway.

Contact: Evanston Ranger District, 307/789-3194.

91 Smith and Morehouse

    10

Get to a campsite early, especially on weekends; better yet, get a reservation. The combination of good fishing on nearby Smith and Morehouse Reservoir, remodeled facilities, and campsites tucked away in an alpine-forest setting (elevation 7,700 ft.) make this one of the area's most frequented campgrounds. Horseback riding is a popular activity on any of the Forest Service trails in the area.

Location: In Wasatch-Cache National Forest; map A2, grid g5.

Campsites, facilities: There are 34 sites with tent sites, picnic tables, and fire rings. Handicapped-accessible vault toilets and water are available.

Reservations, fees: For reservations, call the U.S. Forest Service National Reservation System at 800/280-2267. Sites are $12.

Open: June–Oct.

Directions: Driving east from Salt Lake City on I-80, take the Wanship exit. Travel southeast on State Route 32 to Oakley. Turn east and take Weber Canyon Road for 11 miles to the campground.

Contact: Kamas Ranger District, 435/783-4338.

92 Ledgefork

   10

Many campers come to this spot to hike the trail leading from the campground into the High Uintas Wilderness Area, or to fish for the planted trout in nearby Smith and More-

house Reservoir. Horseback riding is a popular activity on any of the Forest Service trails in the area. Located in a pretty pine forest (elevation 8,000 ft.), this popular place does fill fast, so reservations are advised.

Location: In Wasatch-Cache National Forest; map A2, grid g5.

Campsites, facilities: There are 73 sites with picnic tables and fire rings. Vault toilets and water are available.

Reservations, fees: For reservations, call the U.S. Forest Service National Reservation System at 800/280-2267. Sites are $12, double sites are $24.

Open: June–Oct.

Directions: Driving east from Salt Lake City on I-80, take the Wanship exit. Travel southeast on State Route 30 to Oakley. Drive east for 12 miles to the end of Weber Canyon Road and the campground.

Contact: Kamas Ranger District, 435/783-4338.

93 Bear River

   8

At this unpaved campground close to the end of the Mirror Lake Scenic Byway, all the sites are next to the fishable Bear River, amid a smattering of trees. The restroom is wheelchair accessible, but the rocky sites are not level.

Location: In Wasatch National Forest near Kamas; map A2, grid e7.

Campsites, facilities: There are four established campsites with picnic tables and fire pits. Water and handicapped-accessible vault toilets are available.

Reservations, fees: Sites are $9 and are first come, first served.

Open: June–Oct.

Directions: From Kamas, drive east for 48.3 miles on State Route 150. The campground is on the west side of the highway.

Contact: Evanston Ranger District, 307/789-3194.

East Fork

 7

At East Fork—the last campground on the Mirror Lake Scenic Byway before you leave the forest and enter Evanston, Wyoming—all sites are on the river next to clumps of willows, in mostly open country with young conifers and aspens nearby. The road and sites are unpaved, and trailers are not recommended due to lack of turnaround room. A private gas station and store are just north of the campground.

Location: In Wasatch National Forest near Kamas; map A2, grid e7.

Campsites, facilities: There are seven sites, picnic tables, and fire pits. Water and vault toilets are available.

Reservations, fees: Sites are $9 and are first come, first served.

Open: June–Oct.

Directions: From Kamas, go 50 miles northeast on Highway 150 to the campground.

Contact: Evanston Ranger District, 307/789-3194.

Little Lyman Lake

  6

This campground is located between Big and Little Lyman Lakes, which are (anglers take note) the only stocked lakes on the Blacks Fork of the Bear River. The road and sites are gravel.

Location: In Wasatch National Forest near Kamas; map A2, grid e7.

Campsites, facilities: There are 10 sites with picnic tables and fire pits. Water and vault toilets are available.

Reservations, fees: Sites are $7 and are first come, first served.

Open: June 15–Sept. 15.

Directions: From Kamas, drive east on State Route 150. Take Forest Service Road 058 to the east, and look for the campground turnoff

about 12 miles later. The campground is 65.6 miles from Kamas.

Contact: Evanston Ranger District, 307/789-3194.

China Meadows

  9

This high-country campground on China Meadows Lake is a favorite with folks who like to fish, hike, and horseback ride, though some simply take in the scenery on rafts, canoes, and boats (trolling motors only). Tent camping is permitted. Across the road, the China Meadows Trailhead campground (see below) provides access to Red Castle, a High Uintas scenic basin with alpine lakes.

Location: In Wasatch National Forest near Mountain View, Wyoming; map A2, grid e8.

Campsites, facilities: There are nine sites with picnic tables and fire pits. Water and vault toilets are available.

Reservations, fees: Sites are $7 and are first come, first served.

Open: July–Sept.

Directions: Take I-80 or State Highway 150 north to Evanston, Wyoming, then go 12 miles north on I-80. Take the Fort Bridger exit and follow State Highway 412 south to Mountain View. From there, take State Route 410 south for seven miles and look for the junction with Uinta County Road 246. Go straight on Uinta County Road 246 for 8.2 miles to the Forest Service boundary, where it becomes Forest Service Road 072, and drive 11 miles to the China Meadows campground.

Contact: Mountain View Ranger District, 307/782-6555.

China Meadows Trailhead

  9

With two horse-loading ramps and a six-stall corral, this campground is used as a trailhead for horse-packing trips into the Uinta

Wilderness. It's set at an elevation of 10,000 feet, so there's usually a later opening date. Road conditions limit RVs to those less than 14 feet long. Tent camping is permitted.

Location: In Wasatch National Forest near Mountain View, Wyoming; map A2, grid e8.

Campsites, facilities: There are 12 sites with vault toilets and picnic tables, but no water.

Reservations, fees: Sites are $5 and are first come, first served.

Open: July–Sept.

Directions: Take I-80 or State Highway 150 north to Evanston, Wyoming, then go 12 miles north on I-80. Take the Fort Bridger exit and follow State Highway 412 south to Mountain View. From there, take State Route 410 south for seven miles to the junction with Uinta County Road 246. Go straight on Uinta County Road 246 for 8.2 miles to the Forest Service boundary, where it becomes Forest Service Road 072, then continue 11 miles to the wilderness trailhead. The trailhead campground is 26.2 miles from Mountain View, Wyoming.

Contact: Mountain View Ranger District, 307/782-6555.

98 Marsh Lake

 8

Two forested loops overlook tree-lined Marsh Lake, where owners of rafts and canoes can fish and enjoy the tranquil beauty of the surroundings. Fly fishers like to try their luck from shore. At an elevation of 9,800, this place stays open a little longer than high-country campgrounds like nearby China Meadows (see page 88).

Location: In Wasatch National Forest near Mountain View, Wyoming; map A2, grid e8.

Campsites, facilities: There are 34 sites, 33 with picnic tables (including one 16-foot-long table), plus tent sites, vault toilets, water, stoves, grills, fire rings, and a boat ramp. One site is wheelchair accessible.

Reservations, fees: Reservations are accepted for a limited number of sites, including the wheelchair-accessible site; call the U.S. Forest Service National Reservation System at 800/280-2267. Single sites are $9, doubles are $28.

Open: June–Oct.

Directions: Take I-80 or State Highway 150 north to Evanston, Wyoming, then go 12 miles north on I-80. Take the Fort Bridger exit and follow State Highway 412 south to Mountain View. From there, take State Route 410 south for seven miles to the junction with Uinta County Road 246. Take Uinta County Road 246 for 8.2 miles, where it becomes Forest Service Road 072, and continue for another 8.7 miles to the campground. The campground is 23.9 miles from Mountain View, Wyoming.

Contact: Mountain View Ranger District, 307/782-6555.

99 Bridger Lake

 8

Set in a woodsy area along the shore of Bridger Lake, this is a popular base camp for hikers or starting point for backpackers. Other campers just take their rafts, canoes, or boats with trolling motors onto the water, where they fish for planted trout or simply take in the scenery.

Location: In Wasatch National Forest near Mountain View, Wyoming; map A2, grid e8.

Campsites, facilities: There are 30 sites with tent sites and vault toilets, plus water and a boat ramp. One site is handicapped accessible.

Reservations, fees: Reservations are accepted for a limited number of sites, including the handicapped-accessible site; call the U.S. Forest Service National Reservation System at 800/280-2267. Single sites are $11, doubles are $18.

Open: June–Oct.

Directions: Take I-80 or State Highway 150 north to Evanston, Wyoming, then go 12 miles north on I-80. Take the Fort Bridger exit and follow State Highway 412 south to Mountain View. Then take State Route 410 south for seven miles to the junction with Uinta County Road 246. Go straight on Uinta County Road 246 for 8.2 miles until it becomes Forest Service Road 072, and continue for 7.9 miles to Forest Service Road 126, which heads off to the east. Then take Road 126 to the campground on Bridger Lake.

Contact: Mountain View Ranger District, 307/782-6555.

100 State Line

   7

The sites are rather close together, but they're set in an alpine forest and face State Line Reservoir. Campers use the nearby boat ramp to take to the water with canoes and rafts.

Location: In Wasatch National Forest near Mountain View, Wyoming; map A2, grid e8.

Campsites, facilities: There are 41 sites (one of them wheelchair accessible) with tent sites, picnic tables, fire pits, water, and vault toilets. A boat ramp is available on State Line Reservoir.

Reservations, fees: For reservations, call the U.S. Forest Service National Reservation System at 800/280-2267. Sites are $10.

Open: June–Sept.

Directions: Take I-80 or State Highway 150 north to Evanston, Wyoming. Then go 12 miles north on I-80, take the Fort Bridger exit, and follow State Highway 412 south to Mountain View, Wyoming. Take State Route 410 south until it intersects with Uinta County Road 246, go straight on Uinta County Road 246 for 8.2 miles until it becomes Forest Service Road 072, and continue 5.5 miles to the campground.

Contact: Mountain View Ranger District, 307/782-6555.

101 Hoop Lake

    7

Like most of the high-mountain lakes in Utah, Hoop Lake offers good fishing in a scenic locale. Anglers won't catch any lunkers here, but the fish are usually plentiful. Fish from shore, raft, or canoe. The campground itself is in a pristinely beautiful alpine setting; don't be surprised if you spot a moose. Horseback riders and hikers can find plenty to explore in the nearby High Uintas Wilderness Area.

Location: In Wasatch National Forest near Mountain View, Wyoming; map A2, grid e8.

Campsites, facilities: There are 44 sites with picnic tables and fire pits, a horse corral, and an adjacent trailhead for hiking or horseback riding. Water and vault toilets are available.

Reservations, fees: Sites are $8 and are first come, first served.

Open: June 15–Sept. 3.

Directions: Take I-80 or State Highway 150 north to Evanston, Wyoming. Then go 12 miles north on I-80, take the Fort Bridger exit, and follow State Highway 412 south to Mountain View, Wyoming. From there, take State Route 414 southeast for 23.6 miles, turn right onto gravel Uinta County Road 264, and drive for 3.2 miles. Stay on that road, which turns into Forest Road 78, heading south for seven miles to the campground.

Contact: Mountain View Ranger District, 307/782-6555.

102 Spruces

    8

Though this is the largest of the Wasatch Front campgrounds, it also has some of the best sites, so it fills up fast. Set in a shaded area off the highway, it's serenaded by the constant soothing babble of Big Cottonwood

Creek, which offers some remarkably good trout fishing in the open meadows nearby. A number of popular hiking trails, including the short trek to Donut Falls, lead out of the campground, but don't even think about bringing your dog into the canyon unless you want a citation. An elevation of 7,400 feet keeps things cool here in summer.

Location: In Big Cottonwood Canyon east of Salt Lake City; map A2, grid g3.

Campsites, facilities: There are 86 individual sites and 20 group sites. Facilities include picnic tables, fire pits, wheelchair-accessible flush toilets, restrooms with cold running water, hiking trails, softball diamonds, and an amphitheater. Dogs are not allowed.

Reservations, fees: For reservations, call the U.S. Forest Service National Reservation System at 800/280-2267. Sites are $14.

Open: June 5–Oct. 15.

Directions: From Salt Lake City, take I-15 or I-80 east and look for the signs for Big and Little Cottonwood Canyons. Take Big Cottonwood Canyon Road (State Highway 190) and head southeast from town for 13.7 miles to the campground, on the south (right) side of the road.

Contact: Salt Lake Ranger District, 801/524-5042.

103 Redman

   9

This pine-shrouded retreat is surprisingly peaceful for a campground located so close to a major city. The only sound is the agreeable trickle of flowing water from Big Cottonwood Canyon, and while the sites themselves are dusty and well used, nearby attractions abound: Silver Flat Lake, at the top of the canyon, has a boardwalk trail and fishing piers, and there are several beautiful canyon hiking trails. (Dogs, however, are prohibited, because this area is the city watershed.) At an elevation of 8,300 feet, Redman

sometimes doesn't open until late June due to heavy snow.

Location: In Big Cottonwood Canyon, east of Salt Lake City; map A2, grid g3.

Campsites, facilities: There are 37 individual sites and five group sites; no sites have hookups. Flush toilets, drinking water, picnic tables, and fire grills are available. Dogs are not allowed.

Reservations, fees: For reservations, call the U.S. Forest Service National Reservation System at 800/280-2267. Individual sites are $20; group fees vary.

Open: June 15–Oct. 15.

Directions: From Salt Lake City, follow the signs from Interstates 80, 15, or 215 to Big Cottonwood Canyon. Take Big Cottonwood Canyon Road (State Highway 190) southeast for 16.4 miles to the campground.

Contact: Salt Lake Ranger District, 801/524-5042.

104 Tanners Flat

  10

The pleasing trickle of water from Little Cottonwood Canyon is a natural buffer against noise from other campers or traffic, making this one of the better Wasatch Front campgrounds. At an elevation of 7,200 feet, the sites are shaded by pines; some are guarded by large slabs of granite or literally carved out of oak trees. Campers can enjoy the hiking and mountain-biking trails at nearby Snowbird Ski Resort or take the Snowbird tram to the top of Hidden Peak to view the spectacular summer wildflower displays. Note: Dogs are not allowed, as this area is the city watershed.

Location: In Little Cottonwood Canyon, east of Salt Lake City; map A2, grid g3.

Campsites, facilities: There are 32 family sites and three group sites. There are no hookups. Facilities include restrooms with cold running water, drinking water, picnic tables, fire pits, a trailhead, and a view area. Dogs are not allowed.

Reservations, fees: For reservations, call the U.S. Forest Service National Reservation System at 800/280-2267. Sites are $12; fees for group sites vary.

Open: Memorial Day weekend–Oct., depending on the snow conditions.

Directions: From Salt Lake City, take I-15, I-215, or I-80 into the Salt Lake Valley and follow the signs to Little Cottonwood Canyon. Take Little Cottonwood Canyon Road for 11.7 miles southeast of town to the campground.

Contact: Salt Lake Ranger District, 801/524-5042.

105 Albion

  10

There is no denying the beauty of this campground, with its breathtaking wildflower displays, alpine meadows, and views of granite, glacier-carved mountains. But private homes, ski-lift towers, and power lines, coupled with road dust from the early-summer weekend crowds, do detract from the splendor. Hiking trails leading to Cecret Lake and Sunset Peak are among the most popular on the Wasatch Front. When crowds fill up the parking spaces, expect to be stopped by an attendant and asked to park nearby at the Alta Ski Resort instead. Given the altitude (9,500 ft.), the camping season can be short.

Location: In Little Cottonwood Canyon, east of Salt Lake City; map A2, grid g3.

Campsites, facilities: There are 24 individual sites and two group sites. There are no hookups. Facilities include vault toilets, picnic tables, drinking water, picnic tables, and trailheads. Dogs are not allowed.

Reservations, fees: For reservations, call the U.S. Forest Service National Reservation System at 800/280-2267. Sites are $10.

Open: Late June–mid-Sept.

Directions: Albion is 18.4 miles southeast of Salt Lake City. From Salt Lake City, take I-15, I-215, or I-80 into the Salt Lake Valley and follow the signs to Little Cottonwood Canyon. Take Little Cottonwood Canyon Road (State Highway 210) to the top of the road; follow the pavement to the Alta Ski Resort, then use the dirt road into the campground.

Contact: Salt Lake Ranger District, 801/524-5042.

106 Little Mill

   8

Large Little Mill campground, located on the banks of American Fork Creek in a steep canyon (elevation 6,000 ft.), is popular with Wasatch Front residents looking for a weekend retreat. Other big attractions in the area include the hike to Timpanogos Cave at the national monument just down the canyon, and whiling away the hours fishing on the creek below nearby Tibble Fork Reservoir.

Location: In Uinta National Forest; map A2, grid g3.

Campsites, facilities: There are 79 sites with picnic tables, fire pits, and grills. Restrooms with flush toilets and drinking water are available.

Reservations, fees: For reservations, call the U.S. Forest Service National Reservation System at 800/280-2267. Sites are $10.

Open: May–Oct.

Directions: From Salt Lake City, drive south on I-15 until you reach exit 287. Take the exit and drive east on State Route 92 approximately 12 miles up American Fork Canyon. The campground is located on the south side of the road near a fork.

Contact: Pleasant Grove Ranger District, 801/785-3563.

107 Granite Flat

 10

Located in pines and aspens above scenic Tibble Fork Reservoir, Granite Flat has long been a local favorite. At an elevation of 6,800 feet, it offers hikers and tenters a cool alternative to the sunbaked valley. Favorite summer pastimes here are rafting, canoeing, and fishing at the reservoir or Silver Flat Lake; hiking to Timpanogos Cave; or horseback riding or hiking into the Lone Peak Wilderness Area. Horse-unloading facilities are nearby.

Location: In the North Fork of American Fork Canyon; map A2, grid g3.

Campsites, facilities: There are 44 single-family sites, eight double-family sites, and three group areas, but there are no hookups. Facilities include picnic tables, fire pits, drinking water, and flush toilets.

Reservations, fees: Reservations are taken for group sites only. Single-family sites are $13, double-family sites are $23.88, and group-site fees vary.

Open: May 24–Sept. 30.

Directions: Drive south from Salt Lake City on I-15, taking exit 287. Go east on State Route 92 for approximately 15 miles, traveling up American Fork Canyon. Take North Fork Road (Forest Road 85) past Tibble Fork Reservoir to the campground.

Contact: Pleasant Grove Ranger District, 801/785-3563.

108 Mount Timpanogos

 10

Campers who saw the movie *Jeremiah Johnson* should recognize the alpine splendor of this forested campground. Mount Timpanogos, one of the tallest peaks in the Wasatch Range, guards the campground. Ambitious hikers make the 18-mile round-trip hike to the summit; others enjoy shorter walks to the nearby waterfalls in the Mount Timpano-

gos Wilderness Area. Horseback riders can ride from the stables at the nearby Sundance Ski Area. For another scenic outing, take a drive north to Forest Road 114 and visit Cascade Springs, a wonderful nature area where boardwalks lead past interpretive signs and spring-fed ponds filled with trout.

Location: In Uinta National Forest; map A2, grid g3.

Campsites, facilities: There are 27 sites with tent sites, picnic tables, fire grills, drinking water, and flush toilets.

Reservations, fees: Eleven sites can be reserved; call the U.S. Forest Service National Reservation System at 800/280-2267. Sites are $11.

Open: June 1–Sept. 25.

Directions: From Orem, drive east up Highway 189. Look for the turnoff to the Sundance Ski Area on State Highway 92. Take that road to the north for just over three miles to the campground.

Contact: Pleasant Grove Ranger District, 801/785-3563.

109 Timpanoke

 10

Located at the pinnacle of the Alpine Loop at an elevation of 7,400 feet in forests of aspen and pine, this campground is a popular foliage-viewing spot in the fall. The Loop, in fact, might be the most-traveled scenic autumn drive along the Wasatch Front, so expect heavy traffic in the campground, which is located next to the road. Hiking and horseback riding are favorite activities on the nearby Great Western Trail.

Location: In Uinta National Forest; map A2, grid g3.

Campsites, facilities: There are 26 single-family and six double-family sites with tent sites, picnic tables, fire grills, vault toilets, and drinking water.

Reservations, fees: Reservations are taken for 16 single-family and five double-family sites; call the U.S. Forest Service National Reservation System at 800/280-2267. Single-family sites are $10, doubles are $21.

Open: May 25–Oct. 31.

Directions: Drive south from Salt Lake City on I-15 and take exit 287 to State Route 92. From the mouth of American Fork Canyon, drive nine miles to the campground, staying on State Route 92, now marked as the Alpine Loop.

Contact: Pleasant Grove Ranger District, 801/785-3563.

110 American Campground

  2

This campground is on gravel with small grass strips. But campers are shaded by tall cottonwoods, and there are pleasing touches such as flowers planted around the trees. The sites are close together and bordered by a field on one side and storage units on the other.

Location: In American Fork; map A2, grid g4.

Campsites, facilities: There are 53 RV sites, most of them occupied by year-round residents, with 12 reserved for overnighters. Full hookups, restrooms, showers, laundry facilities, RV waste-disposal, picnic tables, and a public phone are available. Tent camping is permitted and pets are welcome.

Reservations, fees: Reservations are accepted. Sites are $18.

Open: Year-round.

Directions: From Provo, go north three miles on I-15 and take exit 279 to Pleasant Grove. Take the first road to the left over the freeway, and turn left at the sign to the campground.

Contact: American Campground, 418 E. 620 S., American Fork, UT 84003; 801/756-5502.

111 Mountain Spa

   4

There's not an awful lot to this campground;

it's basically contained within a gravel parking area of the Mountain Spa Resort. Still, it has the feeling of being way out in the country, and the resort itself (which, unlike the campground, is open year-round) is an appealingly old-fashioned bathing spa with most activity centered around the bubbling hot springs. Golfers can perfect their game on courses at the Homestead Resort and in Wasatch Mountain State Park.

Location: In Midway; map A2, grid g5.

Campsites, facilities: This RV campground is next to the cabins at the Mountain Spa Resort, where two mineral pools, a café, and a gift shop are open to campers for use. There are seven sites with full hookups and a grassy area for tents, plus restrooms, showers, picnic tables, and a swing set. Leashed pets are allowed.

Reservations, fees: For reservations and fees, call 801/654-0721.

Open: Memorial Day–Labor Day.

Directions: From Salt Lake City, take I-80 east to U.S. Route 40, then take Route 40 south toward Midway. Turn off on River Road and take it to 600 North, then take 600 North to 200 East. Turn onto 200 East, go two blocks, and turn right at the sign to Mountain Spa Resort.

Contact: Mountain Spa Campground, 801/654-0721.

112 Oak Hollow

    8

Oak Hollow is a campground set up for tent campers only, with a leveled, framed dirt pad at each site and picnic tables set on cement pads. Each site is surrounded by scrub oak, which serves as a vegetation screen. The surrounding Wasatch Mountain State Park is famous for its 27-hole golf course (popular with cross-country skiers and snowmobilers in winter), and nearby Deer Creek Reservoir is a prime spot for fishing and other water sports.

Location: In Wasatch Mountain State Park; map A2, grid g5.

Campsites, facilities: There are 40 sites, plus handicapped-accessible restrooms with flush toilets, showers, water, sewage disposal, picnic tables, and fire pits.

Reservations, fees: Reservations are strongly recommended, since this is Utah's most popular state park; call 800/322-3770. Sites are $14; Utah seniors with a Special Fun Tag get a $2 discount Sun.–Thurs., excluding holidays.

Open: May–Oct., depending on snow conditions.

Directions: From Salt Lake City, take I-80 east. Turn onto U.S. Route 40 and follow the signs to Wasatch Mountain State Park. Turn onto River Road and follow it as it turns into Burgi Lane. At another park sign, turn right on Pine Canyon Lane and continue to the park.

Contact: Wasatch Mountain State Park, 435/654-1791.

Mahagony

 9

The campground, one of four in Wasatch Mountain State Park, is built especially for RVs. The paved, level sites have full hookups, with back-ins and pull-throughs. The road is paved as well, and the picnic tables are set on cement pads. Many sites are in an open setting, in tall grass and sagebrush, with good views of the Heber Valley, Deer Creek Reservoir, and the surrounding mountains, and access to a pleasant stream. The park, a favorite getaway from Salt Lake City, has a 27-hole golf course. Fishing and other water sports are popular at Deer Creek Reservoir.

Location: In Wasatch Mountain State Park; map A2, grid g5.

Campsites, facilities: This RV-only campground has 35 sites, full hookups, RV waste-disposal, showers, flush toilets, water, picnic tables, and fire pits. The restrooms are handicapped accessible.

Reservations, fees: Reservations are strongly recommended; call 800/322-3770. Sites are $16. Utah residents 62 and older with a Special Fun Tag get a $2 discount Sun.–Thurs., excluding holidays.

Open: May–Oct., depending on snow conditions.

Directions: From Salt Lake City, take I-80 east. Turn onto U.S. Route 40 and follow the signs to Wasatch Mountain State Park. Turn onto River Road and follow it as it turns into Burgi Lane. At another park sign, turn right on Pine Canyon Lane and continue to the park.

Contact: Wasatch Mountain State Park, 435/654-1791.

Cottonwood

 9

The settings vary in this split campground for tent campers and RVs: Some sites are back in the trees, others are out in the scrub oak and tall grass, and still others border the famed 27-hole golf course. All roads and sites are paved. No tents are allowed in the RV section. This area abounds with hiking trails; the park visitors center can provide information, maps, and travel tips.

Location: In Wasatch Mountain State Park; map A2, grid g5.

Campsites, facilities: This campground is divided into two sections: one for RVs only, with 16 sites and full hookups, 14 with no sewer, and one for tents or self-contained campers, with 15 sites and no hookups. Picnic tables, fire rings, flush toilets, showers, water, and RV disposal are available. The restrooms are handicapped accessible.

Reservations, fees: Reservations are recommended; call 800/322-3770. Sites with full hookups are $16. Sites with partial hookups are $14.

Open: May–Oct.

Directions: From Salt Lake City, take I-80 east. Turn onto U.S. Route 40 and follow the signs to Wasatch Mountain State Park. Turn onto River Road, which becomes Burgi Lane. At another park sign, turn right on Pine Canyon Lane and continue to the park.

Contact: Wasatch Mountain State Park, 435/654-1791.

115 Deer Creek

   8

This remote campground, although part of Wasatch Mountain State Park, is 17 miles southwest of the park's other campgrounds and its golf course. Yet it's not too far from Cascade Springs—a beautiful natural preserve with boardwalks, interpretive signs, bubbling pools and waterfalls, and spring-fed ponds full of trout (but no fishing is allowed). Located on Forest Road 114 approximately five miles south of the campground, the springs are a must-see and a special treat for families.

Location: In Wasatch Mountain State Park; map A2, grid g5.

Campsites, facilities: There are 17 sites with no hookups. Tent camping is permitted. Picnic tables, fire pits, water, and flush toilets are available. The restrooms are handicapped accessible.

Reservations, fees: Reservations are recommended; call 800/322-3770. Sites are $10. Utah seniors with a Special Fun Tag get a $2 discount Sun.–Thurs., excluding holidays.

Open: Apr.–Nov.

Directions: From Provo, drive east up Provo Canyon on Highway 189 and take the Sundance turnoff. Take State Route 92 approximately six miles, then turn east toward Cascade Springs on Forest Road 114. Stay on that road, which takes a turn past Cascade Springs and then heads north, for approximately eight miles, following the signs to Deer Creek.

Contact: Wasatch Mountain State Park, 435/654-1791.

116 Heber Valley RV Park

   8

This mostly RV campground is in a wonderfully scenic, remote spot, right below the dam holding back Jordanelle Reservoir. The terrain is spacious and open, with young trees and new facilities. And while the sites are close together, the place is not always full, so campers aren't so apt to feel crowded. Trout fishing is great on the Provo River and Jordanelle Reservoir.

Location: Next to the Jordanelle Reservoir; map A2, grid g5.

Campsites, facilities: There are 34 sites with full RV hookups, 66 sites with water and electricity, and some tent sites and cabins.

Reservations, fees: Reservations are accepted. Sites with full hookups are $18.95, sites for RVs with no hookups are $13, sites with water and electricity are $15.95, and tent sites are $11. Cabins with kitchen and bath are $39.95

Open: Year-round.

Directions: From Salt Lake City, take I-80 east, turn off on U.S. Route 40, and drive past the Jordanelle Dam. Take State Route 32 toward Francis for about four-tenths of a mile, turn left on a dead-end road, and proceed 2.1 miles to the campground. The campground is 12 miles from the Kamas-Park City interchange.

Contact: Heber Valley RV Park, 435/654-4049.

117 Wolf Creek

  9

The big attractions here are the quiet and the scenery: a forested setting next to a dirt road at an elevation of 9,000 feet. There's also plenty of fishing nearby on the North Fork of the Duchesne River and the Mill Hollow

Reservoir. This is a beautiful area for an autumn drive.

Location: In Uinta National Forest; map A2, grid g6.

Campsites, facilities: There are three single-family and three group sites, with picnic tables, fire pits, drinking water, and vault toilets.

Reservations, fees: No reservations are accepted for the single-family units. Sites are $12.

Open: Late May–Sept.

Directions: From Woodland, take State Route 35 east for 13 miles to reach the campground.

Contact: Heber Ranger District, 435/645-0470.

118 Mill Hollow

  8

Many come to this pine-shaded area to fish on the small reservoir at the campground's edge. Whether from shore, a raft, or a canoe, the rainbow trout (regularly stocked by the Utah Division of Wildlife Resources) can be caught through most of the summer. With an elevation of 8,800 feet, the nights can be cool.

Location: In the Uinta National Forest; map A2, grid g6.

Campsites, facilities: There are 25 sites with picnic tables and fire pits; drinking water and vault toilets are available.

Reservations, fees: Sites are $12 and are first come, first served.

Open: June–Sept.

Directions: From Woodland, drive 12 miles southeast on State Route 35, then turn south on Forest Road 504 and look for the sign to the campground.

Contact: Heber Ranger District, 435/654-0470.

119 Deer Creek State Park

   8

Apart from the abundant amenities at the campground, the Deer Creek Reservoir offers a wide range of recreational activities. Its north end, near the Island Boat Camp, is popular with sailboarders, and consistent winds make it a prime sailing area. Anglers like to fish the waters for bass, walleye, and trout. And relatively warm summer water temperatures make Deer Creek a popular water-skiing park. The campground is set on a flat spot overlooking the reservoir, in the shadow of spectacular Mount Timpanogos.

Location: On Deer Creek Reservoir; map A2, grid g4.

Campsites, facilities: There are 32 sites with no hookups. Facilities include picnic tables, fire grills, restrooms with showers, a sewage disposal and fish-cleaning station, and a concrete boat-launching ramp and adjacent paved parking area. In the reservoir's day-use areas, two concessionaires offer a restaurant, boat rentals, gasoline, and camping supplies.

Reservations, fees: Reservations are available 120 days in advance for a nonrefundable $6 per site; call 800/322-3770 Mon.–Fri. 8 A.M.–5 P.M. Sites are $12. Utah residents 62 years and older with a Special Fun Tag receive a $2 discount Sun.–Thurs., excluding holidays.

Open: May 1–Oct. 1.

Directions: From Heber City, take U.S. Highway 189 southwest for seven miles. The park is located on the east side of the highway.

Contact: Deer Creek State Park, 435/654-0171.

120 Hope

   9

One of the only public campgrounds in Provo Canyon, this scenic spot called Hope (elevation 6,600 ft.) in Uinta National Forest offers visitors hiking on Squaw Peak and anglers looking to try their luck in the popular Provo River an overnight stopping place. Families enjoy visiting nearby

Bridal Veil Falls, where water cascades several hundred feet off the canyon walls.

Location: In Uinta National Forest; map A2, grid h4.

Campsites, facilities: There are 24 sites with picnic tables and fire grills. Drinking water and vault toilets are available.

Reservations, fees: Sites are $7 and can be reserved through the National Recreation Reservation Service (877/444-6777) for a nonrefundable fee of $8.

Open: June–Sept.

Directions: From Orem, head east on Highway 189 toward Provo Canyon for about two miles. Right after entering the mouth of the canyon, look for Squaw Creek Road, or Forest Road 027. Drive five miles south on this dirt road, which climbs quickly above the canyon.

Contact: Pleasant Grove Ranger District, 801/785-3563.

121 Utah Lake State Park

    4

For a campground next to a big city, this one has a surprisingly quiet feel. Many of the tree-shaded sites are grassy, and most are set along the Provo River. A short walk from the premises, anglers can fish the river for white bass and walleye. There's even an Olympic-sized ice rink next to the visitors center (though it's only open in winter). The state park provides access to 96,000-acre Utah Lake, which, while muddy and turbid enough to deter all but the hardiest swimmers or water-skiers, makes a good early-season boating or rafting spot.

Location: On Utah Lake; map A2, grid h3.

Campsites, facilities: There are 71 sites with no hookups. Tent sites are available. Facilities include handicapped-accessible restrooms, showers, a fish-cleaning station, a dump station, four boat-launching ramps, a marina, and a visitors center. The fishing pier is also handicapped accessible.

Reservations, fees: Reservations are available 120 days in advance for a nonrefundable $6 per site; call 800/322-3770 Mon–Fri. 8 A.M. –5 P.M. Sites are $13. Utah residents 62 years and older with a Special Fun Tag get a $2 discount Sun.–Thurs., excluding holidays.

Open: Year-round.

Directions: From I-15 in Provo, take the West Center Street exit and drive five miles west to the campground.

Contact: Utah Lake State Park, 801/375-0733.

122 Lodgepole

   9

This is the kind of pretty canyon campground that can easily be overlooked by campers who would rather be close to a lake. It's located at the bottom of Daniels Canyon at an elevation of 7,800 feet in a grove of aspen and pine. The paved loops lead to private sites tucked away in the trees. Anglers, in particular, appreciate the tranquil beauty of nearby Strawberry and Deer Creek Reservoirs. Though the place isn't fully wheelchair accessible, some sites and restrooms have been modified to accommodate people with disabilities.

Location: In Daniels Canyon; map A2, grid h6.

Campsites, facilities: There are 50 sites with picnic tables and fire pits, flush toilets, and a dump station. Some wheelchair-accessible facilities are available.

Reservations, fees: Reservations are available for 25 sites; call the U.S. Forest Service National Reservation System at 800/280-2267. Sites are $12.

Open: June–Oct.

Directions: From Heber City, drive 16 miles southeast on Highway 40 to the campground, which is on the west side of the road.

Contact: Heber Ranger District, 435/654-0470.

Currant Creek

 10

Few U.S. Forest Service campgrounds in Utah offer such extensive amenities, including some of the best facilities for the disabled in the state. Children like the Western-themed tot lot; and Loop C, with its horse-unloading ramps, feeding troughs, and corrals, was clearly designed with riders in mind. Trout fishing on the reservoir can be excellent, though anglers shouldn't ignore the creek below the dam. Use power boats, canoes, or rafts to explore the reservoir. The campground is tucked away amid quaking aspens, with the paved sites spaced a nice distance apart.

Location: Near Currant Creek Reservoir; map A2, grid h7.

Campsites, facilities: There are 99 sites with tent sites, picnic tables, and fire grills, wheelchair-accessible restrooms with flush toilets, a wheelchair-accessible fishing pier over the reservoir, a playground, running water, a boat ramp, a fish-cleaning station, and a dump station.

Reservations, fees: For reservations, call the U.S. Forest Service National Reservation System at 800/280-2267. Sites are $12.

Open: May 25–Oct. 31.

Directions: From Heber City, drive 41 miles southeast on Highway 40 to the Currant Creek Lodge, then 20 miles north on a rough dirt road around the reservoir. The campground is on the southwest side of the reservoir.

Contact: Heber Ranger District, 435/342-5200.

Deer Creek Park

 6

Set off the road a ways (a nice plus in such a narrow canyon), this campground offers great views of Mount Timpanogos, and decent, plentiful fishing on the Provo River.

Deer Creek Reservoir is another popular place to fish as well as water-ski, and the fairly constant breeze makes it a favorite with sailors and windsurfers, too.

Location: In Provo Canyon near Provo; map A2, grid h4.

Campsites, facilities: There are 90 sites, 65 of which include water and electricity, plus a grassy area for tents. Amenities include chemical toilets, showers, picnic tables, barbecue grills, a public phone, and a small shop offering snacks, firewood, and ice. Dogs are allowed on a leash.

Reservations, fees: Reservations are recommended on summer holidays. Sites with full hookups are $16; all others, including tent sites, are $13. Persons over age 12 in groups larger than two pay an additional $1.50 each.

Open: May–Sept.

Directions: From Provo, take Highway 189 north up Provo Canyon for 10 miles. The campground is right past Bridal Veil Falls and the turnoff to Sundance, in front of the Deer Creek Reservoir dam.

Contact: Deer Creek Park, Rural Rte. 3 Box 620, Provo, UT 84604; 801/225-9783.

Frazier Trailer Park

 3

Provo Canyon is a narrow canyon, with the campgrounds, river, and highway sometimes squeezed all together in one small space. At this shaded trailer park, the sites themselves are close together and situated on gravel; in fact, it feels like a parking lot. Some RV sites are even right next to the highway. The canyon itself, however, is indisputably scenic, and the Provo River is famous for its fly-fishing. Kayak and tube rentals are available nearby, and just a quarter mile down the canyon is the historic Heber Creeper, a steam engine that takes tourists on a panoramic ride up the canyon to Heber Valley and back.

Location: In Provo Canyon near Provo; map A2, grid i4.

Campsites, facilities: There are 40 sites; eight have full hookups, 30 have water and electricity, and two are for tents.

Reservations, fees: Reservations are recommended; call 801/225-5346. Campsites are $15.

Open: Mar. 20–Nov. 1.

Directions: From Provo, take Highway 189 and travel up Provo Canyon for about five miles to the point where the highway narrows into two lanes. The campground is on the right side of the road.

Contact: Frazier Trailer Park, 3362 E. Provo Canyon Rd., Provo, UT 84604; 801/225-5346.

126 Lakeside

 7

This campground, next to the entrance to Utah Lake State Park, is a cut above the usual, with new facilities, attractive landscaping, and well-shaded, grassy sites. Even better, it sits in front of majestic Mount Timpanogos. And nearby Utah Lake is popular with anglers, boaters, and water-skiers.

Location: In Provo; map A2, grid h4.

Campsites, facilities: There are 148 sites with full hookups and 12 sites for tents, with restrooms, showers, laundry facilities, an RV waste-disposal site, picnic tables, a game room, a swimming pool, a public phone, a convenience and gift store, a playground, volleyball and basketball courts, and a horseshoe pit.

Reservations, fees: Reservations are suggested June–Oct. Sites are $21 with full hookups, $18 for partial hookups, $19 for a pull-through, and $16 for tents, plus $2 for each additional person in groups of more than two.

Open: Year-round.

Directions: Take I-15 in Provo to exit 258. Go west for two miles on Center Street to the campground.

Contact: Lakeside Campground, 4000 W. Center St., Provo, UT 84601; 801/373-5267.

127 Provo KOA

 5

The appeal of this semi-urban campground, located two miles from boating and water sports at Utah Lake State Park, is its proximity to the Provo River Parkway, a riverside jogging and hiking path. The campground itself is in a residential area, but the vegetation provides privacy and buffers the noise. The road and sites are gravel and shaded by tall trees, and there's a grassy area for tents.

Location: In Provo; map A2, grid h4.

Campsites, facilities: There are 95 sites; 45 have full hookups, 20 have water and electricity, and 30 are for tents. Amenities include restrooms, showers, laundry facilities, RV waste-disposal, picnic tables, a swimming pool, and a playground.

Reservations, fees: Reservations are accepted. Sites are $24.50 with full hookups, $23 with water and electricity, and $18 for tents.

Open: Year-round.

Directions: From Provo, take I-15 and get off at exit 268. Go west on Center Street for about one mile to 2050 West. Turn right and go to 320 North. The campground is on the right side of the street at 2050 W. 320 North.

Contact: Provo KOA Campground, 2050 W. 320 North, Provo, UT 84601; 801/375-2994.

128 Whiting

 7

This relatively small campground is in a timbered setting, with access to some nice forest hiking trails and a small, fishable stream. At an elevation of 5,400 feet, the place features some especially splendid views in the fall. Whiting is also popular with equestrians who ride on the extensive nearby trail system; three campsites are designed specifically for horse owners. Tent camping is permitted.

Location: In Uinta National Forest; map A2, grid i5.

Campsites, facilities: There are 16 sites for families, three sites for equestrians, and six double-family sites. Picnic tables, fire pits, flush toilets, drinking water, and equestrian facilities are available.

Reservations, fees: For reservations, call the U.S. Forest Service National Reservation System at 800/280-2267. Single-family and horse sites are $11; double-family sites are $22.

Open: May–Oct.

Directions: Drive two miles east of the Utah County town of Mapleton on Forest Road 025.

Contact: Spanish Fork Ranger District, 801/798-3571.

129 Cherry

   9

Though many campers like to fish the stream running through this beautiful forested canyon, the real draw is the nearby Hobble Creek Golf Course, one of Utah's more scenic links. The Springville Art Museum, one of the state's oldest visual-arts centers, is also worth checking out. And with oaks and aspens so plentiful in the canyon, this is a great place to view the changing autumn leaves. The elevation of 5,200 feet means it stays fairly warm here late into the year. Tent and RV camping are permitted.

Location: In Hobble Creek Canyon; map A2, grid i5.

Campsites, facilities: There are 10 single-family, four double-family, and four group sites, with drinking water, picnic tables, fire pits, and handicapped-accessible restrooms with flush toilets.

Reservations, fees: For reservations, call

800/280-2267. Fees are $11 for single-family sites and $22 for double sites.

Open: May 21–Oct. 31.

Directions: From Springville, drive east on State Route 79, which turns into Forest Road 058. The campground is 8.3 miles up the canyon from Springville on the south side of the road.

Contact: Spanish Fork Ranger District, 801/798-3571.

130 Balsam

   9

Located at the end of a paved road in a gorgeous canyon setting, this remote campground is especially scenic in the fall. A small stream offers plenty of fishing, hiking trails are nearby, and there's golfing down the canyon at Hobble Creek Golf Course. Tent camping is permitted.

Location: In Hobble Creek Canyon; map A2, grid i5.

Campsites, facilities: There are 24 single-family sites, one triple-family site, and one group site; amenities include picnic tables, fire grills, flush toilets, and drinking water.

Reservations, fees: For reservations, call the U.S. Forest Service National Reservation System at 800/280-2267. Fees are $11 for single-family sites and $33 for the triple-family site; group prices vary.

Open: May 25–Oct. 31.

Directions: From Springville, head east on State Route 79, which turns into Forest Road 058. The campground is 13.1 miles up the canyon from Springville on the south side of the road.

Contact: Spanish Fork Ranger District, 801/798-3571.

131 Strawberry Bay

    7

This huge, modern facility is the hub of activity at Utah's

most popular trout-fishing spot. Water-skiing is allowed, but the primary activity here is fishing. Many of the paved sites, set largely in sagebrush-covered, open terrain, have views of the nearby Strawberry Reservoir. Sheltered picnic tables come in handy as wind and sun breaks. The marina store offers boat rentals, groceries, motel units, and a small café, making this an ideal spot for both boaters and anglers. Due to its elevation of 7,700 feet, the campground usually opens when the ice leaves the reservoir and closes when the snow flies.

Location: On Strawberry Reservoir; map A2, grid h7.

Campsites, facilities: There are 249 single-family sites without hookups, 26 sites (on Loop B) with hookups, tent sites, and a few group sites, plus wheelchair-accessible restrooms, sheltered picnic tables and fire grills, a day-use shelter, fish-cleaning stations, a full-service marina with gasoline and boat rentals, a dump station, and a boat ramp.

Reservations, fees: Reservations are available through the U.S. Forest Service National Reservation System at 800/280-2267. Sites are $12 for single or large families and $22 with full hookups. Group sites vary.

Open: May–Oct.

Directions: From Heber, drive 23 miles southeast on U.S. Highway 40, then approximately five miles on Forest Road 131. Look for signs for the marina and campground. A small entrance station signals the start of the forest facilities.

Contact: Heber Ranger District, 435/342-5200.

132 Renegade Point

 7

Anglers come to this place to pursue lunker, rainbow, and cutthroat trout in the shallower Meadows area of Strawberry Reservoir. Waterskiing is allowed, but the primary activity here is fishing. Use a canoe or raft along the shore to fish. There's a boat ramp in the area and some shore fishing as well. Renegade Point Campground itself is a little more rustic and out-of-the-way than some Strawberry facilities.

Location: On Strawberry Reservoir; map A2, grid i7.

Campsites, facilities: There are 66 sites, plus picnic tables, fire grills, flush toilets, and drinking water. The restrooms are handicapped accessible.

Reservations, fees: Sites are $12 and are first come, first served.

Open: May 25–Oct. 31.

Directions: Drive 23 miles southeast of Heber City on Highway 40 and then south on Forest Road 131 about eight miles to the campground.

Contact: Heber Ranger District, 435/654-0470.

133 Soldier Creek

 7

Strawberry Reservoir is one of the premier trout-fishing areas in the United States, regularly yielding cutthroat and rainbows up to 10 pounds. And this campground, located on a bay in the newer portion of the expanded reservoir, primarily caters to anglers although rafting and waterskiing is allowed. The property is paved, in somewhat open terrain, with a few picnic shelters. At an elevation of 7,600 feet, these are cooler waters, so water-skiers should consider pulling on their wet suits before taking off.

Location: On Strawberry Reservoir; map A2, grid h7.

Campsites, facilities: There are 163 sites with no hookups. Facilities include picnic tables, fire grills, handicapped-accessible restrooms with flush toilets, drinking water, a small marina, a boat ramp, a fish-cleaning station, a covered group-use area, and a dump station.

Reservations, fees: For reservations, call

the U.S. Forest Service National Reservation System at 800/280-2267. Fees are $9.

Open: May 25–Oct. 31.

Directions: Drive 33 miles southeast of Heber City on Highway 40, then turn south on Forest Road 480 and go 3.5 miles to the campground.

Contact: Heber Ranger District, 435/342-5200.

134 Aspen Grove

 10

Aspen Grove is the most remote, shaded, and scenic of the many campgrounds surrounding huge Strawberry Reservoir. The paved loops at the edge of a high-elevation alpine forest make it a popular weekend retreat during the summer, especially for anglers, boaters, and other water enthusiasts. While the fishing on the reservoir is fantastic, fly fishers shouldn't ignore the Strawberry River below the dam, one of Utah's few blue-ribbon trout streams.

Location: On Strawberry Reservoir; map A2, grid i8.

Campsites, facilities: There are 60 sites with no hookups. Facilities include picnic tables, fire grills, handicapped-accessible restrooms with flush toilets, drinking water, and a nearby boat ramp.

Reservations, fees: Sites are $12 and are first come, first served.

Open: May 25–Oct. 31.

Directions: Drive 34 miles southeast of Heber City on Highway 40 to Forest Road 482, then drive about seven miles on Road 482, past Strawberry Dam to the campground.

Contact: Heber Ranger District, 435/342-5200.

135 Maple Bench

 8

This small campground just off the road often serves as an overflow area when nearby campgrounds fill up early. Located close to a small reservoir that's frequently stocked with trout, Maple Bench is a favorite with canoeing and rafting enthusiasts. The elevation is 5,800 feet and the setting is fairly open, with hiking trails leading out from the campground into the nearby forest. Horseback-riding trails meander through the area as well. Tent camping is permitted.

Location: In Payson Canyon; map A2, grid i3.

Campsites, facilities: There are 10 sites with picnic tables and fire grills. Flush toilets and drinking water are available.

Reservations, fees: Sites are $7 and are first come, first served.

Open: May–Oct.

Directions: From Payson, drive five miles south on Nebo Scenic Loop Road. The campground is on the west side of the road.

Contact: Spanish Fork Ranger District, 801/798-3571.

136 Payson Lakes

 9

Long a favorite with Utah County residents, this fine National Forest Service campground (elevation 8,000 ft.) has a lot to offer. The paved spurs are nice, but the surroundings are even nicer: Visitors can raft, canoe, or fish for trout on the small but well-stocked lake, strolling on the pavement near the water, or driving along Nebo Scenic Loop Road, with its views of towering Mount Nebo in the distance. Horseback-riding trails are nearby.

Location: In Payson Canyon; map A2, grid i4.

Campsites, facilities: There are 82 single-family sites, 10 double-family sites, and three group sites, plus picnic tables and fire grills, drinking water, flush toilets, a paved trail around the lake, and a grassy area nearby. Some sites are wheelchair accessible.

Reservations, fees: Reservations are available for group sites, 26 of the single-family sites, and four of the double-family sites; call the U.S. Forest Service National Reservation System at 800/280-2267. Fees are $11 for single-family and $22 for double-family sites. Group prices vary.

Open: June–Oct.

Directions: Drive 12 miles south of Payson on Nebo Scenic Loop Road, then turn southwest and follow the signs to the lake.

Contact: Spanish Fork Ranger Station, 801/798-3571.

137 Tinney Flat

 9

Less crowded than nearby Payson Lakes (see above), this campground permits tents and is set in an excellent side canyon that is great for exploring in the fall. A trailhead at the campground leads to the adjacent Mount Nebo Wilderness, popular with hikers and horseback riders, and the main road connects to Nebo Scenic Loop Road. There's a small, fishable stream, and the sites are shielded by shade trees.

Location: In Santaquin Canyon; map A2, grid j3.

Campsites, facilities: There are 12 single-family sites, two double-family sites, and three group sites, plus picnic tables, fire grills, drinking water, and flush toilets.

Reservations, fees: For reservations, call the U.S. Forest Service National Reservation System at 800/280-2267. Fees are $11 for single-family sites and $22 for double-family sites. Group prices vary.

Open: June–Oct.

Directions: Driving south from Provo, take exit 248 (for Santaquin) and head east on Forest Road 014. The campground is nine miles east of the town of Santaquin.

Contact: Spanish Fork Ranger District, 801/798-3571.

138 Blackhawk

    9

The former forest supervisor who helped design this relatively new campground was a horseback rider, and it shows. With cribs, unloading docks, and overnight holding space for horses, this is an ideal place for equestrians looking to explore the nearby woods and mountains of the Uinta National Forest. Blackhawk campground itself is at an elevation of 7,100 feet and permits tent camping. Check with the Spanish Fork Ranger District for suggestions on trail rides in the surrounding area.

Location: Near Payson; map A2, grid j4.

Campsites, facilities: Sites are designed for horse owners. There are 12 single-family sites, three double-family sites, and three group sites, with picnic tables, fire grills, drinking water, toilets, and facilities for holding and unloading horses. The restrooms are handicapped accessible.

Reservations, fees: For reservations, call the U.S. Forest Service National Reservation System at 800/280-2267. Sites are $11 for single units and $22 for double units.

Open: June–Oct.

Directions: From Payson, drive 16 miles south on Nebo Loop Scenic Road. The campground is about two miles south of the main road on Forest Road 175.

Contact: Spanish Fork Ranger District, 801/798-3571.

139 Mountain View

     5

Though surrounded by forest, Scofield Reservoir is somewhat devoid of shade. The campground, located near the dam at an elevation of 7,600 feet, features grassy sites with paved parking areas terraced on the reservoir banks. Though this can be a good spot for water-skiing, fishing for rainbow trout is the main attraction.

Location: In Scofield State Park; map A2, grid j6.

Campsites, facilities: There are 34 sites, plus picnic tables, fire grills, showers, handicapped-accessible restrooms, a fish-cleaning station, a boat ramp, and a dump station.

Reservations, fees: Reservations are available 120 days in advance for a nonrefundable $8 per site; call 800/322-3770 Mon.–Fri. 8 A.M.–5 P.M. Sites are $12. Utah residents 62 years and older with a Special FunTag get a $2 discount Sun.–Thurs., excluding holidays.

Open: May 15–Sept. 15.

Directions: From Spanish Fork, drive east on U.S. Highway 6, passing the tiny hamlet of Soldier Summit, then drive 13 miles south on State Route 96 to the campground.

Contact: Scofield State Park, 435/448-9449 (summer), 435/637-2732 (winter).

140 Madsen Bay

     6

The group-use pavilion makes this a popular local family-reunion spot. The campground is located on the north end of Scofield Reservoir in a fairly open setting and permits tent camping. Fishing for rainbow trout at the reservoir and fly-fishing on nearby streams can be excellent. Waterskiing, rafting, or canoeing are also a possiblity.

Location: On Scofield Reservoir; map A2, grid j6.

Campsites, facilities: There are 37 sites, plus picnic tables, grills, modern restrooms, a dump station, a boat ramp, and a group-use pavilion.

Reservations, fees: Reservations are available 120 days in advance for a nonrefundable $8 per site; call 800/322-3770 Mon.–Fri. 8 A.M.–5 P.M. Sites are $10. Utah residents 62

years and older with a Special FunTag get a $2 discount Sun.–Thurs., excluding holidays.

Open: May 15–Sept. 15.

Directions: Drive east on U.S. Highway 6 from Spanish Fork until you pass the small hamlet of Soldier Summit. Look for the signs to Scofield Reservoir. Drive 13 miles south on State Route 96 to the campground.

Contact: Scofield State Park, 435/448-9449.

141 Nephi KOA

    8

This isolated spot high in a scenic canyon has lots of trees and grass to recommend it, along with the more dramatic attractions of the Uinta National Forest four miles away. Anglers can try their luck with the trout in smallish Salt Creek, which runs past the campground. For golfers, there's a city-owned course in Nephi.

Location: East of Nephi; map A2, grid j2.

Campsites, facilities: There are 87 sites; 28 have full hookups, 39 have water and electricity, and 20 are for tents. Cabins are also available. Amenities include picnic tables, barbecue grills, restrooms, showers, laundry facilities, an RV disposal site, pool, a game room, a public phone, a convenience/gift store, and a playground. Pets are allowed on a leash.

Reservations, fees: Reservations are strongly recommended. Sites are $22 with full hookups, $21 with water and electricity, and $16 for tents. Their two cabins are $29. Groups of more than two pay an additional $2.50 for each extra child over four and $3.50 for each extra adult over 18.

Open: May 15–Oct. 1.

Directions: From Provo, go south on I-15 and take exit 225. Then follow State Route 132 east up Salt Creek Canyon for five miles to reach the campground.

Contact: Nephi KOA, P. O. Box 309, Nephi, UT 84648; 435/623-0811.

142 Gooseberry

 9

This campground offers some excellent fishing in the small stream running through it and at nearby Lower Gooseberry Reservoir. It's located in somewhat open country at an elevation of 8,600 feet, and affords beautiful views of the surrounding mountain areas.

Location: In Manti-La Sal National Forest; map A2, grid j5.

Campsites, facilities: There are eight sites, plus picnic tables, fire grills, vault toilets, and questionable drinking water.

Reservations, fees: Sites are $5.

Open: June–Sept.

Directions: From the town of Fairview, drive east on State Route 31 about seven miles, looking for Forest Road 51. Travel north on that road and then slightly east for another two miles to the campground.

Contact: Price Ranger District, 435/637-2817.

143 Price Canyon Recreation Area

 8

Shaded by large ponderosa pines, this campground is a popular place to beat the heat. Nature lovers will appreciate the nearby short and easy Bristlecone Ridge Hiking and Nature Trail, which offers fascinating information on local flora and fauna, along with excellent vistas of the surrounding area.

Location: On Bureau of Land Management property near Price; map A2, grid j7.

Campsites, facilities: There are 18 sites and one group site with picnic tables, fire grills, drinking water, vault toilets, and a nature trail nearby.

Reservations, fees: Reservations are accepted only for the group site. Campsites are $8.

Open: June–Oct.

Directions: Drive 15 miles north of Price on Highway 6/50, then three miles west on a paved and well-marked Bureau of Land Management road into Price Canyon.

Contact: Price Canyon Bureau of Land Management, 435/637-4584.

144 Chicken Creek

 9

Before reaching the campground itself, anglers can find a nice, deep pond, regularly stocked with rainbow trout, behind a small dam. There's also respectable fishing in Chicken Creek itself, which flows nearby. Located in a timbered setting, the campground is remote and quiet. Consider taking the road that heads east from the campground over the San Pitch Mountains into Sanpete County, for the spectacular views of the Wasatch Plateau to the east and the valley below.

Location: In Manti-La Sal National Forest; map A2, grid j3.

Campsites, facilities: There are eight sites, plus picnic tables, fire grills, drinking water, and vault toilets.

Reservations, fees: Sites are $5 and some can be reserved by calling the National Recreation Service at 877/444-6777.

Open: June 1–Sept. 10.

Directions: From Salt Lake City, take I-15 south for 90 miles, exit at Nephi, and follow State Route 28 to Levan. From Levan, travel six miles east on Chicken Creek Canyon Road to the campground.

Contact: Sanpete Ranger District, 435/283-4151.

145 Maple Canyon

 9

This is a fantastic spot in the fall when the canyon's eponymous maples begin to change. The campground is remote but extremely pretty, with large rocks sheltering the sites. A short hiking trail leads into some geologically interesting scenery in the canyon.

Location: In Manti-La Sal National Forest; map A2, grid j3.

Campsites, facilities: There are 12 sites, plus picnic tables, fire grills, and vault toilets, but no drinking water.

Reservations, fees: Sites are $5; some can be reserved by calling the National Recreation Reservation Service at 877/444-6777.

Open: June 1–Sept. 10.

Directions: From Nephi, drive south and east on State Route 132 to Fountain Green. Look for State Route 30 and follow it south about 5.5 miles to the town of Freedom. Take a winding road north and east into Maple Canyon about three miles.

Contact: Sanpete Ranger District, 435/283-4151.

146 Flat Canyon

  8

This pretty little spot is in a wooded area at an elevation of 8,900 feet, a stone's throw from Boulger Reservoir. Though small, the reservoir is regularly stocked with rainbow trout.

Location: On Boulger Reservoir; map A2, grid j6.

Campsites, facilities: There are 12 sites with no hookups. Picnic tables, fire grills, drinking water, and vault toilets are available.

Reservations, fees: Sites are $8 and are first come, first served. Some sites may be reserved. Call the National Recreation Reservation Service at 877/444-6777.

Open: May 15–Sept. 15.

Directions: From Fairview, take State Route 31 east for approximately six miles. Turn south and west on State Route 264 (Forest Road 057) and follow it to the campground, which is on the west side of the road.

Contact: Price Ranger District, 435/637-2817.

147 Old Folks Flat

   8

This is one of the closest campgrounds to Electric Lake and Miller Flat Reservoir. Fly-fishers especially like nearby Huntington Creek, one of the better fishing rivers in the area. Located in an alpine setting next to a paved road at an elevation of 8,100 feet, the campground is easily accessible and not too far from Skyline Drive, a popular and scenic four-wheel-drive route in the fall.

Location: In Manti-La Sal National Forest; map A2, grid j7.

Campsites, facilities: There are nine sites, plus picnic tables, fire grills, drinking water, and handicapped-accessible toilets.

Reservations, fees: Sites are $8 and are first come, first served.

Open: June 1–Sept. 15.

Directions: From Huntington, drive 21 miles northwest on State Route 31 to the campground, which is on the east side of the road.

Contact: Ferron Ranger District, 435/384-2372.

148 Forks of the Huntington

   8

This small retreat is popular with locals for the superb alpine scenery, the fishing at Huntington Creek and nearby Electric Lake, and the easy paved access. The campground sits at an elevation of 7,700 feet.

Location: In Manti-La Sal National Forest; map A2, grid j6.

Campsites, facilities: There are six sites, plus vault toilets, picnic tables, and fire pits, but no water.

Reservations, fees: Sites are $6 and are first come, first served.

Open: June–Sept.

Directions: Drive 18 miles northwest of Huntington on State Route 31 to the campground, which is on the west side of the road.

Contact: Ferron Ranger District, 435/384-2372.

149 Indian Creek

  8

At an elevation of 8,000 feet, this remote campground is in a timbered setting with a small, fishable creek. Its out-of-the-way location recommends it as a place to beat the big crowds. Alert campers can spot a more-than-occasional elk or mule deer in the area.

Location: In Fishlake National Forest; map A2, grid j6.

Campsites, facilities: There are 29 sites, plus picnic tables, fire grills, drinking water, and flush toilets.

Reservations, fees: Sites are $6 and are first come, first served.

Open: June–Sept.

Directions: From Orangeville, travel eight miles on State Route 29, looking for a road that heads north near a gravel pit. That road turns into Forest Road 40, which leads 11 miles to the campground.

Contact: Call the Ferron Ranger District at 435/384-2372.

CHAPTER A3

UINTA MOUNTAINS

MAP A3

One inch equals approximately 11 miles.

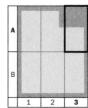

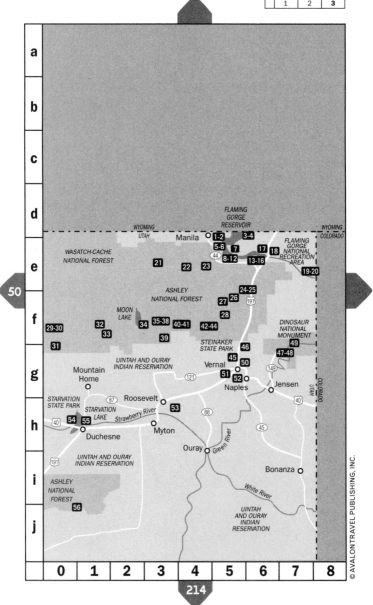

WYOMING
UTAH

Manila

FLAMING
GORGE
RESERVOIR

WYOMING
COLORADO

WASATCH-CACHE
NATIONAL FOREST

FLAMING
GORGE
NATIONAL
RECREATION
AREA

1-2 **3-4**

5-6

7

44 **8-12** **17** **18**

21 **22** **23** **13-16**

19-20

ASHLEY
NATIONAL FOREST

24-25

27 **26** 191

MOON
LAKE

28

DINOSAUR
NATIONAL
MONUMENT

29-30 **32** **34** **35-38** **40-41** **42-44**

33 **39**

49

31

STEINAKER
STATE PARK **46**

47-48

45

50

UINTAH AND OURAY
INDIAN RESERVATION

Vernal

51 **52**

Mountain
Home

121

Naples

Jensen

149

STARVATION
STATE PARK

87 Roosevelt

53

88

COLORADO
UTAH

STARVATION
LAKE

Strawberry River

40

54 **55**

Duchesne

Myton

Ouray

Green River

45

40

191

UINTAH AND OURAY
INDIAN RESERVATION

Bonanza

ASHLEY
NATIONAL
FOREST

White River

56

UINTAH
AND OURAY
INDIAN
RESERVATION

© AVALON TRAVEL PUBLISHING, INC.

50

214

CHAPTER A3

The Uinta Basin of Utah collects and stores a big share of the heavily populated Wasatch Front's water as it flows from the High Uinta Mountains. This is good for tourists. First of all, the population of the Uinta Basin is relatively small, leaving lots of wide-open public land in which to recreate. Secondly, from trout streams or white water rivers to huge reservoirs, water fun of all kinds is king. Add to this mix a fascinating geologic show of dinosaur bones and stunning layers of eons of rock exposed to the elements. It's easy to spend three days or a week exploring the northeast corner of the state.

Three-Day Itinerary: Steinaker State Park 🏕 Dinosaur National Monument 🏕 Utah Field House of Natural History Museum 🏕 Flaming Gorge

Day One
Steinaker State Park is situated on Steinaker Reservoir. The water at the reservoir is usually warmer than many lakes in the area and

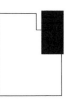

is great for water sports and fishing. Actually, Steinaker or nearby Red Fleet State Park on Red Fleet Reservoir are each great bases for a three-day trip for those who hate making and breaking camp each day. Reservations can be made before arrival at either park (800/322-3770).

Day Two
A trip to Dinosaur National Monument (see directions to Split Mountain Campground, page 133) is a must. Here, partially excavated dinosaur bones have been left in the hillside and enclosed in the visitors center building. The National Park Service has presently ceased excavation to show the public how the bones were found in a jumbled mess, part of a Jurassic "sandbar cemetery" that collected the bones of crocodiles, turtles, and 14 species of dinosaurs as they were washed downstream.

Visit the Utah Field House of Natural History Museum in Vernal, first, if time permits. Here, complete skeletons are reconstructed and further information about the dinosaurs given. Outside, a garden complete with life-size cement reproductions of a pterodactyl, Tyrannosaurus Rex, and other dinosaurs is a hit with kids. Spend the night at either Split Mountain or Green River Campground in the monument. Let the song of the Green River play all night in your dreams. This is the river that John Wesley Powell descended to meet the Colorado River during his historic 1869 voyage. If time permits, take the trail to the Josie Morris Ranch and some outstanding ancient Indian petroglyphs. Josie Morris was a crusty pioneer woman who outlived or ran out several husbands. Her homestead, although run-down, is a glimpse back into a time where settlers scraped out a living in the dry land by clinging to the occasional water source.

Day Three
Return to Vernal and then head north on Highway 191 to Flaming Gorge National Recreation Area. For a scenic drive, take the Drive Through the Ages Scenic Byway (pick up a brochure at the Utah Field House of Natural History Museum or Ashley National Forest Office in Vernal). The 168-mile, five-hour trip leads to 20 geologic

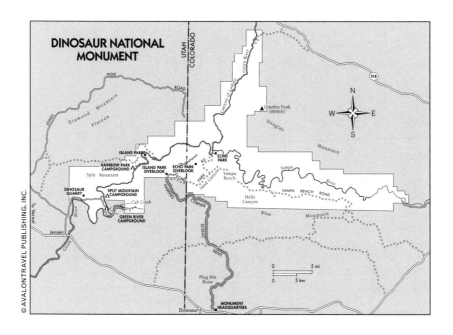

signs along the route that point out various geologic formations. The rest of the day, there are lots of options. Take a tour of the dam. Rent a boat and fish or water-ski in the colorful red-rock canyon. Rent a raft and float the clear river below the dam. The water is calm enough for novices and the river is full of fly fishermen and women angling for trophy-size trout. Pick up a brochure at the dam detailing hiking in the area and explore on foot. Or, head to a campground to fish, swim, or relax. Lucerne Valley and Antelope Flat are large campgrounds near the water. Firefighters Memorial is up in the forest and therefore cooler in hot weather.

Seven-Day Itinerary: Starvation Reservoir 🏕 Dinosaur National Monument 🏕 Steinaker State Park 🏕 Flaming Gorge 🏕 Ashley National Forest

Day One
Travel from Salt Lake on I-80 until the Heber City exit to Highway 40. Take Highway 40 to Starvation Reservoir. This relatively undiscovered body of water has a large grassy area and beach. Fishing is usually spotty, but the setting in buff-colored rock makes it a nice place for other water sports.

Days Two and Three
Continue on Highway 40 about 30 miles to Roosevelt. Take Highway 191 another 30 miles to Vernal. Visit the Dinosaur Natural History Museum (see Three-Day Itinerary, Day Two). After whetting your dinosaur appetite at the museum, head out to Dinosaur National Monument and spend the night (see Three-Day Itinerary, Day

Two). The next day, visit the Josie Morris Ranch and take the Sounds of Silence hike. The trailhead for the two-mile hike is about one mile from the visitors center entrance station on the north side of the road.

Day Four
Return to Vernal and head north on Highway 191 to Steinaker State Park (see Three-Day Itinerary, Day One).

Days Five and Six
Continue north to Flaming Gorge National Recreation Area. Spend two days boating, touring, fishing, hiking, or relaxing (see Three-Day Itinerary, Day Three).

Day Seven
If you're having fun at Flaming Gorge, spend one more day. If you want to see more, then sample the Ashley National Forest on your way back to Salt Lake City. About 16 miles south of Flaming Gorge, look for the Red Cloud Loop Road (Forest Road 020). Arrive early to get a spot in one of the three campgrounds—East Park, Oaks Park, and Kaler Hollow—on the loop. The Red Cloud Loop Road is unpaved in places. It winds its way through a pine and aspen forest. Try fishing in East Park or Oaks Park Reservoirs or in the small feeder streams that lead to them.

1 Vernal KOA

 3

This is a shaded, grassy oasis in an otherwise arid urban setting. Actually, the campground is at the edge of town, in a semi-rural residential section of Vernal surrounded by open fields. But the real bonus is all that's nearby: The Utah Field House of Natural History, Steinaker and Red Fleet State Parks, Dinosaur National Monument, and Flaming Gorge National Recreation Area are all a short drive away.

Location: In Manila; map A3, grid d4.

Campsites, facilities: There are 55 RV sites with full hookups and 35 tent sites, plus restrooms, showers, laundry facilities, RV waste-disposal facilities, picnic tables, a game room, barbecue grills, a swimming pool, a public phone, a convenience and gift store, cable TV, and a playground. Miniature golf, volleyball, and horseshoe facilities are also available. Pets are welcome.

Reservations, fees: Reservations are recommended in the summer. Sites with full hookups are $20 and tent sites are $16.

Open: May 1–Sept. 3.

Directions: In Vernal, take Highway 191 east and go 2.5 miles past the intersection with State Route 191. The KOA is on the west side of the road near the Westin Plaza.

Contact: Vernal KOA, 435/789-8935.

2 Carmel

 8

Due to flash-flood danger, the National Forest Service closes Carmel to camping during most of the warm-weather season, which means that unlike most Utah campgrounds, this is a fall-through-winter kind of place, located near an interesting geological area called Sheep Creek Canyon. Here, erosion has exposed the canyon geology to dramatic effect, revealing a tremendous array of formations from earlier eras amid a series of towering cliffs. When canoeing or rafting, stay near the shore to avoid getting caught in rough water during storms.

Location: In Flaming Gorge National Recreation Area; map A3, grid e4.

Campsites, facilities: There are 15 sites with tent sites, pit toilets, and fire grills, but no drinking water.

Reservations, fees: Sites are free and are first come, first served.

Open: May 15–Oct. 1.

Directions: From Vernal, drive north on Highway 191 for 36 miles. Turn west on State Route 44, go 20 miles, and pick up Forest Service Road 218. Continue west for one mile to the campground, located on the north side of the road.

Contact: Flaming Gorge Ranger District, 435/784-3445.

3 Lucerne Valley

 5

Fishing is the big activity here. Flaming Gorge Reservoir is famous for producing trophy lake trout, and the Lucerne Marina is one of its most-favored launching areas. Swimming and water-skiing are popular pastimes, too; the reservoir is large enough to provide boaters with lots of opportunity to escape the crowds. Unfortunately, the campground—in a sagebrush setting with only a few shade trees—tends to be hot and windy in the summer.

Location: In Flaming Gorge National Recreation Area; map A3, grid d5.

Campsites, facilities: There are 161 sites with picnic tables, fire pits, and water, plus a boat ramp, RV waste-disposal facilities, a public phone, a marina, and an amphitheater.

Reservations, fees: Reservations are accepted for group sites and some single sites. Single-family sites are $13 and group sites are $22.

Open: Mid-Apr.–Oct., though the water is turned off when the temperature is below freezing.

Directions: From Vernal, take Highway 191 north, and then take State Route 44 to Manila. In Manila, follow State Route 43 east for about four miles. Turn right on Forest Service Road 146 and drive four miles to the campground.

Contact: Flaming Gorge Ranger District, 435/784-3445.

4 Gravel Pit/Stateline/Swim Beach

 4

If you're looking to get rustic and close to the water, this place fits the bill, with expansive beaches and swimming options galore. Good for boater who want privacy rather than crowded campgrounds. But be warned: The dispersed camping is on the flats, so summers can be hot.

Location: On Flaming Gorge Reservoir; map A3, grid d5.

Campsites, facilities: This place has undeveloped campsites, with a vault toilet at Gravel Pit and another at Swim Beach. There is no drinking water.

Reservations, fees: Sites are free and are first come, first served.

Open: Mid-May–mid-Sept.

Directions: From Vernal, drive north on Highway 191 to State Route 44. Take that route for four miles to Lucerne Valley. Gravel Pit is 2.1 miles down Lucerne Valley Road on the right, Stateline is 2.4 miles down the road on the left, and Swim Beach is 2.9 miles down on the left.

Contact: Flaming Gorge Ranger District, 435/784-3445.

5 Kingfisher Island

 9

This is a boater's paradise, not to mention a rare chance to get away from car campers and experience the water at its most pristine. To reach the campsites you must climb a moderately steep slope from shore. The sites are terraced, providing nice views of the red rock formations, though the campground, in a sagebrush, juniper, and piñon setting, is rocky and lacks shade. Alert campers can catch a glimpse of the osprey that nest and fish in the area.

Location: In Flaming Gorge National Recreation Area; map A3, grid e4.

Campsites, facilities: There are eight sites with pit toilets, picnic tables, and fire grills, but no water.

Reservations, fees: Sites are free and are first come, first served.

Open: Apr. 1–Dec. 31.

Directions: This campground is accessible by boat only. To get there, travel 17.5 miles up the reservoir from the Flaming Gorge Dam, or seven miles down the reservoir (south) from the Lucerne Valley or Antelope Flat boat ramps.

Contact: Flaming Gorge Ranger District, 435/784-3445.

6 Hideout Canyon

 9

With sites on moderately steep, terraced land in a piñon and juniper forest, this campground offers boat campers some nice amenities, better-than-normal shade, and relative solitude. There's good fishing for kokanee salmon, smallmouth bass, and rainbow and lake trout, and excellent water-skiing in the summer.

Location: In Flaming Gorge National Recreation Area; map A3, grid e4.

Campsites, facilities: There are 18 sites with picnic tables and fire grills, plus flush toilets, water, and boat docks. Three sites are handicapped accessible.

Reservations, fees: Reservations are

available for some sites up to 120 days in advance, July 1 to Labor Day; call the National Reservation System at 800/280-2267. Sites are $18.

Open: Open year-round, but water is only available mid-May–mid-Sept.

Directions: Access here is primarily by boat, though hikers can reach the campground via the lower two miles of the Hideout Trail, which starts near the Dowd Mountain Overlook (take State Route 44 to Forest Road 94 and driving west for four miles). By water, travel 15.5 miles up Flaming Gorge Reservoir, nine miles down the reservoir (south) from the boat ramps at Lucerne Valley and Antelope Flat, or three miles east from the Sheep Creek Bay boat launch.

Contact: Flaming Gorge Ranger District, 435/784-3445.

⑦ Antelope Flat

 8

Because this site is a little farther from the major marinas and less shaded than other area campgrounds, Antelope Flat tends to be less crowded than its neighbor. Campers who do venture here find a real treasure: the swimming beach, though on the primitive side, is one of Flaming Gorge's best, with antelope often wandering by. Boating on Flaming Gorge can be done from here too. And the view of the gorge that gives the reservoir its name is a sight to remember. Shore fishing for smallmouth bass can be excellent.

Location: In Flaming Gorge National Recreation Area; map A3, grid e5.

Campsites, facilities: There are 121 single sites and four group sites, plus picnic tables and fire grills, water, and restrooms with cold running water. An RV waste-disposal site, a boat ramp, a public phone, a fish-cleaning station, an undeveloped swimming area, and a covered picnic pavilion are also available at Antelope Flat.

Reservations, fees: Reservations are available 120 days in advance; call the National Reservation System at 800/280-2267. Sites are $12.

Open: Mid-May–mid-Sept.

Directions: From Vernal, take U.S. Route 191 north to Flaming Gorge National Recreation Area. Then follow Forest Service Road 145 west for four miles to the campground.

Contact: Flaming Gorge Ranger District, 435/784-3445.

⑧ Canyon Rim

 9

Set in a lodgepole forest at an elevation of 7,400 feet, small Canyon Rim Campground is blessed with a convenient location: Visitors will discover that it's close to the Red Canyon Visitors Center, commercial Red Canyon Lodge, and Greens Lake. Take time to enjoy the various natural-history exhibits at the visitors center and the standout views of Flaming Gorge. Following the short nature walk that starts and ends near the center property is also a worthwhile activity.

Location: In Flaming Gorge National Recreation Area; map A3, grid e5.

Campsites, facilities: There are 18 sites with picnic tables, plus fire grills, drinking water, and vault toilets.

Reservations, fees: Sites are $12 and are first come, first served.

Open: Mid-May–mid-Sept.

Directions: From Vernal, take U.S. Route 191 north to Flaming Gorge National Recreation Area. Follow State Route 44 east for about three miles. Turn north on Forest Service Road 095 and continue for about 1.5 miles to the campground.

Contact: Flaming Gorge Ranger District, 435/784-3445.

9 Gooseneck

   8

Solitude is the number-one selling point here; boaters don't often get the chance to enjoy their crafts in such beautiful seclusion. The canyon scenery is superb, and the campground has a nice shaded setting of large ponderosa pines with scattered juniper and piñon trees. Expect a steep climb to the sites, and be aware that at this altitude (6,040 ft.), the reservoir does freeze up some winters.

Location: In Flaming Gorge National Recreation Area; map A3, grid e5.

Campsites, facilities: There are six sites with picnic tables, plus fire grills and pit toilets, but there's no water.

Reservations, fees: Sites are $5 and are first come, first served.

Open: Year-round.

Directions: This campground is only accessible by boat. Travel 8.5 miles up the reservoir from the Flaming Gorge Dam or 16 miles down the reservoir from the marinas at Lucerne Valley or Antelope Flat.

Contact: Flaming Gorge Ranger District, 435/784-3445.

10 Greens Lake

     8

Campers won't lack for things to do at this shaded haven perched at 7,400 feet in the ponderosa pines. Greens Lake, at the campground's edge, has plenty of decent rainbow-trout fishing, as well as opportunities for swimming and exploring in small rowboats and canoes. The Red Canyon Nature Trail and the walk on the Canyon Rim are a bonanza for hikers, with views of a red-rock gorge and of Flaming Gorge Reservoir 1,360 feet below the rim. And the Red Canyon Visitors Center has some interesting exhibits on the area's geology, cultural history, and plant and animal life, along with great views of the gorge.

Location: In Flaming Gorge National Recreation Area; map A3, grid e5.

Campsites, facilities: There are 19 sites with picnic tables and fire grills, plus water, vault toilets, a group area, and trash pickup. The Red Canyon Visitors Center and Nature Trail are nearby, and the trailhead for the Canyon Rim Hiking Trail is at the campground entrance.

Reservations, fees: Sites are $9 and are first come, first served.

Open: May 17–Nov. 1.

Directions: From Vernal, take U.S. Route 191 north to Flaming Gorge National Recreation Area. Follow State Route 44 west for about four miles to Forest Service Road 095, known as Red Canyon Road. Turn north and proceed about a mile to the campground on Greens Lake.

Contact: Flaming Gorge Ranger District, 435/784-3445.

11 Skull Creek

    8

This retreat in the ponderosa pines has a creek trickling melodiously nearby. There's also a trailhead for the Canyon Rim Hiking Trail, which offers some nice views of Flaming Gorge Reservoir. Boating from Flaming Gorge is a nearby option. At the sites, the spurs are somewhat short, suitable for trailers or RVs up to 20 feet long. At an elevation of 7,600 feet, this campground is cooler than many.

Location: In Flaming Gorge National Recreation Area; map A3, grid e5.

Campsites, facilities: There are 17 sites with picnic tables and fire pits, plus water and two vault toilets.

Reservations, fees: Sites are $12 and are first come, first served.

Open: Memorial Day weekend–Labor Day weekend.

Directions: From Vernal, take U.S. Route 191 north to the Flaming Gorge National Recreation Area, and follow State Route 44 west for three miles. The campground is on the north side of the highway.

Contact: Flaming Gorge Ranger District, 435/784-3445.

12 Greendale West

    6

Set in a fairly open part of the national recreation area at an elevation of 6,950 feet, this campground is within walking distance of Flaming Gorge Lodge. The lodge and a motel include a store, a restaurant, and raft rentals for exploring the Green River below the Flaming Gorge Dam. On some summer weekends, campfire programs are available at the nearby Bootleg Amphitheater. This is a good central location for anyone planning to enjoy Green River rafting or acquatic attractions of fishing and boatingon the reservoir itself.

Location: In Flaming Gorge National Recreation Area; map A3, grid e5.

Campsites, facilities: There are eight campsites with picnic tables and fire pits; drinking water and vault toilets are available.

Reservations, fees: Sites are $12 and are first come, first served.

Open: May 20–Dec. 31.

Directions: From Vernal, take Highway 191 north to Flaming Gorge Dam. From there, drive four miles south, staying on the highway. The campground is on the west side of the road near Flaming Gorge Lodge.

Contact: Flaming Gorge Ranger District, 345/784-3445.

13 Firefighters Memorial

     7

For RVers looking for ponderosa-shaded sites with large parking spurs, this is the spot. The only drawback: You'll have to drive to the aquatic attractions of Flaming Gorge Reservoir. Still, this is a nice, fairly quiet retreat—

conveniently close to all the amenities of Flaming Gorge Lodge. Families, especially, will like the self-guided tours of nearby Flaming Gorge Dam. Some visitors like to walk the trail that leads along the Green River from the dam, fly-fishing for trout as they go. The elevation is 6,900 feet.

Location: In Flaming Gorge National Recreation Area; map A3, grid e5.

Campsites, facilities: There are 94 sites with picnic tables and fire pits, plus water, flush toilets, and an amphitheater.

Reservations, fees: For reservations, call the National Reservation System at 800/280-2267. Sites are $12.

Open: May 17–Sept. 12.

Directions: From Vernal, take Highway 191 north to Flaming Gorge National Recreation Area. After the Flaming Gorge Dam, go another 3.5 miles. The campground is right off the highway, just north of Flaming Gorge Lodge.

Contact: Flaming Gorge Ranger District, 435/784-3445.

14 Cedar Springs

    6

This is one of the better area campgrounds for serious boaters, since it's right near the full-service Cedar Springs Marina, which offers boat rentals, boat launching, and overnight boat-trailer parking. But despite some tall piñon and juniper trees, summers can be scorching. Luckily, swimmers and water-skiers can cool off in the reservoir.

Location: In Flaming Gorge National Recreation Area; map A3, grid e5.

Campsites, facilities: There are 23 sites with picnic tables and fire grills, plus water, flush toilets, showers, RV waste-disposal sites, a boat ramp, and a marina.

Reservations, fees: For reservations, call the U.S. Forest Service National Reservation

System at 800/280-2267. Sites are $12. Double sites are $25.

Open: May 17–Sept. 12.

Directions: From Vernal, drive north on Highway 191. About 1.5 miles south of Flaming Gorge Dam, look for a turnoff to Cedar Springs Marina, heading north. The campground is just over a mile north of the highway.

Contact: Flaming Gorge Ranger District, 801/784-3445.

15 Deer Run

     6

This is a nice central location for boat trips on Flaming Gorge Reservoir, raft trips on the Green River below the dam, or tours of the dam and its visitors center. And there's overnight boat-trailer parking (plus boat rentals) at Cedar Springs Marina. Still, the campground can get hot in the summer, even though it's surrounded by 10- to 20-foot piñon and juniper trees.

Location: In Flaming Gorge National Recreation Area; map A3, grid e5.

Campsites, facilities: There are 15 single sites and four group areas, along with picnic tables, fire grills, flush toilets, showers, drinking water, and access to the Cedar Springs Marina.

Reservations, fees: For reservations, call the National Reservation System at 800/230-2267. Rates are $14 for single sites and $25 for group sites.

Open: Apr. 20–Sept. 12.

Directions: From Vernal, drive north toward Flaming Gorge Dam on Highway 191, then go 1.5 miles south of the dam on the same highway. Look for the turnoff to the Cedar Springs Marina.

Contact: Flaming Gorge Ranger District, 435/784-3445.

16 Mustang Ridge

    8

This is one of the only area campgrounds with a view of Flaming Gorge Dam. That, along with the decent swimming beach, good fishing and boating, and shaded sites carved out of a piñon-and-juniper forest, also makes it one of the most popular. Reservations are strongly suggested on weekends. Fishing for smallmouth bass is especially good on the rocky points near the boat ramp. At an elevation of 6,200 feet, the water is cold, even in summer, but that doesn't discourage folks from venturing in.

Location: In Flaming Gorge National Recreation Area; map A3, grid e5.

Campsites, facilities: There are 54 single sites, most built for large trailers and RVs, and 19 group sites, with picnic tables, fire grills, drinking water, flush toilets, and showers. A nearby paved boat ramp, an undeveloped swimming area, and boat-trailer parking are also available.

Reservations, fees: To reserve campsites 1–39, call the U.S. Forest Service National Reservation System at 800/280-2267. Rates are $14 for single sites and $28 for group sites.

Open: May 17–Sept. 12.

Directions: From Vernal, take U.S. Route 191 north to Flaming Gorge National Recreation Area. Just past the prominent Dutch John Service Station, turn left on Forest Service Road 184 (State Route 260). Continue for just under four miles to the campground.

Contact: Flaming Gorge Ranger District, 435/784-3445.

17 Jarvies Canyon

  8

The best thing about this little canyon spot is its remoteness. In a sagebrush, piñon, and juniper setting, far from the car-camping crowds, boaters can water-ski or gaze at the stellar scenery in relative solitude. The sites are terraced, so expect to walk uphill with your camping equipment. And be aware that at this

6,040-foot elevation, the reservoir does freeze some winters.

Location: In Flaming Gorge National Recreation Area; map A3, grid e6.

Campsites, facilities: There are eight sites with picnic tables, fire grills, and pit toilets, but no water.

Reservations, fees: Sites are free and are first come, first served.

Open: Year-round.

Directions: This campground on Flaming Gorge Reservoir is accessible by boat only. Go 4.5 miles upstream from Flaming Gorge Dam or 20 miles from the Lucerne Valley or Antelope Flat boat ramps.

Contact: Flaming Gorge Ranger District, 435/784-3445.

18 Dripping Springs

  8

Fishing is so popular on the Green River that this place probably fills more quickly than any other campground in Flaming Gorge National Recreation Area. Set in a spectacular gorge and full of large, hungry trout, the Green is known for having some of the best fishing in the western United States, and hence draws fly anglers from all over the world. Rafters also like the river access. The campground, in a piñon and juniper forest, is also three miles from the Little Hole boat ramp, which is about seven miles from the boat ramp near Flaming Gorge Dam. But be warned: It can get a little windy here.

Location: In Flaming Gorge National Recreation Area; map A3, grid e6.

Campsites, facilities: There are 21 single sites, four group sites, and two double sites, plus picnic tables, fire grills, drinking water (Memorial Day to Labor Day weekend), and flush and vault toilets.

Reservations, fees: For reservations, call the U.S. Forest Service National Reservation System at 800/280-2267. Sites are $12 from

Memorial Day to Labor Day weekend, and free (but without water) the rest of the year.

Open: Year-round.

Directions: From Vernal, take U.S. Route 191 north to Flaming Gorge National Recreation Area. At Dutch John Service Station, turn right on Forest Service Road 075. Continue about two miles to the campground.

Contact: Flaming Gorge Ranger District, 435/784-3445.

19 Bridge Hollow

   5

Located next to the Green River in the midst of willows and cottonwood trees, this is a great place for anglers to end their float trips, should they elect to raft past Little Hole while floating from Flaming Gorge Dam. Also, the nearby Browne's Park State Waterfowl Management Area is a good place to see all types of migrating birds. And the John Jarvie Historic Site (see Indian Crossing, page 124) is on the banks of the river. Road conditions can be iffy in bad weather, so check out the situation first in Vernal or Dutch John during the off-season.

Location: On Bureau of Land Management property; map A3, grid e7.

Campsites, facilities: There are 13 sites with picnic tables and fire pits. Vault toilets and drinking water are available.

Reservations, fees: Sites are $5 and are first come, first served.

Open: Year-round.

Directions: From Vernal, take Highway 191 north to the town of Dutch John. Continue north for another three miles, then drive east for 20 miles on Clay Basin Road. Look for a turnoff into Jesse Ewing Canyon, drive five miles south through the canyon, and cross the Green River. The campground is near the bridge.

Contact: Vernal District

Office of the Bureau of Land Management, 435/789-1362.

20 Indian Crossing

 5

This Green River campground is popular among anglers and rafters coming from Little Hole, a boat ramp and picnic area (accessible by road from Dutch John) in Flaming Gorge National Recreation Area. Tours of the nearby John Jarvie Historic Site, a ranch once visited by outlaw Butch Cassidy, are available during much of the spring, summer, and fall tourist season. Mr. Jarvie, an innkeeper and ranch owner, was murdered by a pair of transient workers in 1909; today, the property consists of the stone house and dugout that served as his home, along with a blacksmith shop and corrals.

Location: On Bureau of Land Management property; map A3, grid e7.

Campsites, facilities: There are 24 sites with picnic shelters, tables, and fire pits. Vault toilets and drinking water are available May to September.

Reservations, fees: Sites are $2 and are first come, first served.

Open: Year-round.

Directions: From Vernal, take Highway 191 north to Dutch John. Go three more miles, then head east on winding Clay Basin Road for 20 miles, which eventually takes you five miles south into Jesse Ewing Canyon. Cross the bridge over the Green River, then drive west for two miles. The campground is just past the Jarvie Historic Ranch. There are flush toilets and guided tours May–Sept. at the ranch.

Contact: Vernal District Office of the Bureau of Land Management, 435/789-1362.

21 Spirit Lake

 9

The U.S. Forest Service describes this area as "mountainous, lakefront terrain with plenty of shade and lots of mosquitoes." They're not kidding about the mosquitoes: Anyone going into this part of the Uinta Mountains is definitely going to run into them, so come prepared. Though a bit on the rustic side, the campground is a good place to start a day hike or a backpacking trip into the High Uintas Wilderness, Utah's largest. Spirit Lake itself is a pretty spot, with adequate fishing for stocked trout; a commercial lodge there provides cabins, horse rentals, boat and canoe rentals, a café, and a guide service. Due to the 10,000-foot altitude, the campground has a fairly short season, so check the weather before you come.

Location: In Ashley National Forest; map A3, grid e3.

Campsites, facilities: There are 24 family sites with picnic tables, fire grills, and vault toilets, but no drinking water.

Reservations, fees: Sites are $5 and are first come, first served.

Open: June–Labor Day weekend, depending on snow conditions.

Directions: From Vernal, take Highway 191 north to Greendale Junction, then head west on State Route 44 and drive 14.6 miles to Sheep Creek Canyon Road. Follow this road for three miles to the Deep Creek/Spirit Lake junction, then take Spirit Lake Road (Forest Road 001) 10.4 miles to the Spirit Lake turnoff. The campground entrance is 6.25 miles from the turnoff.

Contact: Flaming Gorge Ranger District, 435/784-3445.

22 Browne Lake

 8

Browne Lake is a pretty little spot with some trees and open spaces, at an elevation of 8,200 feet. Though remote and a bit tricky to reach (it's a rough ride for most trailers and RVs, though some do make the trip), this place can be popular, largely due to the trout fishing and canoeing around the lake. History buffs can explore the nearby Ute Mountain fire lookout, a restored historic fire tower. Guided tours are offered at certain times of year; consult the Flaming Gorge Ranger District for details.

Location: In Ashley National Forest; map A3, grid e4.

Campsites, facilities: There are eight sites with picnic tables, fire grills, and vault toilets, but no drinking water.

Reservations, fees: Sites are $5 and are first come, first served.

Open: May–Sept.

Directions: From Vernal, drive north on Highway 191 to Greendale Junction. Take State Route 44 west for about 10 miles to State Route 218. Follow it approximately three miles to a dirt road, Forest Road 221; take this road west about four miles to Forest Road 96, which leads southeast for about one mile to Browne Lake.

Contact: Flaming Gorge Ranger District, 435/784-3445.

23 Deep Creek

   8

Many anglers like to fish the namesake creek near this nicely shaded campground; the water flows through the rolling and steep reaches of the surrounding terrain. Sites here are not far from Browne Lake or from trailheads into the High Uintas Wilderness (popular with horseback riders). The elevation is 7,800 feet.

Location: In Ashley National Forest; map A3, grid e4.

Campsites, facilities: There are 17 sites, plus vault toilets, picnic tables, and fire grills, but no water.

Reservations, fees: Sites are $6 and are first come, first served.

Open: June 1–Oct. 1.

Directions: From Vernal, take Highway 191 north to Greendale Junction, then follow State Route 44 for 11.4 miles to the Deep Creek Road junction. The campground is located 2.4 miles to the southwest on Deep Creek Road.

Contact: Flaming Gorge Ranger District, 435/784-3445.

24 Lodgepole

     7

Away from the visitor traffic of Flaming Gorge Reservoir, this pretty spot nestled in the quaking aspens and lodgepole pines offers a quieter kind of camping. Yet it's conveniently situated so that boaters and anglers can still enjoy Flaming Gorge to the north, as well as Red Fleet and Steinaker Reservoirs to the south. Hiking, riding, swimming, and waterskiing are all popular at nearby Flaming Gorge National Recreation Area.

Location: In Ashley National Forest; map A3, grid e5.

Campsites, facilities: There are 35 sites; five are pull-throughs and 30 are pull-ins. The RV limit is 22 feet. Facilities include picnic tables, fire pits, water, flush toilets, and a Dumpster.

Reservations, fees: To reserve sites 1–3 and 5–11, call the National Reservation System at 800/280-2267. Campsites are $12.

Open: Apr. 25–Oct. 31.

Directions: From Vernal, take Highway 191 north for 30.5 miles. The campground is on the east side of the road.

Contact: Vernal Ranger District, 435/789-1181.

25 Red Springs

    7

On busy weekends, campers arriving too late to snag a site at Flaming Gorge Reservoir often look to this place next. Set in a forest of quaking aspen and lodgepole pine, it's just a few miles from the reservoir, though boaters, swimmers, water-skiers, and anglers shouldn't ignore the less-crowded Red Fleet Reservoir to the south.

Location: In Ashley National Forest; map A3, grid e5.

Campsites, facilities: There are 13 sites with picnic tables, fire pits, and vault toilets, plus drinking water May–Sept.

Reservations, fees: Sites are $10 and are first come, first served.

Open: Apr. 25–Sept. 30.

Directions: From Vernal, take Highway 191 north for 26 miles. The campground is on the west side of the road.

Contact: Vernal Ranger District, 435/789-1181.

26 East Park

   7

Located in a somewhat open setting surrounded by lodgepole pines, this campground sits right next door to East Park Reservoir. Fish from the shore or use a canoe or raft in deeper water. Anglers will find this small reservoir regularly stocked with fish, though they may have better luck coaxing rainbow, cutthroat, and brook trout from the nearby streams. Hiking trails lead north and west from the reservoir through the Ashley National Forest. And there's some enticing alpine scenery along nearby Red Cloud Loop Road.

Location: In Ashley National Forest; map A3, grid f5.

Campsites, facilities: There are 21 sites; five are pull-throughs and 16 are pull-ins. The RV length limit is 22 feet. Facilities include picnic tables, fire grills, and vault toilets, with drinking water June–Sept.

Reservations, fees: Sites are $8 and are first come, first served.

Open: June–Oct.

Directions: From Vernal, drive north on High-way 191 for 20 miles, looking for Red Cloud Loop Road (Forest Road 018) to the north-west. Take that road, following the pavement for about nine miles to the end before turning right on East Park Campground Road (Forest Road 020). Drive on the gravel for one mile to the campground.

Contact: Vernal Ranger District, 435/789-1181.

27 Oaks Park

  8

The elevation of 9,200 feet makes for a short season, but this pretty alpine campground is a great place for a woodsy summer retreat. There are rainbow trout in adjacent Oaks Park Reservoir, along with decent stream fishing from small area creeks. The reservoir, though not large, is fine for rafts, canoes, and small boats.

Location: In Ashley National Forest; map A3, grid f5.

Campsites, facilities: There are 11 single sites with picnic tables, fire grills, and vault toilets. Water is available mid-June to September from a pump-handle well in an undeveloped area north of the campground.

Reservations, fees: Sites are $5 and are first come, first served.

Open: June–Sept.

Directions: From Vernal, take Highway 191 north for 20 miles, then head west on Red Cloud Loop Road (Forest Road 018) for 13 miles. Turn off at the Oaks Park sign and proceed another mile to the campground.

Contact: Vernal Ranger District, 435/789-1181.

28 Kaler Hollow

 8

Group camping is the norm and fishing is the prime pastime at this small campground in the quaking aspens and lodgepole pines. Local streams yield plenty of trout, as do the nearby Oaks Park and East Park Reservoirs.

Another good diversion is the Red Cloud Loop, a scenic stretch of pavement and dirt that basically starts and ends in Vernal. Pick up a "Drive Through the Ages" brochure at the downtown Vernal Visitors Center to learn about the geological history of the area along Highway 191.

Location: In Ashley National Forest; map A3, grid f5.

Campsites, facilities: There are four tables with fire rings at this largely undeveloped site. There's one vault toilet, but no water.

Reservations, fees: Sites are free and are first come, first served.

Open: June 1–Oct. 31.

Directions: From Vernal, take Highway 191 north to Red Cloud Loop Road (Forest Road 018) and head west. The campground is located at the junction of the loop road and Taylor Mountain Road.

Contact: Vernal Ranger District, 435/789-1181.

29 Iron Mine

   9

The number-one bonus of this lovely mountain spot is the trout fishing on the North Fork of the Duchesne River; the campground is right on the banks. Surrounded by fir, quaking aspen, and pine at an elevation of 7,200 feet, it's also convenient to the horseback rentals of nearby Defas Dude Ranch. The Grandview Trailhead, providing hiking and horseback access into the High Uintas Wilderness Area, is just six miles away.

Location: In Ashley National Forest; map A3, grid f0.

Campsites, facilities: There are 22 single sites, two double sites, and one group site, with picnic tables, fire grills, vault toilets, and dumpsters. The RV length limit is 22 feet. Water is available Memorial Day to Labor Day.

Reservations, fees: For reservations, call the National Reservation System at 800/280-2267. Single sites are $6, doubles are $10, and the group site is $25.

Open: Memorial Day–Labor Day; also open during the fall hunting season, but without water.

Directions: From Duchesne, drive west on Highway 40 for approximately 17 miles. Turn north on State Route 208 and go nine miles. Then head west on State Route 35 through the tiny hamlets of Tabiona and Hanna, looking for Forest Road 144 to the north. Take that road north and go another seven miles to the campground.

Contact: Duchesne Ranger District, 435/738-2482.

30 Hades

    9

This is one of the more remote areas in Utah—and, despite the name, one of the prettiest, especially in fall when the aspen leaves begin to change. For those who make the extra effort to get here, the rewards are great: There's ample fishing in the nearby North Fork of the Duchesne River and in the High Uintas Wilderness Area lakes, which you can reach by horseback or on foot.

Location: In Ashley National Forest; map A3, grid f0.

Campsites, facilities: There are 17 sites, 10 of them suitable for RVs up to 22 feet long. There are also picnic tables, fire grills, drinking water, and pit toilets.

Reservations, fees: Sites are $6 and are first come, first served.

Open: Apr. 25–Sept. 10.

Directions: From Duchesne, drive west on Highway 40 for approximately 17 miles. Turn north on State Route 208 and go another nine miles. Then head west on State Route 35 through the hamlets of

Tabiona and Hanna, looking for Forest Road 144 to the north. Drive five miles north on that road. The campground is on the west side of the road, near Defas Dude Ranch. **Contact:** Duchesne Ranger District, 435/738-2482.

31 Aspen Grove

 9

Set in the quaking aspens in another of northern Utah's most gorgeous hideaways, this remote, high-country campground offers hiking and horseback trails that lead to the lakes of the nearby High Uintas Wilderness Area. And there's all the trout fishing you could want on the North and West Forks of the Duchesne River (the North Fork is adjacent to the campground).

Location: In Ashley National Forest; map A3, grid f0.

Campsites, facilities: There are 33 sites, 26 of them appropriate for RVs up to 22 feet long, with picnic tables, fire pits, drinking water, and pit toilets.

Reservations, fees: Sites are $6 and are first come, first served.

Open: June 25–Sept. 10.

Directions: From Duchesne, drive west on Highway 40 for approximately 17 miles. Turn north on State Route 208 and go nine miles. Then head west on State Route 35 through the hamlets of Tabiona and Hanna, looking for Forest Road 144 to the north. Drive 2.5 miles north on that road; the campground is on the west side.

Contact: Duchesne Ranger District, 435/738-2482.

32 Yellowpine

 9

Adjacent to Rock Creek in a wooded setting of lodgepole, quaking aspen, and ponderosa pine, this is another favored fishing spot. An-

glers try their luck in both the creek and the nearby Upper Stillwater Reservoir, five miles up the canyon. A hiking and horseback trail along Rock Creek begins a quarter-mile away from the campground.

Location: In Ashley National Forest; map A3, grid f1.

Campsites, facilities: There are 20 single sites, seven double sites, and two triple-family sites, with picnic tables, fire grills, handicapped-accessible flush toilets, drinking water, Dumpsters, and an RV waste-disposal site.

Reservations, fees: To reserve sites 1–10, call the National Reservation System at 800/280-2267. Rates are $10 for single sites, $16 for doubles, and $30 for triples.

Open: Memorial Day–Labor Day; also open in the fall, but without water.

Directions: From Duchesne, head north on Highway 87. When you reach Mountain Home, take the road that heads north and west (it eventually becomes Forest Road 134). The campground is about 20 miles from Mountain Home along that road.

Contact: Duchesne Ranger District, 801/738-2482.

33 Upper Stillwater

 9

This relatively new facility in a setting of quaking aspen and lodgepole and ponderosa pine provides good access to the High Uintas Wilderness Area; hiking and horseback riding trails lead right there from the campground. Fishing can be decent at Upper Stillwater Reservoir, a relatively new part of the Central Utah Project (a massive effort to bring water from the Colorado River basin to the Wasatch Front), though bank access is somewhat difficult. Anglers also report success on Rock Creek in the areas where it flows into the reservoir and where it leaves the dam.

Location: In Ashley National Forest; map A3, grid f1.

Campsites, facilities: This is one of the state's newest campgrounds, with 14 single sites, six double sites, and one triple site. The RV length limit is 22 feet. Picnic tables, fire pits, running water, and wheelchair-accessible flush toilets are available.

Reservations, fees: Sites are $10 for singles, $16 for doubles, and $30 for the triple, and are first come, first served.

Open: Memorial Day–Labor Day.

Directions: From Duchesne, head north on Highway 87. When you reach Mountain Home, take the road that heads north and west (eventually it becomes Forest Road 134). The campground is about 19 miles from Mountain Home along that road.

Contact: Duchesne Ranger District at 435/738-2482.

34 Moon Lake

    9

Situated next to a rustic old lodge in the midst of lodgepole pines, this popular campground also sits right up against scenic Moon Lake, a man-made reservoir on the edge of the High Uintas Wilderness Area. Use the lake for canoeing or rafting. There's good rainbow-trout fishing here and on the streams flowing in and out of the reservoir (but be careful not to cross into the Ute Indian Reservation downstream without a special Ute license). At an elevation of 8,100 feet, the campground permits tents and is also a trailhead for horseback riding and hikes into the High Uintas.

Location: On Moon Lake in Ashley National Forest; map A3, grid f2.

Campsites, facilities: There are 56 single sites, two group sites, and one double site, with picnic tables and fire grills, flush toilets, running water, and a Dumpster. The RV length limit is 22 feet.

Reservations, fees: Only the two group sites can be reserved; call the National Reservation System at 800/280-2267. Fees are $12 for single sites, $20 for the double, and $40 for the group sites.

Open: May–Sept.

Directions: From Duchesne, drive north on State Route 87 for 33 miles to the campground. Once in the forest, the road turns into Forest Road 131.

Contact: Roosevelt Ranger District, 435/722-5018.

35 Swift Creek

   7

This is one of the horse-friendliest campgrounds in the area, with 16 stalls and two unloading ramps at the Swift Creek Trailhead. The trail itself leads to some fishable waters in the scenic High Uintas Wilderness Area. Closer by, the Yellowstone River offers decent trout fishing. The campground is in a setting of flat-to-rolling canyon bottom with conifer, aspen, and sagebrush, at an elevation of 8,200 feet.

Location: In Ashley National Forest; map A3, grid f3.

Campsites, facilities: There are 13 single sites with picnic tables and fire grills. Drinking water and vault toilets are available.

Reservations, fees: Sites are $9 and are first come, first served.

Open: May–Sept.

Directions: The campground is 32 miles north of Duchesne. From Duchesne, take State Route 87 for 21 miles and turn onto Forest Road 119, which leads to the campground.

Contact: Roosevelt Ranger District, 435/722-5018.

36 Riverview

    7

Situated on the Yellowstone

River at an elevation of 8,000 feet, this is a pleasant and remote place to relax in an alpine setting. Horseback riding through the summer and into the winter is popular. Rainbow-trout fishing on the Yellowstone River can be good, as is hiking the nearby High Uintas Wilderness Area. Backpackers like to take trails to Timothy Lake or, if they're ambitious, up to 13,528-foot King's Peak, the highest point in Utah.

Location: In Ashley National Forest; map A3, grid f3.

Campsites, facilities: There are 19 single sites with picnic tables and fire grills; drinking water and vault toilets are available.

Reservations, fees: Sites are $9 and are first come, first served.

Open: May 17–Sept. 12.

Directions: The campground is 31 miles north of Duchesne. From Duchesne, take State Route 87 for 21 miles to Forest Road 119, which leads to the campground.

Contact: Roosevelt Ranger District, 435/722-5018.

37 Reservoir

   7

The reservoir in question here is tiny but full of rainbow trout, and the nearby Yellowstone River isn't bad for angling either. Nestled in a flat and rolling canyon bottom amid conifers, aspens, and sagebrush, this high-country spot (elevation 8,000 ft.) is a place to enjoy camping on the cool side. Hiking and horsepacking trips lead from here into the High Uintas Wilderness Area, Utah's largest.

Location: In Ashley National Forest; map A3, grid f3.

Campsites, facilities: There are five single sites with an RV length limit of 22 feet, plus vault toilets, picnic tables, water, and fire grills.

Reservations, fees: Sites are $9 and are first come, first served.

Open: May–Sept.

Directions: The campground is 31 miles north of Duchesne. From Duchesne, take State Route 87 for 21 miles to Forest Road 119, which leads to the campground.

Contact: Roosevelt Ranger District, 435/722-5018.

38 Bridge

   8

This campground, in a mixed pine, aspen, and conifer forest at an elevation of 7,800 feet, is not far from the hiking trails and horseback-riding areas of Ashley National Forest. Trout fishing can be quite productive in the Yellowstone River as well as in nearby Water Lily Lake, so don't forget your fishing pole.

Location: In Ashley National Forest; map A3, grid f3.

Campsites, facilities: There are five tent sites with picnic tables and fire pits. Drinking water and vault toilets are available.

Reservations, fees: Sites are $9 and are first come, first served.

Open: May–Sept.

Directions: The campground is about 28 miles north of Duchesne. From Duchesne, take State Route 87 for 21 miles to Forest Road 119, which leads to the campground.

Contact: Roosevelt Ranger District, 435/722-5018.

39 Yellowstone

   8

Because this place is somewhat off the beaten byways, there's some better-than-average fishing in the small canyon reservoir, the scenic Yellowstone River, and nearby Water Lily Lake. The campground itself is in a mixed pine, conifer, aspen, and sagebrush forest at the edge of the High Uintas Wilderness Area. Horseback or hike into the High Uintas.

Location: In Ashley National Forest; map A3, grid f3.

Campsites, facilities: There are 16 single sites with an RV length limit of 22 feet. Picnic tables, fire grills, vault toilets, and drinking water are available.

Reservations, fees: Sites are $9 and are first come, first served.

Open: May–Sept.

Directions: The campground is 28 miles north of Duchesne. From Duchesne, take State Route 87 for 21 miles to Forest Road 119, which leads to the campground.

Contact: Roosevelt Ranger District, 435/722-5018.

40 Wandin

   8

Located on flat-to-rolling terrain in a mixed-conifer forest, this small campground sits right on the edge of the Uinta River at an elevation of 7,800 feet. Trout fishing in the river and hiking or horseback riding in the canyon are the chief lures for visitors here.

Location: In Ashley National Forest; map A3, grid f3.

Campsites, facilities: There are six single sites with picnic tables, fire grills, and vault toilets, but no water. The RV length limit is 22 feet.

Reservations, fees: Sites are $9 and are first come, first served.

Open: June–Sept.

Directions: From Roosevelt, drive 16 miles north on State Highway 121. The road becomes Forest Road 118, which leads north; take it nine more miles to the campground.

Contact: Roosevelt Ranger District, 435/722-5018.

41 Uinta Canyon

   9

This campground, set in a lovely alpine mead-

ow surrounded by aspen and ponderosa pine, is at 7,600 feet. There's fishing for small trout on the Uinta River (which is really more of a creek) and plenty of hiking and horseback riding in the nearby High Uintas Wilderness Area, a rugged expanse of glacier-carved mountain terrain and the largest such area in the state.

Location: In Ashley National Forest; map A3, grid f3.

Campsites, facilities: There are 24 single sites with picnic tables and fire grills, no drinking water, vault toilets, and a Dumpster. The RV length limit is 22 feet.

Reservations, fees: Reservations are accepted. Sites are $9.

Open: May–Sept.

Directions: Drive 16 miles north of Roosevelt on State Route 121, which turns into Forest Road 118; take it north for nine more miles to the campground.

Contact: Roosevelt Ranger District, 435/722-5018.

42 Pole Creek

   9

As the rugged uphill drive here might suggest, this is one of the state's highest campgrounds, at an elevation of 10,200 feet. It's a spectacularly secluded setting of mixed conifers on flat-to-rolling terrain, right next to the highly fishable Pole Creek Lake. Hikers can take one- to two-mile treks to Upper, Middle, and Lower Rock Lakes, just east and south of the High Uintas Wilderness Area boundary. Horseback riding on trails in the High Uintas is a appealing alternative.

Location: In Ashley National Forest; map A3, grid f4.

Campsites, facilities: There are 18 single sites with picnic tables, fire grills, and pit toilets, but no water.

Reservations, fees: Sites are $5 and are first come, first served.

Open: July–Sept.

Directions: From Roosevelt, take State Highway 121 north for 16 miles. Go four miles northeast on Forest Road 118, then turn onto Forest Road 117 and climb for another seven miles to the campground.

Contact: Roosevelt Ranger District, 435/722-5018.

43 Paradise Park

     8

Located next to the small Paradise Reservoir, this is a much-visited boating, swimming, and fishing spot. Hiking and horse trails lead to nearby alpine lakes in the High Uintas Wilderness Area, where brook and cutthroat trout are the main prey. At an elevation of 10,000 feet, the campground is a good place to beat the summer heat.

Location: In Ashley National Forest; map A3, grid f4.

Campsites, facilities: There are 15 pull-in sites with picnic tables, fire grills, and vault toilets, but no water.

Reservations, fees: Sites are $5 and are first come, first served.

Open: June–Oct.

Directions: From Vernal, follow State Route 121 to a junction east of Lapoint. Turn north and follow the signs on Forest Road 104, continuing on the dirt road for another 11 miles to the campground.

Contact: Vernal Ranger District, 435/789-1181.

44 Whiterocks

   9

Set at the bottom of a steep-walled canyon in a forest of blue spruce, aspen, and ponderosa and lodgepole pine, this is clearly a place for folks who like their camping remote. The nearby Whiterocks River offers good trout fishing, and hikers can access a trail a little farther up the canyon. Horseback riding on trails in the High Uintas Wilderness is a appealing alternative.

Location: In Ashley National Forest; map A3, grid f4.

Campsites, facilities: There are 21 single sites and two group sites with picnic tables, fire grills, two double-vault toilets, and drinking water. The RV length limit is 22 feet.

Reservations, fees: Sites are $5 and are first come, first served.

Open: May–Sept.

Directions: The campground is 31 miles northwest of Vernal. From Vernal, drive west on State Route 121. Just past Lapoint, look for a sign on an unnamed road leading to the town of Whiterocks on the Uinta and Ouray Indian Reservation. From Whiterocks, drive north for four miles to the graveled Forest Road 492. Follow that road for another eight miles.

Contact: Vernal Ranger District, 435/789-1181.

45 Steinaker State Park

    4

The warm water at this relatively low-altitude reservoir (5,500 ft.) is a special enticement for water-skiers, boaters, rafters, canoers, and swimmers; the sandy beaches are popular, too. The reservoir also offers some decent fishing for stocked rainbow trout and largemouth bass. The surrounding terrain is largely open, though there are shady spots near the campground.

Location: On Steinaker Reservoir; map A3, grid g5.

Campsites, facilities: There are 31 sites with picnic tables, fire grills, modern restrooms, a boat ramp, two group-use pavilions, and a dump station.

Reservations, fees: Reservations are available 120 days in advance for a $6.25 fee; call 800/322-3770 Mon.–Fri. 8 A.M.–5 P.M. Sites are $10.

Open: Apr.–Nov.

Directions: From Vernal, drive seven miles north on Highway 191, turning to the west after passing the Steinaker Reservoir.

Contact: Steinaker State Park, 435/789-4432.

46 Red Fleet State Park

 8

One of the best parts of visiting scenic Red Fleet Reservoir (apart from the first-rate fishing and boating) is the drive from Vernal. Before heading out of town, pick up a "Drive Through the Ages" brochure at the visitors center on Main Street and use it to trace the interesting geologic history of the route to Flaming Gorge Reservoir. Inside the park boundary is a dinosaur trackway dating back 200 million years.

Location: On Red Fleet Reservoir; map A3, grid g5.

Campsites, facilities: There are 29 sites near the water, with 32 covered picnic tables, two modern restrooms (with no showers), a sandy beach, a boat ramp, a fish-cleaning station, and a sewage dumping station.

Reservations, fees: Reservations are available 120 days in advance for a nonrefundable $6.25 per site; call 800/322-3770 Mon.–Fri. 8 A.M. –5 P.M. Sites are $10. Utah residents 62 years and older with a Special Fun Tag receive a $2 discount Sun.–Thurs.

Open: Open year-round, though winter camping is not recommended due to cold weather.

Directions: From Vernal, drive 10 miles north on Highway 191 and turn east at the state-park sign. Follow the road to the park for about five miles.

Contact: Red Fleet State Park, 435/789-4432.

47 Split Mountain

 8

This is the first campground you come to after entering Dinosaur National Monument from the west. Featuring both open and wooded sites, it's set right on the Green River, with impressive views of the rock formations on either side (hence, Split Mountain). A nature trail with interpretive signs leads from the campground into the surrounding rugged sandstone terrain. At the Dinosaur Quarry, where remains of stegosaurus, apatosaurus, and allosaurus can be viewed, fossils are preserved just as they were found (some were removed in the past, but no longer). The visitors center, open daily except New Year's Day, Thanksgiving, and Christmas, offers information on river-running and fishing as well.

Location: In Dinosaur National Monument; map A3, grid g6.

Campsites, facilities: There are 35 sites, including tent sites, with picnic tables and fire pits. Drinking water, modern restrooms, some pit toilets, firewood, and a ramp for launching boats or rafts onto the Green River are also available.

Reservations, fees: From Memorial Day to Labor Day, this campground offers one group site only. Call 435/789-8277 to reserve it. A nonrefundable fee of $10 will be charged and the site is $25 per night. In the winter, sites are free and are first come, first served.

Open: Year-round.

Directions: From Vernal, drive east on Highway 40 for 13.4 miles to Jensen, then drive 6.5 miles north on State Route 149 to the Dinosaur Quarry Visitors Center. The campground is four miles east of the quarry on State Route 149.

Contact: Dinosaur National Monument, 970/374-3000; Dinosaur Quarry Visitors Center, 435/789-2115.

48 Green River

 8

Though the fossil-filled Dinosaur Quarry (see Split

Mountain, page 133) is the big draw at this Green River campground, the area features some other nice side trips and hiking trails. Just down Cub Creek Road, for example, there's the historic Josie Morris Ranch, commemorating one of the area's first settlers, along with a short walk to some petroglyphs. The campground itself, in a mostly desertlike setting, has some lovely river views.

Location: In Dinosaur National Monument; map A3, grid g6.

Campsites, facilities: There are 100 sites for RVs and tents, with picnic tables and fire pits, drinking water, modern restrooms, and pit toilets.

Reservations, fees: Sites are $12 and are first come, first served.

Open: Memorial Day–Labor Day.

Directions: From Vernal, drive west on Highway 40 for 13.4 miles to Jensen, then north for 6.5 miles to the Dinosaur Quarry Visitors Center. The campground is five miles east of the quarry.

Contact: Dinosaur National Monument, 970/374-3000; Dinosaur Quarry Visitors Center, 435/789-2115.

49 Rainbow Park

  8

This area is mainly used by boaters taking day trips down the Green River to Split Mountain, but the cottonwood-shaded campground is a nice place to spend the night. Nearby, the federally managed Jones Hole Fish Hatchery makes for an interesting visit. Trout fishing on Jones Hole Creek below the hatchery can be challenging: Fly fishers can see big fish in the pools, but getting them to bite may be another story.

Location: In Dinosaur National Monument; map A3, grid g7.

Campsites, facilities: There are four tent sites with picnic tables, fire pits, and pit

toilets, but no drinking water. A boat ramp also provides Green River launch access for rafts.

Reservations, fees: Sites are free and are first come, first served.

Open: May 1–Nov. 30.

Directions: From Vernal, go east on Highway 40 for 13.4 miles to Jensen. Then drive four miles to Brush Creek Road and take it for 4.8 miles to the northwest, looking for an unnamed dirt road that heads north. Take this unlabeled road for 2.2 miles until it intersects with Island Park Road, then take that dirt road for 13.8 miles to the campground. Note: These rugged dirt roads are impassable when wet, and trailers are not recommended.

Contact: Dinosaur National Monument, 970/374-3000; Dinosaur Quarry Visitors Center, 435/789-2115.

50 Fossil Valley

 2

This is a city RV park, with little more to recommend it than decent hookups and some grass and trees. It's next to several grocery stores and restaurants.

Location: In Vernal; map A3, grid g6.

Campsites, facilities: There are 45 sites with full hookups and five tent sites, plus picnic tables, restrooms, showers, laundry facilities, RV waste-disposal facilities, and a public phone. Cable TV is available for $1.50 per night. Pets are welcome.

Reservations, fees: Reservations are recommended in summer. Sites are $19.50 for full hookups and $12.50 for tents, plus an additional $2 for each extra person over age six in groups larger than two.

Open: Apr.–Oct.

Directions: The campground is right in Vernal. Take U.S. Route 40 two miles into town.

Contact: Fossil Valley, 999 W. Hwy. 40, Vernal, UT 84078; 435/789-6450.

51 Manila/Flaming Gorge KOA

     6

Manila's shaded, grassy KOA is in a rural area on a hill five miles above Flaming Gorge Reservoir. This private facility has hookups, whereas area U.S. Forest Service facilities do not, making it popular with boaters and anglers looking for a more-civilized camping experience. Manila, though small, is the largest Utah town near the reservoir.

Location: In Manila; map A3, grid g5.

Campsites, facilities: There are 40 RV sites, 10 tent sites, and six cabins with picnic tables, barbecue grills, restrooms, showers, laundry facilities, RV waste-disposal facilities, a game room, a swimming pool, a public phone, and a convenience/gift store. Pets are allowed with a deposit.

Reservations, fees: Reservations are strongly recommended; some sites are booked a year in advance. Tent sites are $17. All other sites are full hookups and are $21. Cabins are $31.

Open: Mid-Apr.–mid-Oct.

Directions: In Manila, take State Route 43 west for three blocks to the sign for the campground.

Contact: Manila/Flaming Gorge KOA, P. O. Box 157, Manila, UT 84046; 435/784-3184.

52 Dinosaurland KOA

     3

This urban RV park caters to groups, and it hosts trailer rallies each year. Vernal is the gateway to Dinosaur National Monument, with lots of city amenities; alas, it also has the city ambience to go with 'em, meaning business and highway noise all around.

Location: In Vernal; map A3, grid g5.

Campsites, facilities: There are 100 RV sites, 65 with full hookups, plus a large grassy area for tents. Some of the pull-throughs are big enough for extra-wide trailers. Facilities in-

clude restrooms, showers, cable TV, a swimming pool, a convenience/gift shop, a covered picnic pavilion, a playground, miniature golf, and a game-room area. Pets are allowed.

Reservations, fees: Reservations are recommended. Sites with full hookups are $20. Tent sites are $6 for each adult. Prices for hookup sites increase by $2 for every adult in groups larger than two, and all sites charge $1 extra per child ages 7–15.

Open: Apr. 1–Oct. 31, though nine hookup sites are open through the winter.

Directions: The campground is on Highway 191 in Vernal, nine blocks north of the city center. (The highway becomes Vernal Avenue in town.)

Contact: Dinosaurland KOA, 930 N. Vernal Ave., Vernal, UT 84078; 435/789-2148 or 800/245-2148.

53 Pelican Lake

  3

Don't expect big crowds at this small desert pond set in largely open farmland. Pelican Lake once had a reputation as one of the West's best bluegill fisheries, but a variety of water-quality problems has caused fishing to drop off; accordingly, camping has, too. In spring and summer, birders may enjoy driving south on State Route 88 to view migrating winged species at the Ouray National Wildlife Refuge. In fact, there are good numbers of feathered creatures, including red-winged and yellow-headed blackbirds, at Pelican Lake itself.

Location: On Bureau of Land Management property at Pelican Lake; map A3, grid h3.

Campsites, facilities: There are 12 sites with picnic tables and vault (sweet-smelling) toilets, but no drinking water.

Reservations, fees: Sites are free and are first come, first served.

Open: Year-round.

Directions: From Vernal, take Highway 191 south and west to State Route 88. Turn south and proceed 8–10 miles to a bench. Turn left at the bottom and continue to a three-way junction. Turn right and look for signs to Pelican Lake.

Contact: Vernal District Office of the Bureau of Land Management, 435/789-1362.

Mountain View

 6

This campground is situated above a 3,500-acre desert reservoir, providing nice views of the buff-colored rock all around. Scattered shade trees give welcome relief from the sun, and boating and water sports help keep campers cool, too. Ask the ranger about the nearby off-highway-vehicle riding area.

Location: On Starvation Reservoir; map A3, grid h0.

Campsites, facilities: There are 30 sites with no hookups. Facilities include modern restrooms, showers, a nice playground, a group-use area, and a sewage dumping station. A few of the campsites are handicapped accessible.

Reservations, fees: Reservations are available 3–120 days in advance for a $6.25 fee; call 800/322-3770 Mon.–Fri. 8 A.M.–5 P.M. Sites are $12.

Open: May 1–Oct. 15.

Directions: From the west end of Duchesne, take the well-marked paved road to the state park and follow it northwest for four miles.

Contact: Starvation State Park, 435/738-2326.

Lower Beach

 6

Beach lovers clamor for the grassy sites right next to the water at this 3,500-acre reservoir. And while boating and water sports are prime pastimes, the reservoir isn't as crowd-ed as many along the Wasatch Front, so it's worth the drive to beat the crowds.

Location: On Starvation Reservoir; map A3, grid h1.

Campsites, facilities: There are 24 sites with no hookups. Facilities include modern restrooms, showers, a nice playground, a group area, and a sewage dumping station. A few of the campsites are handicapped accessible.

Reservations, fees: Reservations are available 3–120 days in advance; call 800/322-3770 Mon.–Fri. 8 A.M.–5 P.M. Sites are $12.

Open: May 1–Oct. 15.

Directions: From the west end of Duchesne, take the paved, well-marked road that leads to the state park and drive northwest for four miles.

Contact: Starvation State Park, 435/738-2326.

Avintaquin

 9

There's no fishing in this forest campground—a rarity in Utah. That makes it a nice, quiet place to get away from the angling crowds for a simple weekend of hiking or horseback riding. The campground is at an elevation of 8,800 feet in a remote alpine setting of aspen and pine; in the surrounding rolling meadows, wildlife—especially mule deer—is a common sight.

Location: In Ashley National Forest; map A3, grid j0.

Campsites, facilities: There are 13 RV sites and two tent sites, with picnic tables, fire grills, and pit toilets, but no water.

Reservations, fees: Sites are $5 and are first come, first served.

Open: Apr. 25–Sept. 10.

Directions: From Duchesne, drive 32.7 miles southwest on State Route 33. Then go about one mile west on Forest Road 047 to the campground.

Contact: Duchesne Ranger District, 435/738-2482.

CHAPTER 31

ZION CANYON FROM ANGELS LANDING

MAP B1

One inch equals approximately 11 miles.

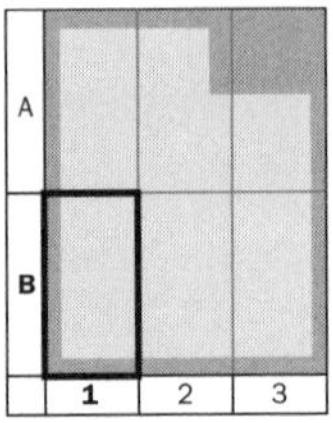

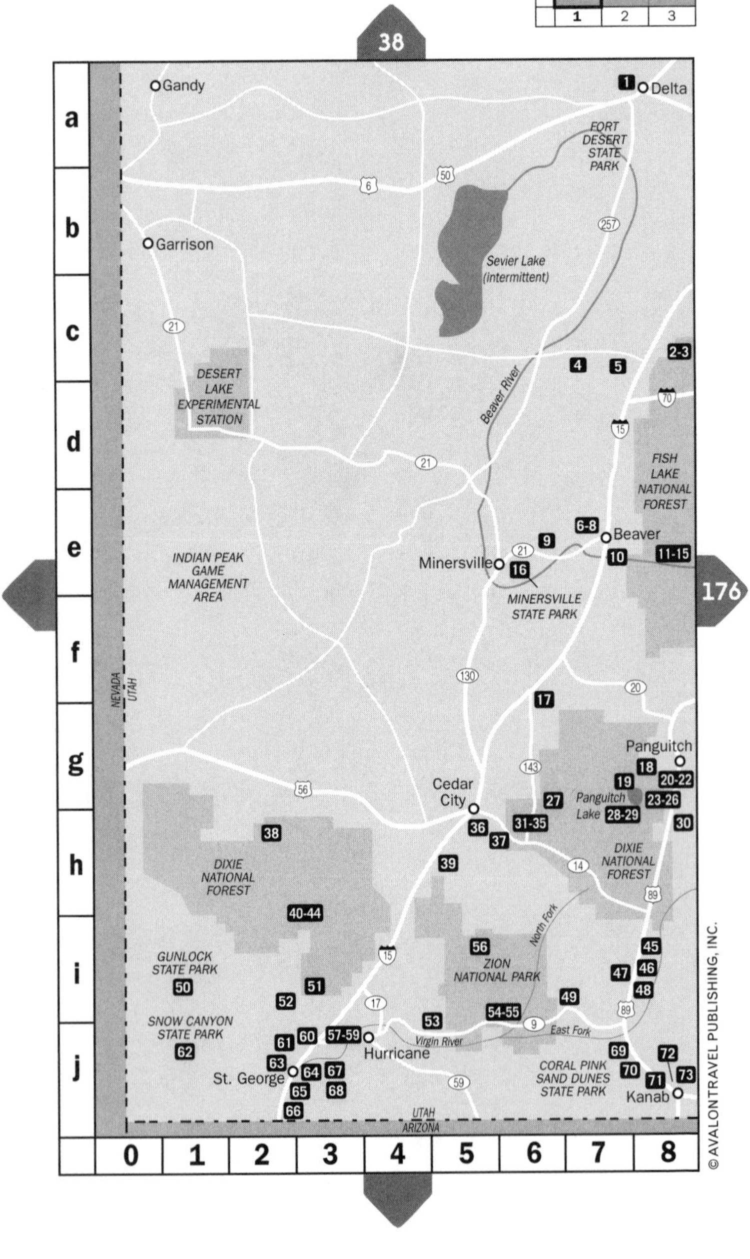

CHAPTER B1

(CONTINUED ON NEXT PAGE)

Utah's Dixie features a colorful tapestry of blue sky, green forests, and a painter's pallet full of reds, oranges, purples, and tans in layers of stone. St. George, a sizeable city, sports palm trees and swimming pools. In the land surrounding the city, a visitor sees elements of the Colorado Plateau, Mohave Desert, and Great Basin ecosystems that overlap here. Summer visitors can walk through alpine wildflower meadows in the morning in Cedar Breaks National Monument at 10,000 feet and later warm their feet in fine sand at Snow Canyon State Park at 2,600 feet. Winter travelers can bask in the sun in light jackets while hiking Dixie Red Cliffs or Coral Pink Sand Dunes State Park or enjoying a round of golf at one of St. George's many courses.

Three-Day Itinerary: Cedar Breaks National Monument ⚑ Zion National Park ⚑

Day One

Travel to Cedar City, 250 miles south of Salt Lake City on I-15. Take

State Route 14 east to the turnoff to Cedar Breaks National Monument on State Road 148. Camp at the Point Supreme Campground in Cedar Breaks National Monument. The snow is usually gone by mid-June. Take the short trail along the rim of the Cedar Breaks Amphitheater. It resembles a miniature Bryce Canyon National Park. The two-mile Alpine Pond Trail passes through a forest of bristlecone and limber pines and visits a pond along the way. If time permits, look into catching a play at Cedar City's annual Utah Shakespeare Festival. Visitors can choose to see a Shakespeare play performed in an outdoor replica of the Globe Theatre or a contemporary play in the Randall Jones Theatre.

Day Two
Return to State Road 14 and take it east 23 miles to Long Valley Junction. Go south along a scenic portion of Highway 89 for 23 miles to Mount Carmel Junction. From here, take State Road 9 to the east entrance to Zion National Park. A fun way to see the park for the first time is on foot. Park just east of the tunnel and take the one-mile Canyon Overlook Trail. With feet firmly planted

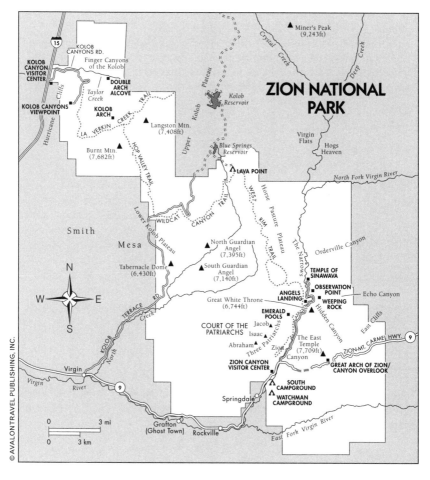

Zion National Park map

and hands on the guardrail, look down the 1,500-foot cliff to the road below and take in the canyon. Giant cottonwood trees grow along the Virgin River. These trees are in turn dwarfed by the magnificent rock walls that define the canyon. Camp at the newly constructed campgrounds. The National Park Service has instituted a shuttle system for travel up and down the canyon floor. This should ease the overcrowding on the road and parking lots. To see the park up close, consider taking a hike on one of the area's many trails.

Day Three
Another day or week in Zion National Park would not be a bad choice. However, if you insist, leave the park at the west entrance. The town of Springdale, located right outside the park, is a rather upscale gateway community. Artists and gourmet cooks have been attracted to it because of the park. Tour a few galleries and

grab a bite for lunch. From Springdale, continue on State Road 9 to I-15. Take I-15 to St. George. Continue through the city and take State Road 18 to Snow Canyon State Park. The campground is popular but can be reserved (800/322-3770). Recent volcanism has coated parts of the brilliant orange sandstone with black lava. Choose one of several hikes through the formations. If things get too hot in the middle of the day, take a trip back into St. George. The Mormon pioneers who settled this area tried to grow cotton (hence the nickname, Utah's Dixie). Visit Brigham Young's winter home or Jacob Hambin's house, or pick up a walking guide to historical homes at the Chamber of Commerce office (St. George Boulevard and 100 East). The old sandstone buildings are surprisingly cool in the summer. If the thought of touring other people's houses doesn't sound like fun, consider this alternative: Drive northwest to the tiny town of Veyo and enjoy a dip in a natural hot springs' pool at Veyo Hot Springs, a rustic resort.

Seven-Day Itinerary: Cedar Breaks National Monument 🐾 Panguitch Lake 🐾 Coral Pink Sand Dunes State Park 🐾 Zion National Park 🐾 Snow Canyon State Park

Day One

Visit Cedar Breaks National Monument (see Three-Day Itinerary, Day One).

Day Two

On State Route 14, 28 miles east of Cedar City, look for Navajo Lake Road. Choose from Te-Ah, Navajo Lake, or Spruces Campgrounds. These campgrounds are in a high-mountain forest and offer good fishing nearby in Navajo and Panguitch Lakes. Hiking, biking, and horseback riding are all possible along trails leading to the 32-mile Virgin River Rim Trail.

Day Three

Retrace your route back to Cedar Breaks National Monument and continue east on State Route 143 to Panguitch Lake. The large lake and its lunker trout are popular with anglers. Tall aspen trees and ponderosa pines grow up to the lake's edge in places. Take your pick of several public and private campgrounds, many of which can be reserved.

Day Four

Take State Route 143 toward Mount Carmel Junction and Highway 89. At the junction, take Highway 89 toward Kanab and Coral Pink Sand Dunes State Park. The road to the state park is less than five miles from the junction. Spend the day playing in the dunes and walk the half-mile nature trail. If it gets too hot in the middle of the day, drive 34 miles or so into Kanab. Visit the Thomas Chamberlain house—home to a wife of the well-known Mormon polygamist. A tour of the historic home gives visitors a glimpse into the life of one of Chamberlain's six wives. The area around Kanab has been used as a backdrop for many Western movies.

Day Five

Return along Highway 89 north to the Mount Carmel Junction, then head west on State Route 9 to Zion National Park (see Three-Day Itinerary, Day Two). If you're having a good time in Zion, why not stay and finish the week here, taking trips into Springdale to eat and shop.

Day Six

To cover more territory, go to Snow Canyon State Park (see Three-Day Itinerary, Day Three).

Day Seven

Time to head for the mountains again. Continue north on State Route 18 to Central. Turn east and drive to one of five campgrounds in the Pine Valley Mountains. Relax in the shade or take a trail into the Pine Valley Wilderness Area, one of Utah's best-preserved native forests. You'll find a small fishing pond where anglers catch planted trout. On your way out, stop by the Mountain Meadows Massacre Site. A marker here recalls a time in 1857 when 120 immigrants on their way to California from Arkansas were massacred by Indians and Mormons in what has remained one of Utah's most infamous and mysterious historical events.

◼ Antelope Valley RV Park

 3

This is a 5.5-acre park just outside of Delta, population 3,000. Delta, the largest town in the Great Basin area, is home to some interesting rock shops as well as the Great Basin History Museum. The campground is dotted with more than 40 full-grown trees, though the campsites are in open desert with little shade.

Location: Near Delta; map B1, grid a8.

Campsites, facilities: There are 96 RV sites with full hookups, plus restrooms, showers, laundry facilities, a public phone, and a playground.

Reservations, fees: Reservations are accepted. Sites are $20.

Open: Year-round.

Directions: From Delta, take Highway 50 west for a quarter of a mile; the campground is just west of the overpass. Delta is located 89 miles southeast of Provo along Highway 6, and 87 miles east of the Nevada border along Highway 50/6.

Contact: Antelope Valley RV Park, 435/864-1813.

◼ Oak Creek Canyon

 8

This campground is next to a small stream planted with rainbow trout in a canyon filled with oak and maple trees, so it's especially lovely in fall. The sites sit in a circle on a gravel road. Short hiking trails crisscross the area. Covered picnic tables and horseshoe and volleyball areas make it an ideal family-reunion spot.

Location: In Fishlake National Forest; map B1, grid c8.

Campsites, facilities: This campground has 19 single sites and four group sites, plus picnic tables, fire grills, vault toilets, running water, a covered picnic pavilion, and an amphitheater. One group site has a wheelchair-accessible restroom.

Reservations, fees: Reservations are only accepted for the group site with a wheelchair-accessible restroom. Sites are $8.

Open: Apr. 21–Sept. 30.

Directions: The campground is 4.5 miles northeast of Oak City on State Route 125. From Delta, drive seven miles east on State Route 125, then turn east to the campground.

Contact: Fillmore Ranger District, 435/743-5721.

◼ Adelaide

 10

Don't be fooled by the diminutive size of the stream that flows through this campground: Corn Creek can produce some mighty big fish. The campground itself, built in the Civilian Conservation Corps era, exudes nostalgia; the bandstand-like pavilion with a rock foundation is still a fine place to sit and talk. The sites are nestled under huge trees in a red-rock canyon that's particularly pretty in the fall. Nearby is the Paiute ATV Trail, one of the longest trails of its kind in the United States.

Location: In Fishlake National Forest; map B1, grid c8.

Campsites, facilities: This handicapped-accessible campground has eight sites, most of which are large enough to handle several cars or RVs, plus picnic tables and fire pits, vault and flush toilets, drinking water, a covered pavilion, and an amphitheater.

Reservations, fees: Sites are $8 and can be reserved by calling the Fillmore Ranger District.

Open: Apr. 21–Oct. 30.

Directions: Take I-15 south from Fillmore or north from Beaver, and look for the Kanosh exit. Drive into Kanosh and follow Forest Road 106 east up Corn Creek Canyon for six miles to the campground.

Contact: Fillmore Ranger District, 435/743-5721.

4 Fillmore KOA

      5

This is a newer KOA, meaning it's mostly out in the open with some small shade trees. The grassy tent sites are set amid sagebrush, and the area is served by a gravel road. The combination of amenities and the out-of-the-way location is nice, and there are great views of the Pavant Mountains to the east and the volcanic cinder cones of the valley to the west. There's direct access to the Paiute ATV Trail, which is used by horses and dune buggies alike. ATV and horse rentals and tours are available from vendors in town, as are tours to favorite area rockhounding spots. And history buffs, take note: In Fillmore, Utah's first capital, the old capitol building is now a museum.

Location: In Fillmore; map B1, grid c7.

Campsites, facilities: There are 54 RV sites with full hookups, a tent-camping area with covered picnic tables, and several one- and two-room cabins. A restroom, a shower, laundry facilities, a convenience and gift store with RV supplies, a swimming pool, a game room, a playground, and RV waste-disposal sites are available. Leashed pets are welcome.

Reservations, fees: Reservations are accepted. Sites are $19.75 for full hookups, $18.75 for water and electricity, and $15.50 for tents; cabins are $27 for one room, $33 for two rooms. Off-season rates are slightly lower. Extra people over five years of age must pay $2 each.

Open: Mar. 1–Dec. 10.

Directions: From Beaver, go north on I-15 for 57 miles. Take exit 163 and go east for one-tenth of a mile to the KOA sign. Turn right and proceed half a mile to the campground.

Contact: Fillmore KOA, HC 61 Box 26, Fillmore, UT 84631; 435/743-4420.

5 Wagons West

    5

This campground is in downtown Fillmore, which was the territorial capital of Utah. The town's red-sandstone capitol building is now a museum that's well worth touring. The campground itself is shaded and grassy and next to a private pioneer-era house. It's also close to the Paiute ATV Trail, popular with horseback riders and ATV users alike. ATV riders can access the trail directly from the campground, while horseback riders must transport their horses to the nearby canyons.

Location: In Fillmore; map B1, grid c7.

Campsites, facilities: There are 42 RV sites with full hookups, and eight tent-camping sites. Restrooms, showers, picnic tables, laundry facilities, cable TV, and RV supplies are available. Pets are allowed.

Reservations, fees: Reservations are accepted. Sites are $17.60 for full hookups and $11 for tents.

Open: Year-round.

Directions: From Beaver, take I-15 north for 57 miles to Fillmore (exit 163), and head for Main Street. Wagons West is at 545 North Main Street.

Contact: Wagons West, P. O. Box 901, Fillmore, UT 84631; 435/743-6188.

6 Beaver KOA

   5

This KOA is a little roomier than most, with unusually well-spaced sites and an open-farmland setting. And though it's not far from the freeway, it's far enough to have a somewhat rural feel. Most sites are shaded and grassy, with gravel patches and interior roads; a fence shields the shaded tent area from the road. There's even a view of the towering Tushar Mountains a few miles to the east.

Location: In Beaver; map B1, grid e7.

Campsites, facilities: This handicapped-accessible campground has 65 RV sites, 27 provide full hookups; 10

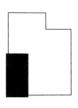

tent-camping sites; and another area for group tenting. Also available are restrooms, showers, laundry facilities, a disposal site, a swimming pool, a grocery and gift shop, fire pits, and a public phone.

Reservations, fees: Reservations are accepted. Sites are $19.75 with full hookups, $18.25 for water and electricity, and $15.50 for tents.

Open: Mar.–Nov.

Directions: Follow I-15 to Beaver and take exit 122 on the north end of town. Turn left and go one mile north on Manderfield Road. The campground, visible from the freeway, is on the west side of Manderfield Road.

Contact: Beaver KOA, P. O. Box 1437, Beaver, UT 84731; 435/438-2924.

7 Delano Motel and RV Park

   1

This is basically a parking-lot RV spot in the middle of a small town: a gravel area off Main Street, behind a motel, with some rough picnic tables and a handful of small trees. Beaver is close to Elk Meadows Ski Resort, however, so the campground is a low-cost winter-lodging alternative. Golfing, fishing, and hunting possibilities abound in nearby Beaver Canyon, which can be reached via a scenic highway (State Rte. 153).

Location: In Beaver; map B1, grid e7.

Campsites, facilities: There are 10 RV sites with pull-throughs and hookups, plus restrooms, showers, and laundry facilities. Pets are allowed.

Reservations, fees: Reservations are accepted. Sites are $12.

Open: Year-round.

Directions: Take I-15 to Beaver, get off at either of the two exits, and head for Main Street. Delano RV Park is at 480 North Main Street, behind the Delano Motel.

Contact: Delano Motel and RV Park, 480 N. Main St., Beaver, UT 84713; 435/438-2418.

8 United Beaver Camperland

  6

Visible from the highway in a farmland setting at the end of town, this campground has some good views of the Tushar Mountains to the east. There are some shaded and grassy sites, and the tent section is on partially open terrain. Heat is usually not a problem, though, because Beaver is at an elevation of 6,000 feet. For winter sports buffs, the Elk Meadows Ski Resort is nearby.

Location: In Beaver; map B1, grid e7.

Campsites, facilities: There are 85 sites with full hookups, plus restrooms, showers, laundry facilities, and an RV disposal site. Facilities are all set on one level for easy wheelchair access.

Reservations, fees: Reservations are accepted. Sites are $17.95 for two people, plus $2 for each additional person.

Open: Year-round.

Directions: Take I-15 to Beaver and get off at exit 109. Turn right on Campground Road and go to the campground at 1603 South.

Contact: United Beaver Camperland, P. O. Box 1060, Beaver, UT 84713; 435/438-2808.

9 Rock Corral

  4

Though in a remote part of Utah's western desert, this dispersed-camping spot in an oak-brush, piñon, and juniper forest offers lots of interesting things to do. The granite rock formations make it one of the area's most scenic campgrounds and have begun to attract rock climbers. And rockhounders and hikers can find plenty of interesting geological specimens in the nearby Mineral Mountains.

Location: On Bureau of Land Management property; map B1, grid e6.

Campsites, facilities: This is a rather primitive area with just a few picnic tables, two fire pits, and pit toilets, but no water.

Reservations, fees: Camping is free and sites are first come, first served.

Open: Year-round.

Directions: From Milford, go south for half a mile on State Route 21. Take a marked turnoff to the east for Rock Corral, and drive another 10 miles to the campground.

Contact: Bureau of Land Management, Cedar City District Office, 435/586-2401.

10 Beaver Canyon

    6

This country campground looks right up at the Tushar Mountains and has a funky Old West feel. In fact, pioneer paraphernalia and artifacts abound. There's a log fort, old wagons and wagon wheels, and a Western-themed children's playground on the property. Even the covered picnic tables in the tent section are made from logs. Most of the campsites are gravel, with little grass or greenery. The Beaver public golf course is located just up the road.

Location: East of Beaver, map B1, grid e7.

Campsites, facilities: There are 31 sites with full hookups, 25 sites with water and electricity only, and 50 tent sites. Restrooms, showers, laundry facilities, a public phone, a playground, fire pits, and firewood are available. Pets are allowed. A Mexican restaurant on the premises offers homemade tamales and chiles rellenos.

Reservations, fees: Reservations are accepted. Sites are $12 with full hookups, $11 with water and electricity, and $10 for tents.

Open: Apr. 15–Nov. 10.

Directions: Take I-15 to Beaver and get off at exit 112 or 109; either way, you'll end up on Main Street. Go to the center of town, pick up State Route 153 heading east, and continue for 1.25 miles until you reach the campground.

Contact: Beaver Canyon Campground, P. O. Box 1528, Beaver, UT 84713; 435/438-5654.

11 Little Cottonwood

  5

Accessible by a paved road, this campground has several features for the disabled, including three specially designed sites, roomy restrooms, and a special ramp leading to the river for fishing. Sites are right next to the Beaver River in a forest of cottonwood and ponderosa pine; the nearby woods have shorter mountain mahogany and juniper trees as well.

Location: In Fishlake National Forest; map B1, grid e8.

Campsites, facilities: There are 14 sites with flush toilets, picnic tables, and fire pits. Two of the sites are handicapped accessible.

Reservations, fees: Sites are $10 and are first come, first served.

Open: May–Nov.

Directions: From Beaver, drive six miles east on State Route 153. The campground is on the right side of the road, with sites situated along the Beaver River.

Contact: Beaver Ranger District, 435/438-2436.

12 Kents Lake

  6

At 8,800 feet, this high-country campground has a somewhat abbreviated season (with water typically available for about four months). The primary pastime is trout fishing on the alpine lake, where anglers are allowed to launch small boats, rafts, or canoes. And for hikers, there's ready access to area trails.

Location: In Fishlake National Forest; map B1, grid e8.

Campsites, facilities: There are 31 sites and two group-use sites with picnic tables and fire grills. Drinking water, vault and flush toilets, and a covered

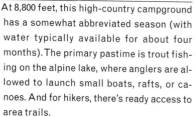

picnic pavilion are also available. The RV length limit is 60 feet.

Reservations, fees: Sites are $8 and are first come, first served.

Open: June–Sept.

Directions: From Beaver, drive east on State Route 153 approximately nine miles. Look for a road marker to Forest Road 137. Drive south on this dirt road for approximately three miles; the campground is on the north side of the road.

Contact: Fishlake National Forest, Beaver Ranger District, 435/438-2436.

13 Mahogany Cove

   5

Easy access, an alpine setting (elevation 7,500 ft.), and impressive views of the nearby Tushar Mountains are the big pluses here. Locals also like being close to the amenities of nearby Elk Meadows Ski Resort and the trout fishing in area streams, lakes, and the Beaver River, which is just one mile away. Half the campground is shaded by ponderosa pine, while the other half is covered with shorter mountain mahogany. In summer, a leisurely scenic drive over the top of the Tushar Mountains into Piute County on the eastern side of the Tushars affords panoramic views of both sides of the range.

Location: In Fishlake National Forest; map B1, grid e8.

Campsites, facilities: There are seven sites with picnic tables and fire pits. Drinking water and vault toilets are available. The RV length limit is 50 feet.

Reservations, fees: Sites are $6 and are first come, first served.

Open: Late May–mid-Oct.

Directions: From Beaver, take State Route 153 southeast for 11.2 miles into Beaver Canyon. The campground is on the north side of the highway.

Contact: Fishlake National Forest, Beaver Ranger District, 435/438-2436.

14 Little Reservoir

    5

The accessible location and pretty alpine scenery (elevation 7,350 ft.) make Little Reservoir one of Beaver Canyon's most popular campgrounds. It's set right next to a fishable lake in a forest of juniper, scrub oak, and ponderosa pine. Little Reservoir is regularly stocked with rainbow trout by the Utah Division of Wildlife Resources and has a wheelchair-accessible dam.

Location: In Fishlake National Forest; map B1, grid e8.

Campsites, facilities: There are eight family sites and two group sites, plus picnic tables, fire grills, drinking water, vault toilets, and wheelchair access for fishing near the dam. There's also a wheelchair-accessible restroom, though the doorway is small. The RV length limit is 40 feet.

Reservations, fees: Sites are $5 and are first come, first served.

Open: May–mid-Oct.

Directions: From Beaver, take State Highway 153 southeast for 11.2 miles up Beaver Canyon; the campground is on the south side of the road.

Contact: Fishlake National Forest, Beaver Ranger District, 435/438-2436.

15 Anderson Meadow

   8

This small alpine campground (elevation 9,500 ft.), set in an aspen-and-mixed-conifer forest, is on the edge of Anderson Meadow Reservoir and is somewhat removed from the traffic of Beaver Canyon. Trout fishing is the primary activity here, though the exceptional setting alone is worth the trip. Pick up a hiking guide to the area at the ranger station in Beaver. The altitude limits water availability—and the camping season—to about four months of the year.

Location: In Fishlake National Forest; map B1, grid e8.

Campsites, facilities: There are 10 sites with picnic tables and fire grills. Drinking water and vault toilets are available. The RV length limit is 24 feet.

Reservations, fees: Sites are $6 and are first come, first served.

Open: June–Sept.

Directions: From the town of Beaver just off I-15, take State Route 153 east for approximately nine miles into Beaver Canyon, looking for a marked turnoff to Forest Road 137. Drive south on this dirt road for approximately five miles to the campground.

Contact: Fishlake National Forest, Beaver Ranger District, 435/438-2436.

Minersville State Park

4

Electrical hookups being a rarity on Utah reservoirs, this is a popular place. The Utah Division of Wildlife Resources manages Minersville as a source of trophy trout; flies and lures are the only tackle allowed. Drawdowns in late summer, which come close to draining the reservoir at times, can make boating difficult; otherwise, the 1,130-acre reservoir is a good boating and water-skiing park. The campground itself has a little landscaped shade, though there's a somewhat desolate feel to the area.

Location: On Minersville Reservoir; map B1, grid e6.

Campsites, facilities: There are 29 sites with electric hookups, modern restrooms with showers, a dump station, and a fish-cleaning station. Boat docks and a launching ramp are nearby.

Reservations, fees: Reservations are available 120 days in advance for a nonrefundable

$6.25 per site; call 800/322-3770 Mon.–Fri. 8 A.M.–5 P.M. Sites are $12. Utah residents 62 years and older with a Special Fun Tag get a $2 discount Sun.–Thurs.

Open: Apr.–Nov.

Directions: To reach the campground, drive 12 miles west of Beaver off State Route 21.

Contact: Minersville State Park, 435/438-5472.

Pit Stop

1

This is the only RV campground in Parowan, the nearest town to Brian Head Ski Resort. It is located behind the Pit Stop Restaurant.

Location: In Parowan; map B1, grid g6.

Campsites, facilities: There are 29 sites with full hookups, plus a few picnic tables, a small store, restrooms, showers, a waste-disposal site, and a public phone. Facilities include ramps for wheelchair access. Pets are allowed.

Reservations, fees: Reservations are recommended for summer weekends. Sites are $14.95 for two people, plus 50 cents for each additional person over age 13.

Open: Year-round.

Directions: Parowan is about 31 miles south of Beaver and about 28 miles north of Cedar City, off I-15. From the interstate, take the Parowan turnoff (exit 78) and go west onto Main Street. The Pit Stop is on the west side of the street, just past the Best Western Motel.

Contact: Pit Stop, P. O. Box 888, Parowan, UT 84761; 435/477-3714.

White Bridge

8

Though it's located a few miles from Panguitch Lake, this is a popular spot. The well-shaded sites are along

a pretty little stream (with good fishing) and the lush vegetation lends a nice sense of privacy.

Location: In Dixie National Forest; map B1, grid g7.

Campsites, facilities: There are 28 sites, plus picnic tables and fire grills, drinking water, vault toilets, and a dump station.

Reservations, fees: For reservations, call the U.S. Forest Service National Reservation System at 800/280-2267. Sites are $10.

Open: June 1–Oct. 1.

Directions: From Panguitch, drive south on South Canyon Road, which turns into Forest Road 36. The campground is on the north side of the road, 10 miles out of town.

Contact: Cedar City Ranger District, 435/865-3700.

19 Hitch-N-Post RV Park and Campground

   2

Sites at the urban Hitch-N-Post campground, including two grassy areas in back for tents, are shaded with medium-size trees. The roads and RV sites are gravel. In a nutshell, this place is not as nice as many camping spots on Panguitch Lake, but it's closer to Bryce Canyon. The campground is 10 miles east of Panguitch Lake and 24 miles west of Bryce Canyon National Park.

Location: On Panguitch Lake; map B1, grid g8.

Campsites, facilities: There are 19 sites with full hookups, 15 sites with water and electricity, and two grass tent-camping areas. Picnic tables, restrooms, showers, laundry facilities, an RV waste-disposal site, and an RV/car wash are also available. Pets are allowed on a leash.

Reservations, fees: Reservations are accepted. Sites are $16 and up for RVs and $12 for tents.

Open: Year-round.

Directions: In Panguitch, take Main Street to the campground at 420 North Main Street.

Contact: Hitch-N-Post RV Park and Campground, P. O. Box 368, Panguitch, UT 84759; 435/676-2436 or 800/282-9633.

20 Paradise Park and Campground

   4

This place is nowhere near as scenic as campgrounds on nearby Panguitch Lake: It's out in the open, in a flat valley of farms and sagebrush, with gravel sites and roads and not much grass. Still, the location is decent: Panguitch is 24 miles from Bryce Canyon National Park, 30 miles from Cedar Breaks National Monument, and 45 miles from Zion National Park. The campground itself is spread over 10 acres. Anglers can try their luck at Panguitch Lake and in small streams in the area.

Location: In Panguitch; map B1, grid g8.

Campsites, facilities: There are 52 RV sites with full hookups (46 are pull-throughs), 16 RV sites with water and electricity (six are pull-throughs), and 25–50 tent-camping sites in a grassy area. Also available are picnic tables, fire pits, restrooms, showers, laundry facilities, and a waste-disposal site, as well as video rentals and a recreation hall. Dry-dock facilities are $10.

Reservations, fees: Reservations are accepted. Sites are $18 with full hookups, $15 with water and electricity, and $10 for tents.

Open: Apr. 15–Nov. 15.

Directions: Take Highway 89 north from Glendale (or south from Junction) for about 11 miles to Panguitch. The campground is in town on the west side of the highway, across the street from the Sevier River.

Contact: Paradise Park and Campground, P. O. Box 655, Panguitch, UT 84759; 435/676-8348.

Red Canyons RV Park

 5

This rural campground has sites in the open, but with covered picnic tables. Campers can view the russet cliffs of Red Canyon in the distance. Mountain bikers will find some good trails in the area, and anglers can head for the small lakes in the surrounding forest, including Pine Lake and Tropic Reservoir.

Location: East of Panguitch on State Route 12; map B1, grid g8.

Campsites, facilities: There are 40 RV sites, all with full hookups, plus a large grassy area with room for 15 tents. New restrooms and showers, covered picnic tables, a convenience store, and an RV waste-disposal site are also available.

Reservations, fees: Reservations are accepted. Sites with full hookups are $18; tent sites are $10. An extra $1 is charged for each additional person in groups larger than two.

Open: Mar. 1–Nov. 1.

Directions: From Panguitch, take Highway 89 south toward Kanab to the Bryce Canyon turnoff (State Rte. 12). From there, travel east for one more mile to the campground.

Contact: Red Canyons RV Park, P. O. Box 717, Panguitch, UT 84759; 435/676-2243.

Panguitch KOA

     5

Set in a rural, sagebrush-covered valley outside of town, this campground looks right up at the mountains of Dixie National Forest. The grassy sites are basically in the open with a few small shade trees. This KOA is in a good location for visitors to the Panguitch Lake area. It's also within an hour of Bryce Canyon National Park and Cedar Breaks National Monument.

Location: South of Panguitch on Highway 143; map B1, grid g8.

Campsites, facilities: There are 35 sites with full hookups, 20 sites with water and electricity, 14 tent sites, 12 cabins, and three group sites. Picnic tables, barbecue grills, restrooms, showers, laundry facilities, a convenience store, a game room, a swimming pool, a playground, and a basketball court are also available. Pets are allowed everywhere but in the cabins.

Reservations, fees: Reservations are recommended from Memorial Day to Labor Day. Sites are $23 with full hookups, $22 with water and electricity, $18.50 for tents, and $38 for cabins.

Open: Apr. 1–Nov. 1.

Directions: In Panguitch, drive south through town; then, instead of following Highway 89 east, take State Route 143 south for five blocks. The KOA is 16 miles before Panguitch Lake.

Contact: Panguitch KOA, Box 384, Panguitch, UT 84759; 435/676-2225.

Lake View Resort

   5

Nestled among the large conifers of Dixie National Forest, this campground has the pleasant feel of an old-fashioned boat camp. Some sites are in the aspens and ponderosa pines and others are in the open; all have a great view of Panguitch Lake, one of Utah's top rainbow-trout producers. Note: The dirt road to the sites is rough and steep.

Location: On Panguitch Lake in Dixie National Forest; map B1, grid g8.

Campsites, facilities: The resort has 20 sites with full hookups; housekeeping cabins are also available. Facilities include picnic tables, fire pits, restrooms, showers, laundry facilities, a public phone, a playground, a convenience store, a restaurant, boat rentals, a boat dock, and gasoline.

Reservations, fees: Reservations are accepted. RV sites are $17; tent sites are $12.

Open: June–Aug.

Directions: From Panguitch, drive 17 miles west on State Route 143. The resort is across the road on the east side of the lake.

Contact: Lake View Resort, Box 397, Panguitch, UT 84759; 435/676-2650.

24 Panguitch Lake Resort

     4

The sites at this campground are best for RVs, since they're right next to each other and out in the open behind the resort. Panguitch Lake, complete with boat tie-ups, is 500 feet away. Views of the lake and mountains are somewhat obstructed.

Location: On Panguitch Lake; map B1, grid g8.

Campsites, facilities: All 88 RV sites have full hookups. The resort has restrooms, showers, picnic tables, a public phone, a fish cleaning station, and a convenience store. Pets are allowed.

Reservations, fees: Sites are $22.50 and are first come, first served.

Open: Apr.–Oct.

Directions: From Panguitch, take State Route 143 to Panguitch Lake. Look for a sign for Panguitch Lake Resort on the north side of the road. The resort is a quarter mile down this road on the south side of the lake.

Contact: Panguitch Lake Resort, P. O. Box 567, Panguitch, UT 84759; 435/676-2657.

25 Panguitch Lake North

    9

Nestled among tall ponderosa pines and wildflowers with a view of Panguitch Lake, this is one of the nicer campgrounds in Utah, and it has the best seat on the lake. Anglers flock to the waters here, one of the state's premier trout-fishing spots. Sites are level and far apart and the road and spurs are paved.

Location: On Panguitch Lake; map B1, grid g8.

Campsites, facilities: This campground with 49 sites offers campers flush and vault toilets, running water, picnic tables, fire grills, a group area, a dump station, an amphitheater, and a ranger station.

Reservations, fees: Reservations for some sites can be made by calling the U.S. Forest Service National Reservation System at 800/280-2267. Rates are $10 or $18, depending on the size of the campsite.

Open: June 1–Sept. 15.

Directions: The campground is located 19 miles southwest of Panguitch. From Highway 89 in Panguitch, take South Canyon Road/State Route 143 to Panguitch Lake. A large sign in the middle of Panguitch directs travelers to the lake. Drive past the southern edge of Panguitch Lake. The campground is on the north side of the road, south and slightly west of Panguitch Lake on Forest Road 80.

Contact: Cedar City Ranger District, 435/865-3200.

26 Panguitch Lake South

   8

This campground with gravel roads and sites is across the lake from Panguitch Lake North (see above). Though less developed than its northern sister, the sites are still far apart and nestled in the trees, and all of them have nice views of the water. Some sites are next to the highway. Panguitch Lake and nearby streams keep trout anglers happy.

Location: On Panguitch Lake; map B1, grid g8.

Campsites, facilities: This campground with 19 sites features vault toilets, picnic tables, drinking water, a dump station, and fire grills.

Reservations, fees: Sites are $7 and are first come, first served.

Open: June 1–Sept. 15.

Directions: The campground is located 19 miles southwest of Panguitch. From Highway 89 in Panguitch, take South Canyon Road/State Route 143 to Panguitch Lake. A large sign in the middle of Panguitch directs travelers to the lake. Drive past the southern shore of Panguitch Lake. The campground is on the south side of the road, south and slightly west of Panguitch Lake.

Contact: Cedar City Ranger District, 435/865-3200.

27 Point Supreme

   8

The camping season is short at Cedar Breaks National Monument, thanks to a 10,000-foot elevation that often leaves the area blanketed by snow into June. The National Park Service tries to open the campground by mid-June, but call in advance just in case the weather isn't cooperating. When summer does finally break through, Cedar Breaks features Bryce Canyon–like amphitheaters, short hiking trails, and scenic overlooks. Wildflower displays in the alpine meadows in July and August are stunning.

Location: In Cedar Breaks National Monument; map B1, grid h6.

Campsites, facilities: This campground has 30 sites, all appropriate for RVs, plus drinking water, picnic tables, fire grills, and handicapped-accessible restrooms with cold running water.

Reservations, fees: Campsites are $10 and are first come, first served.

Open: Mid-June–late Sept.

Directions: Take State Highway 14 east from Cedar City for 23 miles. Point Supreme is a mile north of the Cedar Breaks National Monument Visitors Center.

Contact: Cedar Breaks National Monument, 801/586-9451.

28 General Store Gift Shop and RV Park

   4

This campground is for totally self-contained RVs only, since there are no restrooms other than pit toilets and no showers. Campsites are on the aspen-covered hill behind the store, so campers have a view of the store and trout-filled Panguitch Lake.

Location: On Panguitch Lake; map B1, grid g7.

Campsites, facilities: There are 14 RV sites with full hookups. Portable toilets and drinking water are available. Laundry facilities are located at the store, which sells groceries, sporting goods, and gift items.

Reservations, fees: Reservations are accepted. Sites are $19.

Open: May–Oct.

Directions: From Panguitch, take State Route 143 to Panguitch Lake. The General Store and RV Park are on the south side of the lake, on the left side of the highway when coming from Panguitch.

Contact: General Store Gift Shop and RV Park, P. O. Box 688, Panguitch, UT 84759; 435/676-2464.

29 Rustic Lodge

   4

This year-round resort offers excellent fishing on Panguitch Lake in the spring, summer, and fall, and cross-country skiing, snowmobiling, and ice fishing in the winter. The primitive but pleasant campground is located in a grove of trees, across the street from the lake.

Location: On Panguitch Lake; map B1, grid g7.

Campsites, facilities: The campground has 26 graveled sites, all with full hookups, plus sites for tent camping.

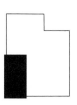

Showers, restrooms, laundry facilities, and fire rings are available. The resort also has a restaurant and cabins.

Reservations, fees: Reservations are recommended. Rates are $16 for RVs, $10 for tents, and $62–85 for cabins.

Open: Year-round.

Directions: From Panguitch, take State Route 143 to Panguitch Lake. Turn right off State Route 143 onto West Shore Road and look for the sign to Rustic Lodge on the left side of the road.

Contact: Rustic Lodge, P. O. Box 373, Panguitch, UT 84759; 435/676-2627.

30 Riverside

   6

While you won't find trees at this campground (elevation 7,000 ft.), you will find grassy campsites on a hill off the highway and weather that's generally cool and breezy. You'll also enjoy nice views of the Sevier River (which flows through the campground) and the orange sandstone cliffs of the Paungausant Plateau to the east. Swimming and fishing for rainbow and brown trout are popular river activities here. Rock shops in such nearby towns as Orderville sell some interesting jewelry. Also close by and worth a visit is the Utah Division of Wildlife Resources' fish hatchery. A little farther afield are Bryce Canyon National Park (21 miles), Zion National Park (51 miles), and Cedar Breaks National Monument (37 miles).

Location: Near Red Canyon; map B1, grid h8.

Campsites, facilities: There are 47 sites with full hookups and 15 with partial hookups, plus 15 tent sites. Other facilities include a laundry room, showers, a restaurant, two picnic pavilions, a waste-disposal station, a recreation hall and field, a public phone, and fire grates.

Reservations, fees: Reservations are accepted. Campsites with full and partial hookups are $19, while tent sites are $13.

Open: Apr.–Oct.

Directions: From Panguitch, travel 15 miles south to Hatch. The campground is one mile north of Hatch on Highway 89.

Contact: Riverside Campground, 594 Hwy. 89, Hatch, UT 84735; 435/735-4223.

31 Cedar Canyon

   7

Set at an elevation of 8,100 feet, this campground sits in amid red rock and forest and offers a cool alternative to the summer heat of the valley below. Campsites are near a stream and are shaded by tall trees. Fishing is available nearby at Navajo and Panguitch Lakes. Cedar Canyon is a great base for campers who come to nearby Cedar City for the annual Utah Shakespearean Festival held every summer from the first week of July through the first week of September. The festival features professional actors, an outdoor replica of Shakespeare's Globe Theatre, and a free "Green Show" with period music and dance. The campground is also located near Milt's Stage Stop, one of the best steak houses in southern Utah. Other activities in the vicinity include an archery range and a children's fishing pond at Iron County–owned Woods Ranch. The 32-mile Virgin River Rim Trail also begins at Woods Ranch, and horseback riders can explore the nearby forest.

Location: In Dixie National Forest; map B1, grid h6.

Campsites, facilities: This campground has 19 sites, vault toilets, picnic tables, drinking water, and fire pits.

Reservations, fees: Sites are $8 and can be reserved. For reservations, call the U.S. Forest Service Reservation System at 800/280-2267.

Open: May 25–Sept. 18.

Directions: From Cedar City, drive 13 miles southeast on State Highway 14. Look for the campground on the north side of the road.

Contact: Dixie National Forest, Cedar City Ranger District, 435/865-3700.

 Te-Ah

   8

Since it's not set right on the lake, Te-Ah tends to fill up later on busy weekends than other Navajo Lake campgrounds. It's also the only campground on the lake that takes reservations in advance, and planning ahead might be a good idea in this popular recreation area. At an elevation of 9,200 feet, the season at this cool, alpine campground is relatively short, usually running from June to mid-September, depending on the weather. Most of the campsites are set in an aspen forest. The road and sites are paved. Hikers should note that the half-mile Pinks Trail, so named because of the path it takes through pink cliffs, begins at the upper portion of the campground. The longer 32-mile Virgin River Rim Trail, which offers great views of the Virgin River Basin and Zion National Park, can also be accessed from the campground. Look for deer and wild turkey in the area. Trails are used by hikers and horseback riders.

Location: In Dixie National Forest; map B1, grid h6.

Campsites, facilities: This 42-site campground features drinking water, picnic tables, flush toilets, a trailer dump station, and fire grills.

Reservations, fees: Reservations are accepted; call the U.S. Forest Service National Reservation System at 800/280-2267. Sites are $10.

Open: June–mid-Sept.

Directions: From Cedar City, drive 28 miles east on State Route 14, then seven miles on Navajo Lake Road. The campground is located just over two miles west of Navajo Lake.

Contact: Cedar City Ranger District, 435/865-3700.

 Navajo Lake

     9

Set high in the pines at an elevation of 9,600 feet, this popular campground on the shore of Navajo Lake fills up quickly, so try to find a spot early in the day, especially on weekends. Anglers will find better places in the state to fish, including nearby Panguitch Lake, but the Utah Division of Wildlife Resources stocks Navajo Lake with rainbow trout on a regular basis, which certainly helps your chances of catching dinner. Nearby, Navajo Lake Lodge offers boating, cabins, a restaurant, and a grocery store. Hiking, biking, and horseback riding can all be found on a trail leading from the campground to the 32-mile Virgin River Rim Trail.

Location: In Dixie National Forest; map B1, grid h6.

Campsites, facilities: This 34-site campground has flush toilets, drinking water, picnic tables, fire grills, and a public boat ramp for access to Navajo Lake. Roads and sites are paved.

Reservations, fees: Campsites are $10 and are first come, first served.

Open: May 25–Sept. 18.

Directions: The campground is located 25 miles east of Cedar City. Take State Route 14 from Cedar City for approximately 20 miles. Continue past Navajo Lake to Navajo Lake Road, and take it three miles south and west to the campground on the southern shore of the lake.

Contact: Cedar City Ranger District, 435/865-3200.

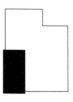

34 Spruces

     9

The 9,200-foot elevation, towering pine trees, and lush alpine nature of the Spruces campground make it a southern Utah favorite that often fills quickly during the busy summer months. Anglers can fish for rainbow trout at Navajo Lake, and boat rentals are available nearby at Navajo Lake Lodge. Hiking, biking, and horseback riding are popular on the trail from the campground that connects to the 32-mile Virgin River Rim Trail. The views of the Virgin River Valley and Zion National Park from this trail are excellent.

Location: In Dixie National Forest; map B1, grid h6.

Campsites, facilities: This 28-site campground offers drinking water, flush toilets, picnic tables, and fire grills. Roads and sites are paved.

Reservations, fees: Campsites are $10 and are first come, first served.

Open: June 15–Sept. 15.

Directions: From Cedar City, drive 25 miles east on State Route 14. Take Navajo Lake Road 2.5 miles west and south. The campground is located on the southeastern shore of Navajo Lake.

Contact: Cedar City Ranger District, 435/865-3700.

35 Duck Creek

   10

This campground at Duck Creek is one of the better public facilities in the area, thanks to its setting amid verdant meadows and pine trees and its easy access to trout fishing on the creek, pond, and Navajo and Panguitch Lakes. At an elevation of 8,600 feet, this is also a great place to beat the scorching summer heat of the southern Utah deserts. In the vicinity is Cedar Breaks National Monument, home to excellent hiking opportunities, a small visitors center, and views of a red-rock amphitheater. Bicycling is also popular in the area.

Location: In Dixie National Forest; map B1, grid h6.

Campsites, facilities: This 93-site campground features drinking water, handicapped-accessible restrooms with flush toilets, picnic tables, a group site, a dump station, an amphitheater, fire grills, and a ranger station. Nearby Duck Creek Village offers a restaurant, laundry facilities, a grocery store, and a gas station.

Reservations, fees: Reservations are accepted for sites in Loop B and the four group areas; call the U.S. Forest Service National Reservation System at 800/280-2267. Sites are $10.

Open: June 15–Sept. 15.

Directions: Drive 29 miles east of Cedar City on State Route 14. The campground is located on the north side of the road.

Contact: Cedar City Ranger District, 435/865-3700.

36 Cedar City KOA

    3

This RV park at the north end of Cedar City is located in a business district, and though it's landscaped with grass and trees, it definitely feels more urban than rural. The colorful mountains of Dixie National Forest which surround the city do create a nice backdrop, and the swimming pool provides relief on warm days. Cedar City is a central location for trips to Cedar Breaks National Monument and Brian Head Ski Resort, which is open year-round for summer and winter recreation. Zion and Bryce Canyon National Parks are an hour away, and the Grand Canyon is two hours away. Cedar City itself is home to the annual Utah Shakespearean Festival, which presents Shakespearean plays in an outdoor replica of the Globe Theatre and modern plays in the Randall Jones Theatre, plus a free nightly "Green Show" with period music, dances, and puppet shows. The festival is held every summer from the first week of July through the first week of September.

Location: In Cedar City; map B1, grid h5.

Campsites, facilities: This handicapped-accessible KOA has 94 RV sites (37 with full hookups and the rest with water and electricity) and 35 tent-camping sites. Restrooms, showers, laundry facilities, an RV waste-disposal site, picnic tables, barbecue grills, a swimming pool, a public phone, a game room, a playground, and a convenience store are also on the premises. Cable TV is available for the higher nightly rate.

Reservations, fees: Reservations are recommended. RV sites with full hookups range from $18–22, while sites with water and electricity are $20. Tent sites are $17.

Open: Year-round.

Directions: Driving south from Beaver on I-15, take exit 62. Turn south onto State Route 130 and continue two miles to the campground. Driving north on I-15, take exit 57. Turn north on State Route 130 and continue four miles to the campground. State Route 130 becomes Main Street in Cedar City.

Contact: Cedar City KOA, 1121 N. Main St., Cedar City, UT 84720; 435/586-9872.

37 Country Aire

   4

Its location on a side road on the edge of Cedar City helps give this suburban RV park a rural feel. One side of the campground faces a residential area, the other overlooks fields. The park is landscaped with flower beds and includes great views of the red hills surrounding the city.

Location: In Cedar City; map B1, grid h5.

Campsites, facilities: The 54 RV sites (28 pull-throughs) at this handicapped-accessible campground include full hookups. Roads and campsites are paved. Amenities include restrooms, showers, laundry facilities, a convenience store, a swimming pool, a playground, and a phone.

Reservations, fees: Reservations are accepted. Campsites are $22.

Open: Year-round.

Directions: North of St. George, take exit 63 off of I-15 and turn right, following the road as it turns into Main Street. The campground is 1.5 miles from the exit on the east side of the street.

Contact: Country Aire, 1700 N. Main St., Cedar City, UT 84720; 435/586-2550.

38 Honeycomb Rocks

  6

Honeycomb Rocks campground is nestled between Upper and Lower Enterprise Reservoirs in a fairly remote part of the state. Campsites are set on a sagebrush plain surrounded by hills. The relatively low 5,700-foot elevation makes for a long season, running from mid-May through the end of October most years. Trout fishing on the reservoirs can be good, and swimmers enjoy the warm lake. The campground gets its name from a nearby rock formation that is full of holes. Horseback riding on trails in the Pine Valley Mountains is possible.

Location: In Dixie National Forest near Enterprise; map B1, grid h2.

Campsites, facilities: The campground features 21 sites with vault toilets, drinking water, and picnic tables.

Reservations, fees: Campsites are $7 and are first come, first served.

Open: May 15–Oct. 31.

Directions: To reach the campground from Enterprise, drive west on State Highway 120 for about seven miles, and then take Pine Creek Road/Forest

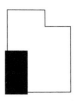

Road 006 south for approximately four miles to the campground.

Contact: Pine Valley Ranger District, 435/652-3100.

Red Ledge

 4

Set next to a small city park, Red Ledge is about the only business in the town of Kanarraville. Shade trees and grass help keep campers cool. Kanarraville is less than 10 miles from the Kolob Canyon entrance to Zion National Park, which gets fewer visitors than the rest of the park.

Location: In Kanarraville; map B1, grid h5.

Campsites, facilities: This campground has 22 RV sites (six pull-throughs) with full hookups. Roads and campsites are graveled. Amenities include restrooms, showers, laundry facilities, a convenience store, and a public phone.

Reservations, fees: Reservations are accepted. Campsites range from $15–17.

Open: Year-round.

Directions: From Cedar City, drive 11 miles south on I-15 and take the Kanarraville exit. Turn left and continue to the campground, which is located in the middle of town at 15 North.

Contact: Red Ledge Campground, P. O. Box 420130, Kanarraville, UT 84742; 435/586-9150.

Blue Spring

   9

Located at an elevation of 6,800 feet near the Santa Clara River, this campground, dotted with pine trees, is part of the Pine Valley Recreation complex, which includes a number of campgrounds and a small lake where visitors canoe and fish. A hiking trail leads into the nearby Pine Valley Wilderness, where horseback riding is also popular (horses can be rented at Pine Valley Lodge). Campers

can use the single- or multiple-family sites. It's best to reserve in advance, as the campsites usually fill up on weekends and holidays.

Location: In Dixie National Forest near Pine Valley; map B1, grid h3.

Campsites, facilities: This 17-site campground includes drinking water, picnic tables, flush and vault toilets, fire grills, two group areas, and a nearby RV waste-disposal site.

Reservations, fees: Reservations are accepted; call the U.S. Forest Service National Reservation System at 800/280-2267. Campsites are $11.

Open: June 1–Sept. 15.

Directions: From St. George, drive 19 miles north to Veyo on State Highway 18. Continue six miles north to Central, then turn east and drive another seven miles to Pine Valley. The campground is less than a mile down the road.

Contact: Pine Valley Ranger District, 435/652-3100.

Equestrian

   9

As the name suggests, this campground is geared toward horseback riding in the surrounding Pine Valley Mountains. Several nice trails lead from the camping area into the hills. Horses can be rented from Pine Valley Lodge, located two miles to the west.

Location: In Dixie National Forest near Pine Valley; map B1, grid h3.

Campsites, facilities: This 18-site campground includes four tent sites, a group site, picnic tables, flush and vault toilets, fire pits, and drinking water.

Reservations, fees: Campsites are $12 and are first come, first served.

Open: June 20–Oct. 31.

Directions: The campground is located two miles east of Pine Valley. To reach Pine Valley, drive 19 miles north of St. George on State Highway 18 to Veyo. Continue six miles north to Central, then turn east and drive another seven miles to Pine Valley and the campground.

Contact: Pine Valley Ranger District, 435/652-3100.

42 North Juniper Park

    9

North Juniper Park (elevation 6,800 ft.) is one of several campgrounds surrounding a small forest lake regularly stocked with rainbow trout by the Utah Division of Wildlife Resources. Pine trees shade the sites. The campground also serves as a starting point for trips into the nearby Pine Valley Mountains, where hikers and horseback riders will find trails aplenty.

Location: In Dixie National Forest near Pine Valley; map B1, grid h3.

Campsites, facilities: This 12-site campground has a dump station, vault toilets, drinking water, picnic tables, and fire grills.

Reservations, fees: Campsites are $11 and are first come, first served.

Open: June 20–Oct. 31.

Directions: The campground is located three miles east of Pine Valley. To reach Pine Valley, drive 19 miles north of St. George on State Highway 18 to Veyo. Continue six miles north to Central, then turn east and drive another seven miles to Pine Valley and the campground.

Contact: Pine Valley Ranger District, 435/652-3100.

43 South Juniper Park

    9

A small lake stocked with rainbow trout makes this a great place to fish. The campground (elevation 6,800 ft.) is located at the base of the Pine Valley Wilderness, which is popular with hikers and horseback riders looking to beat the heat. One of the oldest Mormon churches in Utah is located nearby in the town of Pine Valley.

Location: In Dixie National Forest near Pine Valley; map B1, grid h3.

Campsites, facilities: This 11-site campground has flush toilets, drinking water, fire pits, and picnic tables.

Reservations, fees: Campsites are $11 and are first come, first served.

Open: June 20–Oct. 31.

Directions: The campground is located three miles east of Pine Valley. To reach Pine Valley, drive 19 miles north of St. George on State Highway 18 to Veyo. Continue six miles north to Central, then turn east and drive another seven miles to Pine Valley. Look for the sign just after North Juniper Park Campground.

Contact: Pine Valley Ranger District, 435/652-3100.

44 Pines

   9

Pines (elevation 6,800 ft.) is one of a string of campgrounds surrounding a small, trout-filled lake at the base of the Pine Valley Mountains. Shade from pine trees helps give desert travelers respite from the heat. Hiking and horseback-riding trails crisscross the area as well.

Location: In Dixie National Forest near Pine Valley; map B1, grid h3.

Campsites, facilities: This 13-site campground has flush and vault toilets, drinking water, a dump station, picnic tables, and fire pits.

Reservations, fees: Campsites are $11 and are first come, first served.

Open: June 20–Oct. 31.

Directions: The campground is located three miles east of Pine Valley. To reach Pine Valley, drive 19 miles north

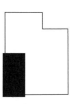

of St. George on State Route 18 to Veyo. Continue six miles north to Central, turn east, and drive another seven miles to Pine Valley and the campground.

Contact: Pine Valley Ranger District, 435/652-3100.

 Bauer's Canyon Ranch

    4

This campground in rural Glendale sits on 1,000 acres in a valley. It's next to a creek and across the highway from a country store, a cider mill, and an apple orchard. While the scenery looking back at Zion National Park is great, the campsites are mostly out in the open, a hot prospect in the summer, and the road and parking spots are gravel. The RV sites are grassy and the tent area is grassy and shaded.

Location: In Glendale; map B1, grid i8.

Campsites, facilities: This handicapped-accessible campground has 20 RV sites, all with full hookups. There is a grassy area for tents. The park has restrooms, showers, laundry facilities, picnic tables, an RV waste-disposal site, and a public phone. Pets are allowed.

Reservations, fees: Reservations are accepted. RV sites are $15; tent sites are $10.

Open: Mar. 1–Nov. 1.

Directions: The ranch is in the middle of Glendale, which is 20 miles from Zion National Park. It's on the west side of Highway 89, the main road through this small town.

Contact: Bauer's Canyon Ranch, Box 65, Glendale, UT 84729; 435/648-2564.

46 Tortoise and Hare Trailer Court

 4

This campground is in the quaint little town of Orderville. It's near Zion National Park (16 miles), Coral Pink Sand Dunes State Park (25 miles), Cedar Breaks National Monument (35 miles), and Bryce Canyon National Park (55 miles). There are several rock shops in town.

Location: In Orderville, east of Zion National Park; map B1, grid i8.

Campsites, facilities: The 15 RV sites all have full hookups. There are restrooms, showers, laundry facilities, picnic tables, and a gift store.

Reservations, fees: Reservations are accepted. Sites are $11 for two people and $1 for each additional person.

Open: Apr.–Nov.

Directions: The campground is located on the east side of Orderville right on Highway 89. Orderville is 22 miles north of Kanab between Glendale and Mount Carmel. It's 16 miles from the east entrance to Zion National Park.

Contact: Tortoise and Hare Trailer Court, P.O. Box 161, Orderville, UT 84758; 435/648-2312.

47 Zion/Bryce KOA

    8

Located on a ranch in a mountain valley, this KOA rates a nine for scenery but an eight because of the closely spaced campsites. New trees provide a bit of shade. Since it's a bit off the highway, it's quieter than some campgrounds in the area. Guided horseback rides organized by the KOA go up a side canyon the locals call Little Bryce because it has the sculpted red-rock formations characteristic of Bryce Canyon National Park. Rides cost $15 per hour per person, and riders must be over eight years of age. Hiking is also popular in this area.

Location: In Glendale; map B1, grid i7.

Campsites, facilities: This handicapped-accessible campground has 65 RV sites, 19 with full hookups. There are also 22 tent-camping sites and three cabins. All sites are grass and gravel. Amenities include restrooms, showers, laundry facilities, an RV waste-disposal site, picnic tables, a game room, barbecue grills, a public phone, a playground, and a convenience and gift store. Pets are allowed.

Reservations, fees: Reservations are recommended between June–Sept. Campsites are $20 for full hookups, $17 for RV sites, and $17 for tent sites. For groups of more than two, an additional $3 is charged per person.

Open: May 1–Oct. 15.

Directions: Glendale is located about 41 miles south of Panguitch and 26 miles north of Kanab. The KOA is five miles north of Glendale on Highway 89, a quarter mile north of the state rest area on the west side of the highway.

Contact: Zion/Bryce KOA, 800/648-2035.

48 East Zion Trailer Park

 2

Though this RV park is little more than a large gravel area with limited services, it's just 11 miles from Zion National Park. The view of the Zion formations from Mount Carmel is impressive.

Location: In Mount Carmel Junction; map B1, grid i8.

Campsites, facilities: The 20 RV sites all have full hookups. Roads and sites are dirt. Facilities include picnic tables, an RV waste-disposal site, a public phone, and a small grocery store.

Reservations, fees: Reservations are accepted. Sites are $15.

Open: Mar.–Nov.

Directions: The campground is located in Mount Carmel Junction at the intersection of Highway 89 and State Route 9. It's about 11 miles from the east entrance to Zion National Park.

Contact: East Zion Trailer Park, Junction

Hwy. 89 and Utah 9, Orderville, UT 84758; 435/648-2326.

49 Mukuntuweep RV Park and Campground

     4

While the campground itself isn't that exciting, the scenery surrounding it—namely the massive sandstone walls of Zion National Park—is spectacular. The RV area has small trees that provide some shade. The tent area is in a grassy spot under juniper trees. This campground is a good alternative to the crowded national park and Springdale facilities. Hiking and horseback riding are available minutes away from the campground inside the park.

Location: Near Mount Carmel Junction; map B1, grid i7.

Campsites, facilities: There are 50 RV sites with full hookups; 20 of these are pull-throughs. A grassy area can accommodate about 185 tents. Amenities include restrooms, showers, laundry facilities, an RV waste-disposal site, a game room, barbecue pits, a playground, and a convenience and gift store. Pets are allowed. There is also a Mexican restaurant on site.

Reservations, fees: Reservations are accepted. RV sites are $19; tent sites are $15. For groups of more than two, an additional $3 is charged per person.

Open: Apr.–Oct.

Directions: The campground is located 13 miles west of Mount Carmel Junction and half a mile from the east entrance to Zion National Park. Mount Carmel Junction is 17 miles north of Kanab on Highway 9. The campground is on the south side of the highway, across the street from a Mexican restaurant.

Contact: Mukuntuweep RV Park and Campground, 435/-648-2154.

50 Gunlock State Park

     4

Set in a dry and often warm part of Utah on 240-acre Gunlock Reservoir, this primitive camping area offers guests a place to enjoy a swim when the weather heats up. The reservoir is also a popular early-season water-skiing area. Anglers enjoy fishing for bass and crappie.

Location: On Gunlock Reservoir; map B1, grid i1.

Campsites, facilities: This primitive campground includes a few picnic tables and pit toilets. There is no drinking water. A boat ramp is available for launching.

Reservations, fees: Campsites are free and are first come, first served.

Open: Year-round.

Directions: Drive 15 miles northwest of St. George on State Route 18. From Veyo, head south to the tiny town of Gunlock. The campground is just south of town on the east bank of Gunlock Reservoir.

Contact: Snow Canyon State Park, 435/628-2255.

51 Oak Grove

  9

It takes a bit of effort to reach this small campground set in a grove of oak trees, but the extra time is worth it if you want to be close to all the hiking and horseback-riding opportunities in the Pine Valley Wilderness.

Location: In Dixie National Forest; map B1, grid i3.

Campsites, facilities: This eight-site campground has drinking water, vault toilets, picnic tables, and fire grills.

Reservations, fees: Campsites are $5 and are first come, first served.

Open: Late May–Oct.

Directions: Drive north of St. George on I-15 for 11 miles to the town of Leeds. Take the

Leeds exit and drive to the north end of town, looking for signs to Silver Reef ghost town. Take Forest Road 32 for nine miles up a dirt road to the campground.

Contact: Pine Valley Ranger District, 435/652-3100.

52 Baker Dam

  5

A piñon forest surrounds this primitive campground. The big draw is trout fishing in the reservoir and a nearby stream. Anglers should check with the Utah Division of Wildlife Resources in Cedar City for fishing information. Use rafts, boats, or canoes to fish the reservoir.

Location: On Bureau of Land Management property west of St. George; map B1, grid i2.

Campsites, facilities: This 20-site campground has vault toilets, picnic tables, fire grills, and drinking water.

Reservations, fees: Campsites are $6 and are first come, first served.

Open: Year-round.

Directions: To reach the campground, drive 25 miles north of St. George on State Route 18. Look for the small brown Bureau of Land Management sign for Baker Reservoir on the right side of the road. Turn here and follow the road to the campground.

Contact: Bureau of Land Management, Cedar City District Office, 435/586-2401.

53 Zion Canyon

     5

This campground in the town of Springdale is adjacent to a motel operated by the same owners. Sites are under large shade trees; some are grassy while others are in sand. A few of the tent camping sites are next to the Virgin River, where many guests like to swim. The river can be a slow stream in late summer or a raging torrent in early spring, and relatively clear or cloudy red. Springdale, home to quite a few artisans, is a great place to browse through the many craft and souvenir shops. The town also has some eclectic restaurants.

Location: In Springdale; map B1, grid j5.

Campsites, facilities: This handicapped-accessible campground has 200 RV sites, 70 with full hookups, plus 65 tent-camping sites. Amenities include restrooms, showers, laundry facilities, an RV waste-disposal site, picnic tables, and a large grocery and gift store. Barbecue grills are available upon request. There is an extra charge for cable television. Pets are allowed with RV campers only.

Reservations, fees: Reservations are recommended from Easter through October, but are accepted by mail only. Write to P.O. Box 99, Springdale, UT 84767. RV sites are $20; tent sites are $16. Groups larger than two people must pay $3.50 for each individual over the age of 16 and $2 for children under 15. Children under 3 are free.

Open: Year-round.

Directions: The campground is off Highway 9 in Springdale, across from Flanigan's Restaurant. The south entrance to Zion National Park a half mile away.

Contact: Zion Canyon Campground, P. O. Box 99, Springdale, UT 84767; 435/772-3237.

Watchman

 6

This campground, nestled next to the Virgin River and shaded by old cottonwood trees, is the only one in Zion National Park open year-round. The town of Springdale is next door, and traffic whizzing by on State Highway 9 can be somewhat noisy, but the sound of the flowing river and rustling trees helps to mute the noise. The Zion Nature Center is within walking distance and offers an excellent junior ranger program for children. Nearby hiking trails and a paved bicycle route are added amenities. Horse rentals are available further up the canyon. The river is a great place to cool off in the warmer months. A shuttle, available at the campground, takes visitors through Zion Canyon. Cars are no longer permitted in the canyon, making the whole experience much quieter and calmer.

Location: In Zion National Park; map B1, grid j5.

Campsites, facilities: The handicapped-accessible campground has 229 sites, 140 of which are appropriate for RVs. Facilities include picnic tables, restrooms with cold running water, drinking water, a group area, and a dump station.

Reservations, fees: Campsites are $14 and can be reserved. Sites with full hookups are $16.

Open: Year-round.

Directions: The campground is located near Zion National Park's south entrance on State Highway 9, about 21 miles east of Hurricane.

Contact: Zion National Park, 435/772-3256 or 800/365-2267.

55 South

 8

Set amid cottonwood trees near the Virgin River, this campground can be one of the coolest places in the park when temperatures begin to hover near the 100s in the summer months. Hiking and bicycling trails add to the popularity of this spot, so try to arrive early during the peak summer season. Horses can be rented at the nearby lodge. Take the shuttle from the campground up Zion Canyon, as cars are not allowed.

Location: In Zion National Park; map B1, grid i5.

Campsites, facilities: This handicapped-accessible campground consists of 140 sites, all appropriate for RVs. Amenities include picnic tables, fire grills, restrooms with cold running water, a dump station, and drinking water. Zion National Park's only group area is located here.

Reservations, fees: Campsites are $14 and are first come, first served.

Open: Apr. 15–Sept. 15; call in advance.

Directions: The campground is located just east of Zion National Park's south entrance on State Highway 9, about 21 miles east of Hurricane.

Contact: Zion National Park, 435/772-3256.

56 Lava Point

   8

Lava Point is located in one of the more remote parts of Zion National Park, making it a good, if primitive, alternative to the hustle and bustle of the larger campgrounds near the park's south entrance. Be sure to bring your own water supply when camping here. Nearby Kolob Reservoir offers good fishing in the summer and fall. Hiking trails from the campsites will take you deep into the park. Arrive early, as the sites fill up quickly. The 7,900-foot elevation limits the camping season to summer and early fall.

Location: In Zion National Park; map B1, grid i6.

Campsites, facilities: This primitive campground with six sites has vault toilets, picnic tables, and fire grills. No water is available.

Reservations, fees: Campsites are free and are first come, first served.

Open: June–mid-Oct., depending on snow conditions.

Directions: Drive 26 miles north from Virgin on Highway 9. Turn west just before Blue Springs Reservoir and continue to the campground.

Contact: Zion National Park, 435/772-3256.

57 Silver Springs RV Park

    2

Located in La Verkin, which is close to Zion National Park and year-round golf in St. George, this is a good place to stay cool in the hot summer months. Many of the RVers here are permanent residents.

Location: In La Verkin; map B1, grid j3.

Campsites, facilities: This handicapped-accessible campground has 12 RV sites, all with full hookups. A grassy area can accommodate some tents. Amenities include restrooms, showers, laundry facilities, an RV waste-disposal site, picnic tables, barbecue grills, swings, a swimming pool, cable TV, and a convenience store. Pets are welcome with overnight visitors.

Reservations, fees: Reservations are recommended for holidays. RV sites are $16; tent sites are $8.

Open: Year-round.

Directions: From St. George, take I-15 north for approximately 10 miles. Exit east on State Route 9 and continue 10 miles to La Verkin. The campground is at the north end of town.

Contact: Silver Springs RV Park, 435/635-7700.

58 Willow Wind

   4

This well-manicured RV park across the street from the supermarket (the largest business in Hurricane) has grass, trees, and a view of the fields and sandstone walls that mark the entrance to Zion National Park some 30 miles away. The tent-camping area is mostly out in the open.

Location: In Hurricane; map B1, grid j3.

Campsites, facilities: This campground has 95 RV sites with full hookups. A grassy, shaded area can accommodate about 25 tents, making this a good bet for groups of tent campers. Roads are gravel, but the sites have cement pads. The park has restrooms, showers, laundry facilities, an RV waste-disposal site, barbecue pits, two public phones, cable TV, and picnic tables (though not at every site). There is a five-acre pet run.

Reservations, fees: Reservations are recommended in the spring and fall. Sites with full hookups are $20 for the first two people and $1 per person thereafter. Tent sites are $12 for the first two people and $1 per person thereafter.

Open: Year-round.

Directions: From I-15, take State Route 9 east toward Hurricane for nine miles. The park is at the west end of Hurricane, across from Lin's Supermarket.

Contact: Willow Park, 1151 W. 80 South, Hurricane, UT 84737; 435/635-4154.

59 Brentwood Utah RV Park

     5

This well-maintained resort is perhaps the nicest RV park near the entrance to Zion National Park, which is located about 30 miles away. Tall mulberry trees shade sites. Activities, including swimming and golf, are just outside your door (or tent flap). The Virgin River, which runs through Zion Canyon, is also nearby. The tent-camping area is fenced off and separate from the RV area.

Location: In Hurricane; map B1, grid j3.

Campsites, facilities: This handicapped-accessible campground has 188 RV sites with full hookups, plus grassy spaces for 15 tents. Amenities include restrooms, showers, laundry facilities, some moveable picnic tables, a game room, a bowling alley, a waterslide park, indoor miniature golf, an indoor swimming pool, and cable TV. Pets are allowed. There is a nine-hole pitch-and-putt golf course on site. The park also boasts a tennis court.

Reservations, fees: Reservations are accepted. RV sites are $19 and tent sites are $12. Groups with more than four people are charged an additional $2 per person.

Open: Year-round.

Directions: Take the Hurricane exit off I-15 north of St. George and drive east on State Route 9 for five miles. Brentwood is on the north side of the road, about four miles west of Hurricane.

Contact: Brentwood Utah RV Park, 150 N. 3700 W., Hurricane, UT 84737; 435/635-2320.

60 Harrisburg Lakeside RV Resort

      5

Though most of the guests at this resort are club members, overnighters are welcome. The resort is just outside of Quail Creek State Park and overlooks the historic old town of Harrisburg, an early Mormon pioneer settlement. Quail Creek Reservoir, a short walk from the campground when it's full, is a popular boating and fishing destination. The campground has grass and trees, though it's primarily developed for RVs. Hikers can head for the many trails available nearby at the Dixie Red Cliffs Recreation Area.

Location: In Leeds; map B1, grid j3.

Campsites, facilities: This RV park has 150 RV sites, all with full hookups. Amenities include showers, a restroom, laundry facilities, a swimming pool, a convenience store, a gas station, picnic tables, a barbecue grill, an RV waste-disposal site, and a clubhouse.

Reservations, fees: Reservations are accepted. Campsites are $20. Cable TV costs extra.

Open: Year-round.

Directions: From Cedar City, take exit 23 off of I-15. From St. George, take exit 22 off of I-15. The resort is two miles south of Leeds on the frontage road.

Contact: Harrisburg Lakeside RV Resort, P. O. Box 2146, St. George, UT 84771; 435/879-2312.

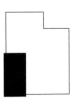

61 Leeds RV Park

 5

This campground with grass and trees is a rural alternative to St. George. The grassy tent area is separate from the RV area. Quail Creek State Park, Zion National Park, and the Dixie Red Cliffs Recreation Area are all close by. Leeds is a historic town with several sandstone buildings dating from early pioneer days. Stop by the Silver Reef Museum to learn more about its pioneer and mining history.

Location: In Leeds; map B1, grid j2.

Campsites, facilities: This campground has 43 RV sites with full hookups, plus eight tent sites. Roads and campsites are gravel. Amenities include restrooms, showers, picnic tables, and a public phone.

Reservations, fees: Reservations are accepted. RV sites with full hookups are $15; tent sites are $10.

Open: Year-round.

Directions: From St. George, drive about 15 miles north on I-15. Take the Leeds exit and follow the signs to the park.

Contact: Leeds RV Park, P. O. Box 461149, Leeds, UT 84746; 435/879-2450.

62 Shivwits

 10

This campground is located in stunning Snow Canyon State Park, where the red and tan Navajo sandstone and black lava rock are a study in colorful contrasts. Campers can explore lava tubes, hike along a nature trail near the campground, or take longer hiking adventures through the red-rock landscape. Children enjoy playing on the shifting coral-pink sand dune and crawling around on the rocks in the campground. Due to its mild winter temperatures, this is an especially popular off-season camping area. In fact, Snow Canyon's off-season is usually in the summer when temperatures regularly top more than 100°F. The tent-camping sites are among the best in this part of the state. There is a horseback-riding concession available in the park.

Location: In Snow Canyon State Park; map B1, grid j1.

Campsites, facilities: This handicapped-accessible campground has 14 sites with full hookups and 21 sites with no hookups. Amenities include showers, modern restrooms with running water, a dump station, a covered group area, and such recreational facilities as volleyball courts and horseshoe pits.

Reservations, fees: Reservations can be made 120 days in advance by calling 800/322-3770 Mon.–Fri. 8 A.M.–5 P.M. A $5 nonrefundable reservation fee is charged for each site reserved. Campsites with hookups are $17, while sites with no hookups are $11. Utah residents 62 years and older with a Special Fun Tag receive a $2 discount Sun.–Thurs.

Open: Year-round.

Directions: The campground is about 11 miles northwest of St. George on State Highway 18.

Contact: Snow Canyon State Park, 435/628-2255.

63 Settlers RV Park

 3

As with other RV parks in St. George, this is definitely a winter-oriented urban facility, since summer temperatures often top 100°F (the swimming pool is the place to be on hot days). The park is neat and clean, with a few trees and cement patios. Some spaces are used by permanent residents, but overnighters are welcome. St. George is home to eight public golf courses.

Location: In St. George; map B1, grid j2.

Campsites, facilities: This campground has 155 RV sites, all with full hookups. Sites are gravel with cement patios. Amenities include restrooms, showers, picnic tables, laundry facilities, a game room, barbecue grills, a swimming pool, a public phone, cableTV, and a playground.

Reservations, fees: Reservations are recommended, especially during the winter. Campsites are $22.80.

Open: Year-round.

Directions: From I-15, take exit 8 to St. George and turn east on St. George Boulevard. Turn south on River Road and drive to 100 South. Look for the Settlers RV Park sign by Shoneys Restaurant.

Contact: Settlers RV Park, 1333 E. 100 South, St. George, UT 84790; 435/628-1624.

64 McArthur's Temple View RV Resort

 2

This urban campground is landscaped with palm trees and shrubs, and is a short walk away from St. George's city park, shopping district, and fast-food restaurants. The view from the resort—beyond the business area—is of the colorful lava-topped mesa that guards the city. A warm climate and year-round golfing opportunities make this a popular winter destination. Snow Canyon State Park (19 miles away) and the Jacob Hamblin Home (five miles away) are nearby attractions. Jacob Hamblin was a Mormon pioneer who was an active negotiator with the Native Americans in the 1800s. Snow Canyon has great hiking, including a trail down a lava tube. Kids will like the nearby amusement park with its car rides, miniature golf, and batting cages.

Location: In St. George; map B1, grid j3.

Campsites, facilities: This large, handicapped-accessible campground has 266 sites with full hookups, including 55 pull-throughs and a grassy area for tents. RV sites are gravel and cement. Amenities include a heat-

ed swimming pool and Jacuzzi, a clubhouse, a game room, billiards, a dance floor, shuffleboard, a TV room, volleyball, and laundry facilities.

Reservations, fees: Reservations are accepted. RV sites are $23.95 for two people; tent sites are $18.95 for two people. Each additional person is $2. The weekly rate is $143.70.

Open: Year-round.

Directions: In St. George, take exit 6 off I-15, then go two blocks north on Main Street to the campground on the east side of the road.

Contact: McArthur's Temple View RV Resort, 975 S. Main St., St. George, UT 84770; 800/776-6410.

65 St. George Campground and RV Park

 5

This campground and RV park in a residential section of St. George has lots of permanent residents, but includes space for overnighters as well. It's nicely landscaped with a lawn and shade trees, and there's a swimming pool perfect for hot days. More vegetation around the perimeter of the park provides a buffer from I-15. Red Cliffs Mall is across the freeway.

Location: In St. George; map B1, grid j3.

Campsites, facilities: The 120 RV sites all have full hookups. There are five tent sites. Also here are restrooms, showers, laundry facilities, barbecue grills, cableTV, a swimming pool, and a small store. Pets are welcome. Some of the facilities are handicapped accessible.

Reservations, fees: Reservations aren't necessary during the summer (off-season) months. In the winter, sites are offered on a first-come, first-served basis. RV sites are $16; tent sites are $12. Seniors 55 and older receive a $1 discount.

Open: Year-round.

Directions: In St. George, take exit 10 off I-15. The north frontage road leads to Middleton Drive. The campground is at 2100 N. Middleton Drive.

Contact: St. George Campground and RV Park, 2100 N. Middleton Dr., St. George, UT 84770; 435/673-2970.

66 Redlands RV Park

 5

This RV park two miles north of St. George looks and feels like a resort, thanks to its fancy clubhouse and swimming pool. Some overnighters are placed side by side in a gravel lot shaded by trees, so ask for one of the more generously spaced sites. Each campsite has two mature trees and lots of grass. Views are of the red desert and sandstone hills surrounding St. George. The park is a mile from a golf course and just down the street from a shopping mall. The Pine Valley Mountains are about 15 miles north, and Zion National Park is 40 miles away.

Location: Near St. George; map B1, grid j3.

Campsites, facilities: This large, handicapped-accessible, 200-site campground has 120 pull-throughs. Because each site is grassy, tent campers can use them as well. Also here are restrooms, laundry facilities, showers, cable TV, a recreation hall, shuffleboard, a swimming pool, a therapy pool, an RV and car wash, and a grocery store that sells RV supplies.

Reservations, fees: Reservations are recommended for the winter months. Fees are $21.95 for RV campers and $15.95 for tent campers. An additional $2 is charged per person for groups larger than two.

Open: Year-round.

Directions: From just north of St. George, take exit 10 off I-15. Turn south on Green Springs Drive and continue to Telegraph Street. Turn west on Telegraph Street and head to the campground at 650 West Telegraph Street.

Contact: Redlands RV Park, P. O. Box 2000, Washington, UT 84780; 800/553-8269.

67 Quail Creek State Park

 6

This campground in Quail Creek State Park is somewhat exposed, but views of the reservoir help compensate for the lack of shade. The reservoir is home to a rare combination of rainbow trout and largemouth bass, making it a popular year-round fishing and boating destination. Campsites are along the reservoir. All sites have shaded picnic areas. Swimming and water-skiing are favorite warm-weather activities. Hiking is available at the Bureau of Land Management's Dixie Red Cliffs Recreation Area. The Silver Reef ghost town area, about two miles west, has a restored museum that's worth a look. Golfers can travel three miles to any of eight public golf courses in St. George.

Location: On Quail Creek Reservoir; map B1, grid j3.

Campsites, facilities: This handicapped-accessible campground with 23 sites has modern restrooms but no showers, a fish-cleaning station, and two covered group-use areas.

Reservations, fees: Reservations can be made 120 days in advance by calling 800/322-3770 Mon.–Fri. 8 A.M.–5 P.M. A $5 nonrefundable reservation fee is charged for each site reserved. Campsites are $10. Utah residents 62 years and older who have a Special Fun Tag receive a $2 discount Sun.–Thurs.

Open: Year-round.

Directions: Take I-15 north from St. George to the Hurricane exit. Follow State Route 9 three miles east to the campground.

Contact: Quail Creek State Park, 435/879-2378.

68 Dixie Red Cliffs

     9

This small campground, set as it is in scenic southern Utah under cottonwood trees, is a real find. Quail Creek flows right through the middle of the picnic area. The campsites, surrounded by the red cliffs which give the place its name, are spaced a good distance apart. One hiking trail leads to waterfalls and swimming holes (be careful of broken glass when wading), while another crosses slickrock to a view of an old ghost town. A third takes hikers to an ancient Anasazi ruin. Golf is available nearby in St. George and Washington, as are boating, fishing, and water-skiing at Quail Creek State Park.

Location: Near Quail Creek Reservoir; map B1, grid j3.

Campsites, facilities: This handicapped-accessible campground with 10 sites has picnic tables, drinking water, and vault toilets.

Reservations, fees: Campsites are $8 and are first come, first served.

Open: Year-round.

Directions: Take I-15 approximately 11 miles north of St. George to the town of Leeds. Take the Leeds exit and follow the signs 4.5 miles southwest to the campground and recreation area.

Contact: Bureau of Land Management, 435/673-4654.

69 Coral Pink Sand Dunes State Park

  10

True to its name, Coral Pink Sand Dunes State Park is home to beautiful coral-pink sand dunes. Sunrise and sunset on the dunes are pretty spectacular, so don't forget your camera. And if you have children in tow, be sure to bring buckets, shovels, and other sand toys so they can frolic on the dunes (but be aware that the sand dunes are popular with dune buggies and all-terrain vehicles). The park also has a short nature trail, as well as an area off-limits to vehicles. The campground itself is located far from the roads in a piñon-juniper forest, and includes nicely spaced sites.

Location: Near the Utah-Arizona border; map B1, grid j7.

Campsites, facilities: This 22-site campground has picnic tables, fire grills, drinking water, restrooms with showers, sewage-disposal facilities, and a picnic area.

Reservations, fees: Reservations can be made 120 days in advance by calling 800/322-3770 Mon.–Fri. 8 A.M.–5 P.M. A $5 nonrefundable reservation fee is charged for each site reserved. Campsites are $13. Utah residents 62 years and older who have a Special Fun Tag receive a $2 discount Sun.–Thurs.

Open: Year-round.

Directions: Drive 22 miles northwest of Kanab on Highway 89. Look for the park sign leading to a turnoff to the south. Turn and follow the road 12 miles to the campground.

Contact: Coral Pink Sand Dunes State Park, 435/648-2800.

70 Ponderosa Grove

  7

Though primitive and lacking the facilities of the nearby Coral Pink Sand Dunes State Park campground (see above), this is a good overflow area. It's popular with the all-terrain-vehicle set. Photographers should consider getting up early to take advantage of the great morning light on the dunes, which feature fine, shifting, coral-pink sands.

Location: Near Coral Pink Sand Dunes State Park; map B1, grid j7.

Campsites, facilities: This campground has seven campsites capable of holding RVs up to 20 feet long,

plus vault toilets, picnic tables, and fire grills. No water is available.

Reservations, fees: Campsites are $5 and are first come, first served.

Open: May–Nov.

Directions: Drive 14 miles northwest of Kanab on Highway 89. Take the county road to Coral Pink Sand Dunes State Park, then follow signs to the campground.

Contact: Bureau of Land Management, Kanab Field Office, 435/644-4800.

Crazy Horse Campark

 6

Kanab, home of Crazy Horse Campark, is a small Utah town with a colorful past. A number of old Westerns were filmed here, including the TV show *Gunsmoke*. Visitors can tour the Johnson Canyon Movie Set, where this long-running series was shot. Also in Kanab is Lopeman's Frontier Movie Town, a re-creation of an old frontier town. The Campark picks up this Western theme in its game room, where you'll find everything from an old movie set to Old-West storefronts and a general store. Half the sites at the Campark are shaded with tall trees, a rarity in this exceedingly hot area. Tent-camping sites are in the sand. Views from the Campark are of the red cliffs behind Kanab and the neighboring golf course. Kanab is close to Lake Powell (60 miles), the North Rim of the Grand Canyon (75 miles), and Bryce Canyon National Park (77 miles).

Location: In Kanab; map B1, grid j8.

Campsites, facilities: There are 56 RV sites with full hookups, 26 sites with water and electricity, and eight tent-camping sites. There is also a grassy area for additional tents. Amenities include restrooms, showers, laundry facilities, picnic tables, an RV waste-disposal site, a game room, barbecue grills, a swimming pool, and a convenience store and gift shop. Cable TV is avail-

able in the sitting area. Pets are allowed on a leash.

Reservations, fees: Reservations are recommended in the summer months. Sites with full hookups are $16. Sites with water and electricity are $14.95. Tent sites are $10.52. An additional $1 fee is charged for visitors over the age of six in groups larger than two.

Open: Year-round.

Directions: Drive east on Highway 89 through the town of Kanab. The campground is on the north side of the road.

Contact: Crazy Horse Campark, 625 E. 30 South, Kanab, UT 84741; 435/644-2782.

Kanab RV Corral

 4

This campground, located on Main Street in the middle of Kanab, is surrounded by businesses and homes, which means it can be a bit noisy. A strip of trees forms the perimeter of the campground, and the sites are red cinder with narrow plots of grass. It's better suited as an RV park than as a place to pitch a tent. Kanab is close to Lake Powell (60 miles) and Coral Pink Sand Dunes State Park (22 miles). It's also a jumping-off point to Zion National Park, Bryce Canyon National Park, Cedar Breaks National Monument, and Grand Canyon National Park, all of which are within 100 miles.

Location: In Kanab; map B1, grid j8.

Campsites, facilities: This handicapped-accessible campground has 40 RV sites with full hookups. Amenities include restrooms, showers, laundry facilities, an RV waste-disposal site, picnic tables, and a swimming pool. Pets are allowed.

Reservations, fees: Reservations are accepted. RV sites are $20 for two people. For groups larger than two, there is a $2-per-person charge. The maximum number of people per site is six.

Open: Year-round.

Directions: In Kanab, go south on Highway 89A (Main St.) for less than a block. The campground is by a fire station.

Contact: Kanab RV Corral, 483 S. 100 East, Kanab, UT 84741; 435/644-5330.

73 Hitch 'N Post

 4

This campground, set beneath tall shade trees, is in the middle of the business section of Kanab, with a laundromat across the street and several fast-food restaurants within walking distance. Views are of the red cliffs surrounding town.

Location: In Kanab; map B1, grid j8.

Campsites, facilities: This campground has 23 sites, all with full hookups. Roads and campsites are gravel. There is a separate grassy area for tent camping, plus restrooms, showers, fire rings, picnic tables on cement pads, and an RV waste-disposal site.

Reservations, fees: Reservations are accepted. Sites with full hookups are $16; tent sites are $10. An additional $2 is charged for each person in groups with more than two people.

Open: Year-round.

Directions: The campground is in the middle of Kanab, half a block east of the junction of Highways 89 and 89A.

Contact: Hitch 'N Post, 196 E. 300 South, Kanab, UT 84741; 435/644-2142 or 800/458-3516.

CHAPTER B2

HIKERS IN BRYCE NATIONAL PARK

MAP B2

One inch equals approximately 11 miles.

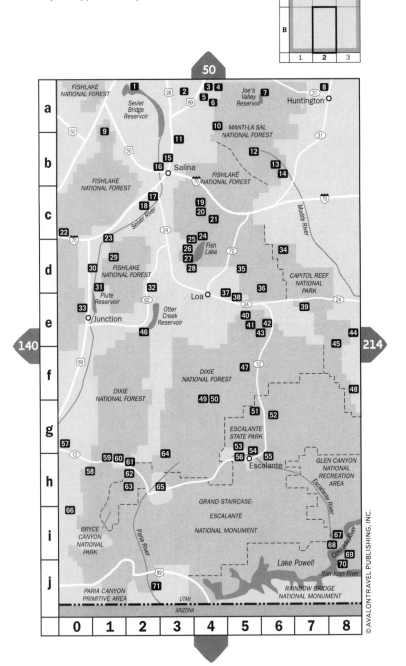

CHAPTER B2

(CONTINUED ON NEXT PAGE)

This part of Utah offers the most variety of camping and outdoor experiences in the state. Explore high-mountain lakes, red-rock canyons, history, and prehistory.

Visiting Bryce Canyon National Park, a red-rock amphitheater, and Lake Powell, the second-largest man-made lake in the United States, may mean rubbing shoulders with visitors from all over the world, but it's worth it. Finding a private corner all to oneself is not impossible, however, as there are relatively unexplored regions just a few hours away.

For example, the new Grand Staircase-Escalante National Monument lies in this part of the state. Not only is it one of the nation's newest national monuments, it's a place where it's easy to find solitude. The monument is largely roadless and in many places is accessible only by foot.

Three-Day Itinerary: Capitol Reef National Park 🏕 Anasazi State Park 🏕 Bryce Canyon

Day One

Capitol Reef National Park, approximately 215 miles south of Salt Lake City, can be seen in an hour by following State Route 24 through the park. Shortly before entering the park from Torrey, Utah, drivers may sense a kind of vertigo as anything resembling a horizontal horizon disappears. Instead, the vistas are of red, purple, and orange rock layers thrust into the sky and gouged out by water. The scenery demands more than a drive, however. Take a short (one mile, one-way) hike to Hickman Bridge or Capitol Gorge to see how the forces of nature have sculpted the sandstone canyons and rock formations, some of which resemble the domed rotunda of our nation's capitol. Spend the night in a pioneer orchard near the visitors center that is now Fruita Campground. Deer may be seen nibbling grass here in the winter. Campers, on the other hand, can sample apples from the trees in season and see living-history demonstrations that include a horse-drawn cider press.

Day Two

Travel south on State Highway 12 from Torrey to Boulder. This half-hour trip begins what may be the most varied and interesting stretch of highway in the Unit-

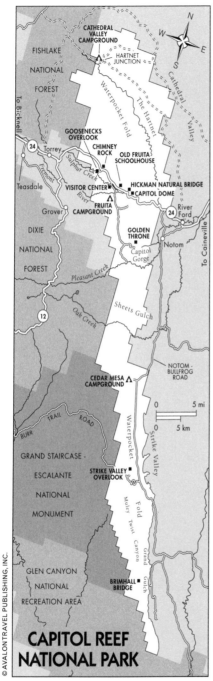

CAPITOL REEF NATIONAL PARK

ed States. From the red-rock desert, you'll climb into an alpine forest complete with high lakes and mountain campgrounds. The summit is over 9,000 feet high. Stop at viewpoints to look down at Capitol Reef or across to the towering Henry Mountains to the east. In Boulder, take a half hour and stop in at the Anasazi State Park visitors center. Learn about the Prehistoric Basket Makers who once lived in the area. The name Anasazi comes from a Navajo word thought to mean "ancient enemies." This name is presently not considered politically correct, hence the use of "Prehistoric Basket Makers" when referring to the ancient people. Take another few minutes to tour the stone ruins that are partially covered by a protective roof. A reconstructed dwelling near the visitors center gives modern-day tourists a feeling for what life in the stone apartments was like. A large collection of artifacts is housed in the center.

There are many options as to where to spend the rest of the day. For an adventure, inquire at Anasazi Village State Park about hikes in the canyons within Grand Staircase-Escalante National Monument. (Be aware that the monument is not supervised as closely as state and national parks. Visitors are more or less on their own in the backcountry.) Park personnel can show hike locations on a map or indicate books that have been published concerning these hikes. Information is available at the state park or at an interagency visitors center in Escalante.

Another option is to spend the rest of the day strolling or fishing along the stream to Calf Creek Falls, not far from Anasazi State Park.

Calf Creek is a green oasis nestled in the bottom of a spectacular sandstone canyon. While there is a small campground at Calf Creek, it fills up nearly every night. Plan to spend the night at Kodachrome Basin State Park, 60 miles to the east. Highway 12 from Boulder to Escalante has been cut out of slickrock with interesting turns and twists. At various points, the road drops off almost vertically on both sides with no guardrails. It's a thrilling ride!

The Kodachrome Basin campground is situated in a remote rock amphitheater featuring pinnacles that are actually petrified geysers. Several hiking trails explore this scenic area. See the park brochure for directions to a short drive and hike to Grosvenor Arch, a landmark in the Grand Staircase-Escalante National Monument. Reservations for camping at Kodachrome Basin (P. O. Box 238, Cannonville, UT 84718) are recommended.

Day Three

Finish the three-day trip with a visit to Bryce Canyon National Park on Highway 12 about 15 miles from Kodachrome Basin State Park. Here, the scenery changes again. Bryce is at a higher elevation with an entirely different look than Capitol Reef or Grand Staircase-Escalante. While Bryce can be viewed from scenic overlooks along the rim of the canyon, a relatively level, paved trail connects Fairyland and Bryce Points and can be walked in five or six hours. For a real hands-on treat, descend into the coral-colored canyon via the 1.8-mile round-trip Navajo/Queen's Combination Trail below the rim between Sunset and Sunrise Points. The trail leads through

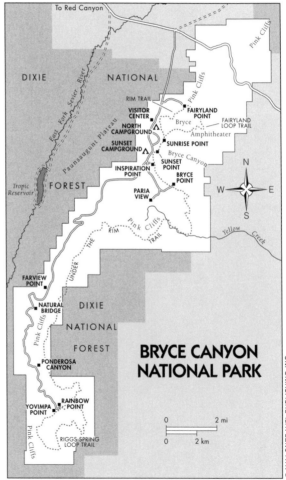

Grand Staircase-Escalante National Monument

Designated in 1996 by President Bill Clinton, the new monument is managed by the Bureau of Land Management instead of the National Park Service. The BLM is in the process of conducting inventories of the new monument. Just about the only proof a tourist sees that it exists, however, are some signs along the highway. An unimproved road across the monument to Grosvenor Arch and Cottonwood Canyon is usually passable in a sedan. Large vehicles should not attempt it, however, due to occasional steep inclines and narrow sections with drop-offs. The road is treacherous when wet or snowy. For hiking in the Escalante Canyons, consult the rangers at Escalante Petrified Forest State Park, Kodachrome Basin State Park, or Anasazi State Park, or pick up a guidebook to the Escalante region.

a maze of weathered formations past tall ponderosa pines and waxy-leafed manzanita bushes. The steep hike out of the canyon can be a workout for couch potatoes. A meal in the classic Bryce Canyon Lodge, built in 1919, is a treat, but it's closed in winter.

Spend the night in the campground at Bryce Canyon National Park. Or, for a smaller campground, try Red Canyon Forest Service Campground just outside the western entrance to Bryce. If you want a more commercial tourist experience, spend the night at the campground at Ruby's Inn, just south on State Route 63. The campground is right outside the park and features Dutch-oven dinners and a rodeo.

Seven-Day Itinerary: Fishlake National Forest 🏕 Capitol Reef National Park 🏕 Anasazi State Park 🏕 Lake Powell 🏕 Bryce Canyon National Park 🏕 Marysville 🏕 Fremont Indian State Park

One week is, unfortunately, not enough time to truly see Capitol Reef National Park or explore the waters of Lake Powell. In fact, the forests and canyons of this part of the world offer the opportunity to get out of the car and either sit, fish, hike, horseback ride, raft, bike, or boat for days at a time. If time does not permit, however, a sampling of one or more of the many activities is possible.

Day One

Start the trip with a day of camping and fishing or hiking in the Fishlake National Forest. Johnson Reservoir and Fish Lake are cool, forested waters, with Fish Lake offering the best angling. Horseback riders, bicyclists and hikers can take the Pelican Canyon Trail (five miles one-way) to the top of 11,000-foot Fish Lake High Top Mountain and usually have the trail to themselves. Recreationists are rewarded at the summit with meadows full of flowers and views of other forested mountains as far as they can see.

Day Two

Spend at least two days in Capitol Reef National Park (see

Lake Powell

Lake Powell is a destination in and of itself. The reservoir contained in Glen Canyon National Recreation Area hosts water sports and vehicles of every stripe, including houseboats, powerboats, personal watercraft, and fishing. Visitors can access the Lake from Page (Arizona), Bullfrog Marina, Hite Crossing, or Halls Crossing Marina. Each of these access points is far from the others by road. Camping at Bullfrog and Halls Crossing is out in the open and close to the water. The only way to really experience the lake is by boat or personal watercraft. Hundreds of miles of rocky coastline and secluded sandy coves beckon sightseers. Perhaps a natural wonder of the world with a span of 467 feet, Rainbow Bridge can be visited by boat.

Three-Day Itinerary, Day One). The Fruita Campground with its historic pioneer buildings is a must. However, if the campground is full, or you want a more private experience, try the Sunglow Forest Service Campground south of Bicknell, about 11 miles west of the park. Hikes in the Capitol Reef range from relatively easy walks along a sandy wash in Capitol Gorge to more strenuous hikes on sandstone formations like those accessed by the trails to Cassidy Arch or Navajo Knobs.

Day Three

From Capitol Reef National Park, it's tempting to take State Road 95 to Lake Powell. But think again. This trip is better saved for a loop trip to see Canyonlands and Arches National Parks. Instead, visit Anasazi State Park (see Three-Day Itinerary, Day Two) and spend the night in Escalante Petrified Forest State Park. Escalante Petrified Forest, 30 miles from Boulder on spectacular Highway 12, is situated next to the Wide Hollow Reservoir. The guided trail at the park leads hikers through an ancient forest containing enormous petrified logs.

Day Four

Drive another 30 miles southwest of Escalante Petrified Forest State Park to the town of Cannonville. Take the turnoff to Kodachrome Basin State Park (see Three-Day Itinerary, Day Two) and spend the day hiking. A horseback-riding concession rents horses and offers buggy rides in the park. Spend the night at the park's campground.

Day Five

Plan on spending a day in Bryce Canyon National Park (see Three-Day Itinerary, Day Three).

Day Six

Leave the beaten path at the end of your trip. Head north on U.S. 89 to Marysville. Stop in and see the historic Moore's Old Pine Hotel, now a bed-and-breakfast (800/887-4565), and pick up a driving-tour guide to Bullion Canyon. Follow memory lane for the next one or two hours and see the relics of a gold boomtown dating from the Spanish Conquistador era to its heyday in 1881. During the summer, take a raft trip on the Sevier River or rent a four-wheeler and ride on a portion of the mountainous Piute ATV Trail. Call ahead and make reservations to spend the night at Fremont Indian State Park's top-notch Castle Rock Campground (435/527-4631).

Day Seven
At the Fremont Indian State Park visitors center, visitors are invited to interpret the rock art they will see along the park's trails. The Fremont Indians, prehistoric contemporaries of the Prehistoric Basket Makers, left an abundance of rock art at this site. Spend another night here or continue north on I-15 to visit Territorial Statehouse State Park in Fillmore, the geographic center of the state. Politics and Mormon leader Brigham Young moved the state capital to Salt Lake City at statehood. Today the old brick statehouse includes a museum and interpretive displays explaining Utah's quest for statehood.

1 Yuba Lake State Park

     5

Because of its low elevation and relatively long season, Yuba Reservoir is popular with boaters and swimmers; in fact, this place can get pretty crowded on summer-holiday weekends. There are also some off-road-vehicle trails in the area. The campground is out in the open and can be hot in the summer, though the picnic shelters on some sites provide shade. Fishing for perch and walleye is generally on the slow side.

Location: On Yuba Reservoir; map B2, grid a2.

Campsites, facilities: There are 27 sites, plus picnic tables, fire grills, drinking water, showers, a dump station, and a group-use pavilion.

Reservations, fees: Reservations are available for a nonrefundable $6.50 per site; call 800/322-3770 Mon.–Fri. 8 A.M.–4 P.M. Sites are $13. Utah residents 62 and older with a Special Fun Tag get a $2 discount Sun.–Thurs., excluding holidays.

Open: Year-round.

Directions: Drive 30 miles south of Nephi on I-15, taking the Yuba Lake State Park exit to the east.

Contact: Yuba Lake State Park, 435/758-2611.

2 Ponderosa

    9

With its timbered setting at 6,200 feet, this is not just a good place to see brilliant autumn hues; thanks to a nearby trailhead, it's also a prime spot to start a trek to the top of Mount Nebo, the tallest peak in the Wasatch area (allow all day for the 18-mile hike). Also try hiking around Devils Kitchen, locally dubbed Little Bryce Canyon because of the eroded red spires of earth that contrast sharply with the alpine surroundings. The fishing in these parts is fairly decent, too.

Location: Near Payson; map B2, grid a3.

Campsites, facilities: There are 22 single-family sites, plus picnic tables, fire grills, vault toilets, and drinking water.

Reservations, fees: For reservations, call the U.S. Forest Service National Reservation System at 800/280-2267. Sites are $12.

Open: May–Oct.

Directions: From Nephi, drive east on Highway 132 and look for Nebo Scenic Loop Road (Forest Road 15). Take this road north for seven miles, turn onto Forest Road 48, and look for the campground just off that road.

Contact: Spanish Fork Ranger District, 801/798-3571.

3 Manti Campground

 5

This campground with plenty of grass and shade has an activities director who plans hay rides, nature hikes for kids, pool games, and other activities all summer. Catered birthday parties for groups with reservations are also available. This is a good place to stay during the annual Manti Mormon Miracle Pageant in late summer. The popular pageant draws Mormon faithful from all over the West. Canoeing, rafting, fishing, and golfing opportunities await just a few miles southeast of the campground in Palisade State Park.

Location: In Manti; map B2, grid a4.

Campsites, facilities: There are 20 RV sites with full hookups, 34 back-ins with water and electricity, and 16 tent-camping sites. The campground, part of a national chain of the same name, has restrooms, showers, an RV waste-disposal site, laundry facilities, a gift shop and small store, a video-game room, fire pits, a swimming pool, and a playground. Pets are allowed for an additional $1 per night.

Reservations, fees: Reservations are accepted. Fees are $20 for campsites with full hookups, $18 for those with water and electricity, and $16 for tent-camping sites. Each additional person over four years old in groups of more than two is charged an extra $2.50 per night.

Open: Apr.–Oct.

Directions: This campground is located on Highway 89 in Manti, a quarter mile north of the Manti Mormon Temple.

Contact: Manti Campground, 435/835-2267.

Lake Hill

  7

The small reservoir next to this forested campground offers visitors a place to fish for stocked trout and a good spot to enjoy a canoe trip.

Location: In Manti-La Sal National Forest; map B2, grid a4.

Campsites, facilities: This 12-site campground has drinking water, vault toilets, picnic tables, and fire grills.

Reservations, fees: Reservations are accepted. Individual sites are $7; group sites are $40.

Open: June–Oct.

Directions: The campground is 8.5 miles southeast of Ephraim in Ephraim Canyon, on the south side of the road.

Contact: Sanpete Ranger District, Ephraim, 435/283-4151; National Recreation Reservation Service, 877/444-6777.

Palisade State Park

  7

This campground is set near a sandy beach on 70-acre Palisade Reservoir. Since the lake is small, only nonmotorized sailboats and canoes are allowed, making it a haven for swimmers and anglers. Some campers like the proximity of the golf course, which is walking-distance away. Other popular nearby attractions are the ATV area at Six-Mile Canyon, the four-wheel-drive road on Skyline Drive across the top of Manti Mountain, and the hiking trails in Manti-La Sal National Forest.

Location: On Palisade Reservoir; map B2, grid a4.

Campsites, facilities: This handicapped-accessible campground has 53 sites, plus a nine-hole golf course, picnic tables, fire grills, modern restrooms with hot showers, a group camping area, and a covered group-use pavilion.

Reservations, fees: Reservations can be made 120 days in advance by calling 800/322-3770 Mon.–Fri. 8 A.M.–5 P.M. A $6.50 nonrefundable reservation fee is charged for each site reserved. Campsites are $13. Utah residents 62 years and older with a Special Fun Tag receive a $2 discount Sun.–Thurs., excluding holidays.

Open: Year-round.

Directions: From Manti, drive nine miles south on Highway 89 to Sterling. Look for the sign to Palisade State Park, turn east, and follow the road for two miles to the campground.

Contact: Palisade State Park, 435/835-7275.

Manti Community

  8

Yearns Reservoir provides good fishing for planted rainbow trout and a quiet place for a canoe trip. Nearby Skyline Drive at the top of the canyon offers some of the state's most scenic views for four-wheel-drive enthusiasts. The tree-shaded campsites are a short walk from the reservoir.

Location: On Yearns Reservoir; map B2, grid a4.

Campsites, facilities: This campground has nine sites, plus drinking water, picnic tables, a small amphitheater, vault toilets, and fire grills.

Reservations, fees: Reservations are accepted. Individual sites are $7; group sites are $40.

Open: June–Oct.

Directions: The campground is seven miles east of Manti on Manti Canyon Road.

Contact: Sanpete Ranger District, Ephraim, 435/283-4151.

7 Joe's Valley

 6

This campground is out in the open on Joe's Valley Reservoir, which is surrounded by buff- and tan-colored cliffs. Nearby streams and small reservoirs provide good fishing, and the reservoir itself is popular with boaters and water-skiers. A small store, snack bar, and gas station are part of the marina complex.

Location: On Joe's Valley Reservoir; map B2, grid a6.

Campsites, facilities: This 46-site campground offers newly renovated handicapped-accessible restrooms, drinking water, a cement boat-launching ramp, picnic tables, and fire grills.

Reservations, fees: Reservations are accepted through the National Recreation Reservation Service at 877/444-6777. Fees are $8 for individual sites and $10 for multiple-family sites.

Open: Memorial Day–mid-Oct.

Directions: Drive 17.6 miles west from Orangeville on State Route 29 to Joe's Valley Reservoir. Signs point the way to the campground at the west end of the reservoir.

Contact: Ferron Ranger District, 435/384-2372.

8 Huntington State Park

 5

Sites at this campground in Huntington State Park are located in a grassy area near the shore of a reservoir. Fishing, boating, water-skiing, and swimming are prime activities in the park, but ATV users and hikers also come here to enjoy the nearby San Rafael Swell. Wasatch Plateau, located just 17 miles away, is the place to go for cooler weather in the summer; it offers good fishing, mountain biking, and hiking on Forest Service land. The

Museum of San Rafael in Castle Dale focuses on the local area and features dinosaur, natural-history, and Native American exhibits.

Location: On Huntington Reservoir; map B2, a7.

Campsites, facilities: This handicapped-accessible campground has 22 sites, showers, a picnic area, a covered group-use area, modern restrooms, a boat ramp, and a sewage-disposal station.

Reservations, fees: Reservations can be made 120 days in advance by calling 800/322-3770 Mon.–Fri. 8 A.M.–5 P.M. A $6.50 nonrefundable fee is charged for each site reserved. Campsites are $12 in summer, $10 in winter when the showers are no longer available. Utah residents 62 years and older with a Special Fun Tag receive a $2 discount Sun.–Thurs., excluding holidays.

Open: Year-round.

Directions: The park is located two miles north of Huntington on State Route 10.

Contact: Huntington State Park, 435/687-2491.

9 Maple Grove

 8

Rustic, remote Maple Grove campground is well worth the drive for the peace and quiet. It's popular with local groups and families looking for a place to hold a reunion. There is some fishing available in the small stream that flows next to the campsites. Camping spots are generously spaced, and a few are tucked back into a forest well off the road. A pretty, dark-colored cliff guards the area. This is a staging area for the Paiute ATV Trail.

Location: In Fishlake National Forest; map B2, grid b1.

Campsites, facilities: This handicapped-accessible campground has 19 individual campsites and three group sites. Drinking water, picnic tables, and vault toilets are available.

Reservations, fees: Reservations are accepted for group sites only. Individual sites are $8.

Open: Apr. 21–Oct. 30.

Directions: Driving south from Nephi on I-15, take the Scipio exit and turn east onto State Route 50. Follow 50 through Scipio and continue east for 16 miles to a sign for the campground. Turning west onto Forest Road 101, follow it left near the foothills and then right over a cattle guard.

Contact: Fillmore Ranger District, 435/743-5721.

Twelvemile Flat

7

At an elevation of 10,000 feet, this campground offers a cool alpine respite during the hot summer months—and since it's off the beaten path, campers can enjoy the solitude, too. The area is especially pretty in the fall, when the oaks and aspens change color. Anglers can try their luck in the small reservoirs.

Location: In Manti-La Sal National Forest; map B2, grid a4.

Campsites, facilities: This 16-site campground has picnic tables, vault toilets, drinking water, and fire grills.

Reservations, fees: Reservations are accepted for family sites through the ranger district office. Call the National Recreation Reservation Service at 877/444-6777. Individual sites are $7 per night; group sites are $40 per night.

Open: July–Sept.

Directions: From Mayfield, located three miles south of Highway 89, head east on the county road. At the Manti-La Sal National Forest boundary, the road becomes Forest Road 022; follow it to the campground near the top of Wasatch Plateau.

Contact: Manti-La Sal National Forest, Sanpete Ranger District, Ephraim, 435/283-4151.

Lund's Campground

2

Gunnison is a quiet place full of small-town pleasures, including old-fashioned shakes and malts at one of several drive-through restaurants in town. Expect parking-lot camping on gravel sites with some shade. Yuba Reservoir and the Painted Rocks Recreation Area are approximately five miles to the north.

Location: In Gunnison; map B2, grid b3.

Campsites, facilities: This 15-site RV park has full hookups, restrooms, showers, picnic tables, and a public phone. Pets are allowed.

Reservations, fees: Reservations are accepted. Campsites are $13.

Open: Mar.–Nov.

Directions: The campground is located at 240 South Main Street in Gunnison, on the west side of the road.

Contact: Lund's Campground, 240 S. Main St., Gunnison, UT 84634; 435/528-3366.

Ferron Reservoir

9

Due to the 9,500-foot elevation, the camping season is short but sweet at Ferron Reservoir. The dam has undergone recent repairs to help improve this pine-shrouded lake as a fishery. There are good views of Emery and Sanpete Counties from the top of Manti Mountain, which is part of Skyline Drive, a four-wheel-drive road that stretches across the top of Manti Mountain from Salina to Spanish Fork Canyon. Campsites are nestled in the trees within walking distance of the reservoir. Horses can be rented nearby.

Location: On Ferron Reservoir; map B2, grid b5.

Campsites, facilities: This 32-site campground has

drinking water, vault toilets, picnic tables, and fire grills.

Reservations, fees: Campsites are $6 and are first come, first served.

Open: June–Sept.

Directions: To reach the campground, take Forest Road 22 west of Ferron for 28 miles. (Forest Road 22 connects the towns of Ferron on the east side of Manti Mountain and Mayfield on the west).

Contact: Ferron Ranger District, 435/384-2372.

13 Ferron Canyon

     6

While officially a picnic area, overnight camping is allowed at this forested site along Forest Road 22. Millsite State Park, which is located approximately four miles to the east, is the place to go for golfing, boating, and fishing. Explore the reservoir by boat, raft, or canoe.

Location: In Ferron Canyon; map B2, grid b6.

Campsites, facilities: There are three campsites and a group picnic area. Amenities include vault toilets, fire grills, and picnic tables, but no drinking water.

Reservations, fees: Campsites are free and are first come, first served.

Open: June 15–Sept. 20.

Directions: Take Forest Road 22 about nine miles northwest of Ferron to the campground.

Contact: Manti-La Sal National Forest, Ferron Ranger District, Ferron, 435/384-2372.

14 Millsite State Park

     7

Located at the mouth of Ferron Canyon, 435-acre Millsite Reservoir is surrounded by buff- and tan-colored cliffs. Fishing, golf, and water sports are the most popular activities. The park is four miles from the alpine splen-

dor of Manti Mountain, where four-wheel-drive enthusiasts enjoy motoring up the canyon and across the famed Skyline Drive in the fall. The golf course is especially scenic and usually uncrowded.

Location: On Millsite Reservoir; map B2, grid b6.

Campsites, facilities: This handicapped-accessible campground with 22 sites has two covered group-use areas, modern restrooms with showers, picnic tables, and fire grills. A boat-launching ramp, nine-hole golf course, and sandy beach are located nearby.

Reservations, fees: Reservations can be made 120 days in advance by calling 800/322-3770 Mon.–Fri. 8 A.M.–5 P.M. A $6.50 nonrefundable reservation fee is charged for each site reserved. Campsites are $12 during the warm season and $9 in the winters when showers are not available. Utah residents 62 years and older who have a Special Fun Tag receive a $2 discount Sun.–Thurs., excluding holidays.

Open: May 15–Oct. 15, and open without water the rest of the year.

Directions: Drive four miles west of State Route 10 near the Emery County town of Ferron, and follow the signs to the campground.

Contact: Millsite State Park, 435/687-2491.

15 Salina Creek RV and Campground

  1

The freeway location makes this a convenient overnight stop for campers coming from the east along I-70 from Arches National Park into Bryce Canyon and Zion National Parks. The facility is basically a gravel parking lot behind a gas station with hookups and level places for RVs. There is only one shaded picnic table.

Location: Near Salina; map B2, grid b3.

Campsites, facilities: This campground has 21 pull-through RV sites with full hookups, but no tent-camping areas. Amenities include restrooms, showers, laundry facilities, a grocery and gift store, and a public phone. Pets are allowed.

Reservations, fees: Reservations are accepted. Campsites are $15.50.

Open: Year-round.

Directions: Take the Salina exit off of I-70 and drive north on State Street. The campground is in a parking lot behind a gas station and convenience store on the west side of the road.

Contact: Salina Creek RV and Campground, 1801 S. State St., Salina, UT 84654; 435/529-3711.

16 Butch Cassidy

    2

Though located along a busy road, this campground offers shaded RV sites, a swimming pool, and a nice, grassy area for tents. Nearby attractions and activities abound, including Salina Canyon and the start of Skyline Drive, a four-wheel-drive-only road that winds its way across the top of the Wasatch Plateau for about 100 miles to Spanish Fork Canyon. The Paiute ATV and Great Western Trails provide good access for all-terrain vehicles and horseback, mountain, and dirt-bike riding.

Location: In Salina; map B2, grid b3.

Campsites, facilities: There are 60 level, gravel RV sites with full hookups (most of them pull-throughs), plus two grassy acres for tents. Amenities include restrooms, showers, picnic tables, an RV waste-disposal station, a swimming pool, a game room, laundry facilities, a grocery and gift shop, and a playground.

Reservations, fees: Reservations are recommended in June and July. Campsites with full hookups are $16.75 per night. Tent sites are $6 per night. These rates are based on two-person occupancy. An additional $2 per person for adults and $2 for children ages

7–15 is charged for groups of more than two. The rates for campsites increase during the June, July, and August summer season.

Open: Apr.–Oct.

Directions: Take the Salina exit off of I-70 and head north on State Street for about a block. The campground is on the west side of the road at 1100 South State Street.

Contact: Butch Cassidy Campground, 1100 S. State St., Salina, UT 84654; 435/529-7400 or 800/551-6842.

17 JR Munchies

   1

This campground is basically a parking area for RVs, with fencing and small trees offering only a bit of shade. However, it is close to Richfield's public golf course and the Paiute ATV Trail. And Fremont State Park, with its archaeological museum, Indian rock art, and hiking trails, is located on I-70 a few miles southwest of Richfield.

Location: In Richfield; map B2, grid c2.

Campsites, facilities: This campground has 21 sites with full hookups, plus restrooms, showers, laundry facilities, an RV waste-disposal site, a public phone, a store, and a gas station. Pets are allowed.

Reservations, fees: Reservations are accepted. Campsites are $14.

Open: Year-round.

Directions: The campground is located at the south end of Richfield at 745 South Main Street.

Contact: JR Munchies Campground, P. O. Box 387, Richfield, UT 84701; 435/896-9340.

18 Richfield KOA

      3

This well-kept private campground has nicely spaced campsites and plenty of grass and shade, plus a swimming

pool. The perimeter is surrounded by vegetation, which adds to the peaceful feeling of the place. Nearby attractions include Richfield's public golf course and the Paiute ATV and Great Western Trails.

Location: In Richfield; map B2, grid c2.

Campsites, facilities: This campground has 83 RV sites with full hookups, but campers only pay for the services they desire. There are also approximately 50 tent sites on a large lawn. Amenities include restrooms; showers; laundry facilities; a store with groceries, gifts, and RV supplies; a game room; an RV waste-disposal site; a playground; a swimming pool; a public phone; and a fire pit for large groups. Pets are allowed.

Reservations, fees: Reservations are accepted. Campsites are $18 for two people. Each additional adult is $3, and children ages 3–17 are $2. Additional fees are charged for water ($1), sewer use ($1), and electricity ($2).

Open: Mar.–Oct., with limited facilities the rest of the year.

Directions: Take I-70 to Richfield and get off on exit 37 or 40. From Main Street, turn west on 600 South Street into a residential area. Drive through two stop signs. The front entrance to the KOA passes through a permanent trailer park.

Contact: Richfield KOA, 435/896-6674.

19 Gooseberry

   8

This campground, with shaded, generously spaced campsites, is located on the banks of Gooseberry Creek and near a number of small, trout-filled reservoirs. The nearby Great Western Trail makes this an ideal base for horseback riding, ATV adventures, and mountain biking.

Location: On Gooseberry Creek; map B2, grid c4.

Campsites, facilities: There are five camp-

sites and one group area. Amenities include picnic tables, fire grills, drinking water, and vault toilets.

Reservations, fees: Individual campsites are $5 and are first come, first served. Call the ranger district about the group site.

Open: June 15–Sept. 15.

Directions: From Salina, take I-70 southeast for seven miles to exit 61. Turn south and continue 11 miles to the campground.

Contact: Richfield Ranger District, 435/896-9233.

20 Tasha

 8

Elk and deer hunters love this place, as do equestrians who ride in the nearby forests. Campsites overlook Johnson Reservoir and are near a meadow.

Location: Near Johnson Reservoir, map B2, grid c4.

Campsites, facilities: Designed for campers with horses, this campground has 10 family campsites and one group area. Facilities include picnic tables, fire grills, and drinking water, but no restrooms.

Reservations, fees: Campsites are free and are first come, first served.

Open: May–Oct.

Directions: The campground is located north and west of Johnson Reservoir. To reach it, drive about 15 miles north of State Route 24 on State Route 25, following the signs to the camp.

Contact: Fishlake National Forest, Loa Ranger District, 435/836-2811.

21 Frying Pan

   8

Anglers and water-sports enthusiasts will find plenty to do at this campground near Johnson Reservoir. The trout fishing is good in the reservoir, and there are also a number of small streams in the area. A herd of moose also calls these parts home. Horseback riding trails are available in nearby Forest Service lands. The campsites are somewhat out in the open, but they have nice views of the reservoir and the southern end of the Wasatch Plateau.

Location: Near Johnson Reservoir; map B2, grid c4.

Campsites, facilities: There are 11 family campsites and one group site, plus vault toilets, picnic tables, drinking water, and fire grills.

Reservations, fees: Reservations are only accepted for the group site, which can be reserved by calling the U.S. Forest Service National Reservation System at 800/280-2267. Campsites are $8.

Open: May 27–Sept. 30.

Directions: The campground is located west of Johnson Reservoir. To reach it, drive about 13 miles north of State Route 24 on State Route 25.

Contact: Loa Ranger District, 435/836-2811.

22 Castle Rock

   7

This campground is a popular spot for all-terrain-vehicle users who can access hundreds of miles of marked trails on the nearby Paiute ATV and Great Western Trails. Hikers will enjoy the trails leading to ancient Native American rock-art sites. The visitors center and museum offer modern displays geared to challenge the imaginations of youngsters. A restored pithouse is located near the visitors-center parking area. Campers can fish in the creek flowing through the campground.

Location: In Fishlake National Forest; operated by Fremont Indian State Park; map B2, grid c0.

Campsites, facilities: This 31-site campground includes a picnic area, fire grills, a group area, modern restrooms, and drinking water, plus a large visitors center and museum.

Reservations, fees: Reservations can be made 120 days in advance by calling 800/322-3770 Mon.–Fri. 8 A.M. –5 P.M. A $6.50 nonrefundable reservation fee is charged for each site reserved. Campsites are $9. Utah residents 62 years and older with a Special Fun Tag receive a $2 discount Sun.–Thurs., excluding holidays.

Open: Apr.–Oct.

Directions: To reach the campground, take I-70 south from Richfield. Take exit 17, then follow signs to campground.

Contact: Fremont Indian State Park, 435/527-4631.

23 Flying U

  1

Flying U Campground is little more than a gravel parking lot with hookups and a few trees. Fremont Indian State Park, located about 10 miles away, offers good hiking trails to Native American rock-art sites, not to mention an excellent museum. There is also a small farm-implements "museum" adjacent to the campground with displays of old farm equipment that was once used in the area.

Location: In Joseph; map B2, grid c1.

Campsites, facilities: This RV park has eight campsites with full hookups, plus restrooms, laundry facilities, groceries, a public phone, and an RV waste-disposal site. Pets are allowed.

Reservations, fees: Reservations are accepted. Campsites are $7–10.

Open: Memorial Day–Oct. 1.

Directions: Driving south on I-70 from Richfield, take exit 26 and head east on Main Street. The campground is located on the east side of the road in the middle of town.

Contact: Flying U Campground, 45 S. State St., Joseph, UT 84739; 435/527-4758.

24 Bowery Haven

    9

Located next to Fish Lake, this resort campground offers boat rentals and launching, plus good trout and perch fishing. One of the area's best restaurants is located at the lodge. Anglers who catch a nice trout or two can have the chef prepare the fish for dinner. The campsites have good views of the scenic lake. Hiking and horseback-riding trails are found throughout the area.

Location: On Fish Lake; map B2, grid d4.

Campsites, facilities: This campground has 69 RV sites with full hookups; 24 of these are pull-throughs. There are also restrooms, showers, picnic tables, laundry facilities, groceries (including fishing tackle), and fire pits, plus a large field for recreational activities. Horseshoes can be rented. The marina has a boat ramp.

Reservations, fees: Reservations are accepted. Campsites are $15.

Open: May–Sept.

Directions: From Richfield, drive north on I-70. Take the Sigurd exit and head southeast on Highway 24 for 46 miles to the junction with State Route 25. Drive just over nine miles north to the northwest corner of Fish Lake and the campground.

Contact: Bowery Haven, 1500 N. Hwy. 25, Fish Lake, UT 84701; 435/638-1040.

25 Bowery

     9

As the name implies, the big draw at this campground is the fishing at Fish Lake. Rainbow trout, lake trout, and yellow perch make this natural lake one of Utah's most popular summer destinations. A paved trail on the west side of the lake offers good hiking op-

portunities. The campground, located in a mixed forest of pine and aspen, overlooks the lake in a beautiful setting. Don't be surprised if you see deer wandering through the campground in the early morning.

Location: On Fish Lake; map B2, grid d4.

Campsites, facilities: This campground has 31 family campsites and 12 group sites, as well as drinking water, picnic tables, fire grills, and vault toilets.

Reservations, fees: For reservations, call the U.S. Forest Service National Reservation System at 800/280-2267. Campsites are $10.

Open: May–Oct.

Directions: From Richfield, drive north on I-70 to the Sigurd exit. Drive 46 miles southeast on State Route 24, looking for the junction to State Route 25. Turn north on State Route 25 and drive nine miles to Fish Lake. The campground is on the west side of Fish Lake.

Contact: Loa Ranger District, 435/836-2811.

26 Fish Lake Lodge and Lakeside Resort

    8

Set beside lovely Fish Lake, this log-cabin resort has the feel of an old Yellowstone Park lodge. Pine trees surround the campsites. The forested Fish Lake area, including nearby Johnson Reservoir, encompasses 13,700 acres, with 3,000 acres of lakes and reservoirs. Moose and mule deer roam through the region. Anglers can take a boat or raft onto the water and cast for plentiful yellow perch and trout; several commercial lodges on the lake offer boat rentals and guides. Equestrians enjoy exploring the open meadows and hills, and hikers can follow a paved two-mile trail along the lake's western edge.

Location: On Fish Lake; map B2, grid d3.

Campsites, facilities: There are 11 pull-through RV sites and 13 back-in RV sites, all with full hookups. The resort has a full-service marina with gas, groceries, and tackle and boat rental. Restrooms, showers, laundry facilities, and a public phone are available.

Reservations, fees: Reservations are accepted. The fee is $16.

Open: May–Oct.

Directions: From Richfield, drive north on I-70. Take the Sigurd exit and drive 24 miles southeast on State Route 24. Look for the signs to Fish Lake and drive about eight miles northeast on State Route 25 to the resort, located on the west side of the lake.

Contact: Fish Lake Lodge and Lakeside Resort, 10 E. Center Hwy. 25, Fish Lake, UT 84701; 435/638-1000.

27 Mackinaw

 9

If you're looking for a cool climate on the way from Bryce Canyon or Zion National Park to Capitol Reef National Park, this alpine campground is a wonderful place to spend the night. Mackinaw is set on a beautiful hill overlooking Fish Lake. The trout and perch fishing is excellent, and several commercial lodges on the lake offer anglers boat rentals and guides. Canoes and rafts are used near shore. Keep an eye out for moose and mule deer in the area. A hiking trail traverses the lake's western edge, and the rolling open country makes for enjoyable off-trail horseback riding.

Location: On Fish Lake; map B2, grid d3.

Campsites, facilities: There are 53 campsites and 15 group areas. Facilities include vault toilets, picnic tables, fire grills, and drinking water. When the temperature dips below zero in late September, the water may be turned off.

Reservations, fees: Call the U.S. Forest Service National Reservation System at 800/280-2267 to reserve a site. The fee is $10 when the water is turned on; otherwise it's free.

Open: May–Sept., although the camp's water may be turned off when the temperature dips below freezing.

Directions: From Richfield, drive north on I-70. Take the Sigurd exit and drive about 24 miles southeast on State Route 24, looking for the signs to Fish Lake. Drive about eight miles north on State Route 25 to the campground, located on the west side of the lake.

Contact: Fishlake National Forest, Loa Ranger District, 435/836-2811.

28 Doctor Creek

 9

Just a short drive from the Fish Lake shoreline, this campground is a little more secluded than some of the others in the area. Surrounded by pine and aspen, it's especially pretty in the fall when the leaves change color. Located at the outlet end of Fish Lake, Doctor Creek is more of a slough than a true creek. For details on boating, fishing, and hiking opportunities at Fish Lake, see the Mackinaw campground, above.

Location: Near Fish Lake; map B2, grid d3.

Campsites, facilities: There are 29 campsites and two group areas. Facilities include vault toilets, picnic tables, fire grills, and drinking water. When the temperature dips below zero in late September, the water may be turned off. There is an RV waste-disposal station at the group area.

Reservations, fees: Call the U.S. Forest Service National Reservation System at 800/280-2267 to reserve a site. The fee is $10 when the water is on. Camping is free when the water is turned off.

Open: May–Sept., although the water may be turned off when the temperature dips below freezing.

Directions: From Richfield, drive north on I-70. Take the Sigurd exit and drive about 24 miles southeast on State

Route 24, looking for the signs to Fish Lake. Drive about six miles north on State Route 25 to the campground, located just south of the lake.

Contact: Fishlake National Forest, Loa Ranger District, 435/836-2811.

29 Monroe Mystic Hot Springs

    5

This quiet, grassy campground is well off the beaten path. Tall trees shade the campsites, and kids get a playground with a trampoline. The hot tubs here are pretty primitive.

Location: In Monroe; map B2, grid d1.

Campsites, facilities: There are 32 RV campsites with full hookups, plus two tepees, one camping cabin, and a large grassy area for tent camping. Picnic tables, a playground, a small store, restrooms, and mineral hot springs are available.

Reservations, fees: Reservations are accepted. The fee is $15 for full-hookup sites, $10 for tent sites, and $35 for tepees and the camping cabin. Hot springs are free to campers. Sevier County residents can rent a hot tub for $3; non-residents pay $5.

Open: Year-round.

Directions: From Richfield, take I-70 south to the town of Monroe. In Monroe, turn east on 100 North. The campground is in three blocks, at the end of a gravel road.

Contact: Monroe Mystic Hot Springs, 475 E. 100 N., Monroe, UT 84754; 435/527-3286.

30 Wildflower RV

     4

From this RV park in Marysvale, it's approximately 10 miles to the boating and fishing at Piute Reservoir. Rainbow trout grow to two and three pounds here, but be forewarned: During dry summers, local farmers can draw the lake down to little more than a stream. When the water's up, both this lake and Otter Creek Reservoir (25 miles from Marysvale) make good spots for water-skiing and canoeing. Otter Creek Reservoir also has a boat ramp.

Location: In Marysvale; map B2, grid d1.

Campsites, facilities: There are six RV sites with full hookups. Restrooms, showers, and a playground are available. Pets are allowed.

Reservations, fees: Reservations are accepted. The fee is $15.

Open: Apr.–Oct.

Directions: From the town of Marysvale, drive four miles north on Highway 89 to the campground.

Contact: Wildflower RV, P. O. Box 183, Marysvale, UT 84750; 435/326-4301.

31 Piute State Park

   4

This campground doesn't get too crowded, and when you see it you'll understand why. It's extremely primitive and the few facilities show signs of disrepair. The terrain is mostly open, but there are a few small trees and some sagebrush. Piute Reservoir offers wide-open expanses of water when it's full, making this an excellent place to boat, raft, and water-ski. When the water is low, however, just getting your boat in the water can be problematic. The reservoir is stocked with rainbow trout, so the fishing is good. This camp attracts many duck hunters in the fall.

Location: On Piute Reservoir; map B2, grid e0.

Campsites, facilities: Primitive dispersed camping is available. Limited facilities consist of pit toilets, picnic tables, and a small cement boat ramp.

Reservations, fees: Campsites are free and are first come, first served.

Open: Year-round.

Directions: From Marysville, drive 12 miles south on Highway 89. Turn east onto the dirt road to the reservoir.

Contact: Otter Creek State Park, 435/624-3268.

Lizzie and Charlie's RV Park

 5

The popularity of the Piute ATV Trail has made this a hot spot for RV folks and their ATVs. If you don't own your own ATV, rent one in Marysvale. Don't be surprised if the regulars put together a Dutch-oven dinner in the covered pavilion on weekends.

Location: In Marysvale: map B2, grid d1.

Campsites, facilities: There are 20 tent sites and 48 RV sites with full hookups. Restrooms, showers, laundry, water, and a covered pavilion for picnickers are also available.

Reservations, fees: Reservations in the summer are recommended. Sites are $12.

Open: Memorial Day–Labor Day.

Directions: In Marysvale, located just off Highway 89.

Contact: Lizzie and Charlie's RV Park, 435/326-2011.

Circleville RV Park

  2

With its open gravel terrain, this campground resembles . . . well, a parking lot with a few trees. It's like you've pulled into an old drive-in theater, with a view of the Tushar Mountains replacing the movie screen. Fishing in the area is the big draw here. Anglers can try for trout at Piute Reservoir, eight miles away, or at Otter Creek Reservoir, 12 miles away. Some small streams nearby also offer fishing prospects.

Location: In Circleville; map B2, grid e1.

Campsites, facilities: There are 35 RV sites; 12 have water and electric hookups, six have full hookups. Restrooms, showers, laundry facilities, picnic tables, picnic pavilion, camp store, an RV waste-disposal station, and two barbecue grills are available. Leashed pets are allowed off the lawn.

Reservations, fees: Reservations are accepted. Full-hookup sites are $16; sites with water and electricity are $13. Tent sites are $3 per person over the age of 4.

Open: June–Oct.

Directions: The campground is located at the south end of Circleville, on the east side of Highway 89.

Contact: Circleville RV Park, 435/577-2437.

Cathedral Valley

 9

This quiet, primitive camp is a great place to escape the crowds. Remote Cathedral Valley lies on the back side of Capitol Reef National Park, offering sweeping views of the high sandstone plateaus to the south that most visitors see up close. The "cathedrals" are towering plateaus and buttes that stand like lonely fortresses in a rugged red-rock desert. From Cathedral Valley Campground, a quarter-mile (one-way) hiking trail leads to the top of a plateau and dead-ends at a cliff, where you can enjoy a 360-degree panorama of the sprawling terrain. Other scenic hikes, four-wheel-drive tours, and mountain-biking routes can be found throughout the park. One popular four-wheel-drive tour, the challenging Cathedral Valley Loop, begins just off of State Route 24, at River Ford Road, approximately 12 miles east of the visitors center.

Location: In Capitol Reef National Park; map B2, grid d6.

Campsites, facilities: There are six campsites with vault toilets, picnic tables, and fire grills. No drinking water is available.

Reservations, fees: All sites are free and are first come, first served. Backcountry camping is permitted in much of the park; obtain a free permit from park headquarters.
Open: Year-round.
Directions: From Torrey, drive 23 miles east on State Route 24. Look for a turnoff to the unpaved Cathedral Valley Road just before reaching the town of Caineville. Drive 28 miles north into Cathedral Valley. The dirt road can be rugged; four-wheel drive is recommended.
Contact: Capitol Reef National Park, 435/425-3791.

35 Elkhorn

 9

Popular with folks enjoying a four-wheel-drive trip into Capitol Reef National Park's Cathedral Valley, which is 40 minutes away, this remote campground offers peace and quiet away from the crowds. Fishing opportunities abound, including the small Neff Reservoir and Round Lake, both of which are stocked with rainbow trout. Anglers can also visit Forsythe Reservoir, Mill Meadow Reservoir, and the Fremont River, but in the recent past they have been closed to fishing as resident trout have been found to carry whirling disease. Get in touch with the Utah Division of Wildlife Resources, 801/538-4700, for the latest conditions.
Location: In Fishlake National Forest; map B2, grid d5.
Campsites, facilities: There are six campsites and one group site. Vault toilets, drinking water, picnic tables, and fire grills are available.
Reservations, fees: Campsites are $10 for single sites and $20 for the group site and can be reserved.
Open: May 27–Sept. 30.
Directions: From Loa, drive 11 miles northeast on State Route 72. Turn south on For-

est Road 206 and drive nine miles to the campground.
Contact: Fishlake National Forest, Loa Ranger District, 435/836-2811.

36 Aquarius Mobile and RV

 4

Even though this rural RV park is in the middle of the town of Bicknell, it doesn't get too loud. The campground is approximately 15 miles from Capitol Reef National Park and numerous hiking trails. Horseback riding is available at the Rim Rock Ranch Motel. Nearby is the Perry Egan Fish Hatchery, a brood-stock facility for the Utah Division of Wildlife Resources. Here you can see workers prepare eggs for shipment to other hatcheries in the facility; some of the trout raised here grow to more than six pounds. Visit the Sunglow Café to sample its pickle, pinto bean, or oatmeal pie. The restaurant at the Aquarius Motel also serves good down-home fare.
Location: In Bicknell; map B2, grid e5.
Campsites, facilities: There are 12 RV sites with full hookups. An RV waste-disposal site is available. Pets are allowed.
Reservations, fees: Reservations are accepted. Campsites are $7.50.
Open: Year-round.
Directions: Follow State Route 24 into Bicknell; in town, it becomes Main Street. The campground is located at 294 West Main Street.
Contact: Aquarius Mobile and RV, P. O. Box 304, Bicknell, UT 84715; 435/425-3835.

37 Sunglow

 9

Though small, this scenic mountain campground can be a fine alternative to nearby Capitol Reef National Park. It's set on a gravel road amid red-rock canyons. Large cottonwood trees shade the sites and a stream runs near the camp. Although you won't find trails, you may enjoy hiking up the narrow canyon or scrambling up rocks to watch the sunset. Visit the nearby Perry Egan Fish Hatchery to see large brood-stock trout, which grow up to six pounds and provide eggs for other Utah hatcheries. Anglers can fish trout in the many tiny alpine lakes that dot Boulder Mountain, a 10-mile drive from the campground.

Location: In Fishlake National Forest; map B2, grid d4.

Campsites, facilities: There are five family campsites and three group areas. Drinking water, picnic tables, and vault toilets are available.

Reservations, fees: Campsites are $10 for single sites and $20 for the group areas and are first come, first served.

Open: May 15–Oct. 30.

Directions: From Bicknell, drive a half mile south on State Route 24. Follow Forest Road 143 approximately 11.5 miles east to the campground.

Contact: Fishlake National Forest, Loa Ranger District, 435/836-2811.

38 Thousand Lakes RV Park

 5

With its summertime wagon rides and old-fashioned Dutch-oven dinners on weekends, this campground preserves a real Western flavor. And how's this for a nice touch? Each guest receives a homemade muffin in the morning. You can rent a four-wheel-drive vehicle and take a trip from Thousand Lakes Mountain into Capitol Reef National Park, which is one mile away. Here you can enjoy a 3.5-mile round-trip hike out to the monolithic Chimney Rock formation, which is located just east of the park entrance. Anglers fish for trout at the many alpine lakes on Boulder Mountain to the

south. Horseback-riding trails are found on Boulder Mountain.

Location: Near Torrey; map B2, grid e5.

Campsites, facilities: There are 36 sites with full hookups, 13 sites with water and electric hookups, nine tent sites, and two camping cabins. Thousand Lakes RV Park also provides visitors with restrooms, showers, laundry facilities, a pool, picnic tables, an RV waste-disposal site, a public phone, a grocery and gift shop, a horseshoe pit, and a playground. Barbecue grills are available for rental.

Reservations, fees: Reservations are accepted. Sites with full and partial hookups cost $15–18, and tent sites on the grassy area are $12. Camping cabins are $28.

Open: Apr.–Oct.

Directions: The campground is located one mile west of Torrey on State Route 24.

Contact: Thousand Lakes RV Park, P. O. Box 750070, Torrey, UT 84775; 435/425-3500.

39 Fruita

 10

Capitol Reef National Park's Fruita campground is, in fact, set in the midst of an old fruit orchard, which was first planted in the 19th century by Mormon settlers. Apple, peach, cherry, mulberry, and Potawatamee plum trees grow here, and when the fruit ripens in midsummer, visitors can pick it fresh. If you want to pick a whole basket, however, you'll have to pay for it. Several good hiking trails, including a 1.75-mile (one-way) trek to Cohab Canyon and a 1.25-mile (one-way) walk to the Fremont River Overlook, begin at the campground. In winter, deer and chukar partridge frequent the area. Near the camp you can visit several living-history displays, including an old blacksmith shop and the Fruita School House, which has been refurbished with timeworn desks, a wood-burning stove, and old-fashioned school books.

Location: In Capitol Reef National Park; map B2, grid e7.

Campsites, facilities: There are 70 campsites. Restrooms with cold running water, picnic tables, an amphitheater, fire grills, and an RV waste-disposal station are available. One restroom is heated for winter use. Group areas can accommodate up to 100 people.

Reservations, fees: Campsites are $10 and are first come, first served. Backcountry camping is permitted in much of the park; obtain a free permit from park headquarters.

Open: Year-round.

Directions: Drive 11 miles east from Torrey on State Route 24 to the park visitors center. From there, drive 1.3 miles south on the marked road to the campground.

Contact: Capitol Reef National Park, 435/425-3791.

Singletree

  10

What you see is what you get at this high-alpine camp, and what you see can be spectacular. At an elevation of 8,200 feet, the panoramic views encompass the Water-pocket Fold, Capitol Reef National Park, and the Henry Mountains to the east. Most of the campsites are shaded by large pine trees. A short hike brings you to Singletree Falls and provides glimpses of Capitol Reef's scenic terrain below. Other trails through the dense forest are ideal for hiking or horseback riding. Anglers find terrific opportunities to cast for large brook trout at Boulder Mountain's many small lakes and reservoirs. A particularly good bet for fishing is nearby Bown Reservoir.

Location: In Dixie National Forest; map B2, grid e5.

Campsites, facilities: There are 26 individual campsites and some group sites. Drinking water, picnic tables, fire grills, and flush toilets are available.

Reservations, fees: Reservations can be made through the U.S. Forest Service National Reservation System, 800/280-2267. Campsites are $10.

Open: Memorial Day–mid-Sept.

Directions: From Teasdale, drive 17 miles southeast on State Route 12 to the campground.

Contact: Dixie National Forest, Teasdale Ranger District, 435/425-3702.

41 Pleasant Creek

   8

This is a good, cooler summer alternative to campgrounds at Capitol Reef National Park, which is 25 miles away. It's an older facility, however, and some of the campsites show signs of wear and tear. Set on Boulder Mountain at 8,700 feet, the campground is close to some decent fishing lakes and streams; check with the Teasdale Ranger Station for suggestions on where the brook trout are biting. The thick alpine forest is crisscrossed with fine hiking routes, four-wheel-drive roads, and horse trails.

Location: In Dixie National Forest; map B2, grid e5.

Campsites, facilities: There are 17 campsites. Picnic tables, vault toilets, drinking water, and fire grills are available.

Reservations, fees: Campsites are $9 and are first come, first served.

Open: Memorial Day–mid-Sept.

Directions: From Teasdale, drive 22 miles southeast on State Route 12 to the campground.

Contact: Dixie National Forest, Teasdale Ranger District, 435/425-3702.

42 Lower Bown

 6

Though primitive, this Boulder Mountain campground stays quiet because it's off the main highway. Piñon and juniper trees provide some shade, but the terrain is more open than elsewhere in the area. Bown Reservoir is a small lake with good fishing when the water is high. It's an ideal spot for anglers to launch a raft and cast for large brook trout. During some years, however, the quality can vary when the reservoir is drawn down for irrigation purposes. In late fall the camp may be quite chilly, especially when the snow flies.

Location: On Lower Bown Reservoir; map B2, grid e6.

Campsites, facilities: There are three sites for RVs and tents. Vault toilets, picnic tables, and fire grills are available, but there is no drinking water.

Reservations, fees: Campsites are free and are first come, first served.

Open: Memorial Day–early Oct.

Directions: From Teasdale, drive 22 miles southeast on State Route 12. Look for Forest Road 181 just past the Pleasant Creek campground. Take that road approximately five miles east to the campground.

Contact: Dixie National Forest, Teasdale Ranger District, 435/425-3702.

43 Oak Creek

 8

This campground is located near the top of Boulder Mountain in a nice grove of pine trees. Set at 8,800 feet, a chill sets in here in the fall. The camp has a well-used look, and it becomes quite dusty in the summer. Small alpine lakes dot Boulder Mountain. Anglers can cast for some of the state's largest brook trout and a few planted rainbow trout. Pick up a map showing hiking and horse trails at the Teasdale Ranger Station.

A scenic 13-mile drive to the south takes visitors to Anasazi State Park, which features a museum and the ruins of a 12th-century Native American village.

Location: In Dixie National Forest; map B2, grid f5.

Campsites, facilities: There are 10 campsites. Picnic tables, vault toilets, drinking water, and fire grills are available.

Reservations, fees: Campsites are $9 and are first come, first served.

Open: Memorial Day–mid-Sept.

Directions: From Teasdale, drive 24 miles southeast on State Route 12 to the campground.

Contact: Dixie National Forest, Teasdale Ranger District, 435/425-3702.

44 Lonesome Beaver

 8

Spruce, fir, and aspen trees shade this campground in the beautiful but rugged Henry Mountains. Set at an elevation of 8,000 feet, it can get cold here in the fall and the snow usually flies by late October. From camp, hikers can access the Mount Ellen Trail, one of the best trails in southern Utah. It winds 1.25 miles along a boulder-strewn ridge to an 11,506-foot peak. From the top you get a 360-degree view of Lake Powell, Canyonlands National Park, and the Waterpocket Fold. Horseback riding trails are found in the Forest Service area of the Henry Mountains.

Location: In the Henry Mountains; map B2, grid e8.

Campsites, facilities: There are five campsites for tents and RVs. Vault toilets, picnic tables, fire grills, and drinking water are available.

Reservations, fees: Campsites are $4 and are first come, first served.

Open: May–late Oct.

Directions: From Hanksville, drive 33 miles south on signed dirt roads to the Sawmill Basin and the campground. Roads are unnamed; for precise directions stop at the Hanksville BLM office before heading out.

Contact: Bureau of Land Management, Hanksville, 435/542-3461.

45 Cedar Mesa

  8

Set in the remote southern end of Capitol Reef National Park, this primitive desert campground is close to spectacular backcountry hiking in nearby Muley Twist Canyon. Here hikers and four-wheelers can explore seldom-visited washes and narrow slot canyons, and gaze upon panoramic views of the surrounding Henry Mountains and Waterpocket Fold. It's a rugged, undeveloped corner of this national park that tends to be relatively uncrowded, except on busy weekends. If you decide to stay here, come prepared to rough it.

Location: In Capitol Reef National Park; map B2, grid f7.

Campsites, facilities: There are five campsites. A pit toilet, picnic tables, and fire grills are available, but there is no water.

Reservations, fees: Campsites are free and are first come, first served. Backcountry camping is permitted in much of the park; obtain a free permit from park headquarters.

Open: Year-round.

Directions: From Torrey, drive 20 miles east on State Route 24. Look for a signed road to the tiny hamlet of Notom. Follow this dirt road about five miles south to Muley Twist Canyon and the campground.

Contact: Capitol Reef National Park, 435/425-3791.

46 Otter Creek State Park

     6

Locals say the rainbow trout at Otter Creek Reservoir grow fast and grow big—some up to six pounds. Angling is the thing at this clean and comfortable campground. There's a dock to launch your boat or raft onto the water and a fish-cleaning station for whatever you catch. Campsites are mostly paved, but you'll find some grass as well. Bryce Canyon National Park is about an hour's drive away. Take the scenic 56-mile drive that leads from Otter Creek into the town of Antimony and then over to State Route 12 and the park entrance. Hikers can trek around Otter Creek Reservoir.

Location: On Otter Creek Reservoir; map B2, grid e2.

Campsites, facilities: There are 30 campsites. Modern restrooms with showers, picnic tables, fire grills, a fish-cleaning station, and an RV waste-disposal station are available. Boat and courtesy docks are located nearby.

Reservations, fees: Reservations, which are strongly recommended on summer weekends, can be made 120 days in advance by calling 800/322-3770 Mon.–Fri. 8 A.M.–5 P.M. A $6.50 nonrefundable reservation fee is charged for each site reserved. The campsite fees are $9–11. Utah residents 62 years and older with a Special Fun Tag receive a $2 discount Sun.–Thurs., excluding holidays.

Open: Year-round.

Directions: From the town of Antimony, drive four miles northwest on State Route 22 to the park.

Contact: Otter Creek State Park, 435/624-3268.

47 Blue Spruce

   8

Although the desert surrounding Escalante can get scorching hot in the summer months, this alpine area provides a cool alternative to the low-lying regions. The elevation is 7,800

feet. Anglers can try to catch rainbow trout at nearby Posy and Tule Lakes.

Location: In Dixie National Forest; map B2, grid f5.

Campsites, facilities: There are six campsites. Drinking water, picnic tables, fire grills, and vault toilets are available.

Reservations, fees: Campsites are $6 and are first come, first served.

Open: June–mid-Sept.

Directions: From Escalante, drive 17 miles north on Forest Road 153 to the campground.

Contact: Dixie National Forest, Escalante Ranger District, 435/826-5400.

48 McMillan Springs

  8

Come here and you just might catch a glimpse of the wild bison herd that often wanders through the Henry Mountains. Set in a ponderosa pine and piñon-juniper grove, the remote camp is a good place to enjoy peace and quiet. Sites are spaced far apart, affording privacy. The 2.5-mile Mount Ellen Trail is nearby. From Mount Ellen's summit, hikers are treated to excellent views over the Waterpocket Fold and Canyonlands National Park.

Location: In the Henry Mountains; map B2, grid f8.

Campsites, facilities: There are five sites for tents and RVs. Drinking water, picnic tables, and vault toilets are available.

Reservations, fees: Campsites are $4 and are first come, first served.

Open: May–Nov.

Directions: From Hanksville, drive 33 miles south on dirt roads to the west side of the Henry Mountains, following signs to the campground. Roads are unnamed; for precise directions, stop at the Hanksville BLM office before heading out.

Contact: Bureau of Land Management, Hanksville, 435/542-3461.

49 Barker Reservoir

   9

This forested campground gets mighty cold in the fall, especially when the first snow hits. It's set at 9,550 feet beside a small reservoir. With panoramic views over the red-rock desert surrounding Escalante, campers will feel as though they are on the top of the world. Anglers can launch a raft onto the water and fish for rainbow trout.

Location: Near Escalante; map B2, grid g4.

Campsites, facilities: There are seven campsites for tents and RVs. Picnic tables, fire pits, and vault toilets are available, but there is no drinking water.

Reservations, fees: Campsites are $7 and are first come, first served.

Open: June–mid-Sept., depending on snow conditions.

Directions: From Escalante, drive five miles west on State Route 12. Head north approximately 11 miles on Forest Road 149 to the campground.

Contact: Dixie National Forest, Escalante Ranger District, 435/826-5400.

50 Posy Lake

    8

When the desert lowlands surrounding Escalante heat up, it's time to head for the cool forest. This alpine camp sits beside tiny Posy Lake, where you can paddle a raft out to the deeper water and hope to catch a rainbow trout for dinner. It's a pleasant drive from the buff red-rock desert to the cool greens of the higher elevations.

Location: Near Escalante; map B2, grid g4.

Campsites, facilities: There are 22 campsites for tents and RVs. Drinking water, picnic tables, fire grills, and vault toilets are available.

Reservations, fees: Campsites are $8 and are first come, first served.

Open: June–mid-Sept., depending on snow conditions.

Directions: From Escalante, drive 11 miles north on Forest Road 153. Turn west on Forest Road 154 and drive one mile to the campground.

Contact: Dixie National Forest, Escalante Ranger District, 435/826-5400.

51 Calf Creek Falls Recreation Area

     9

Campsites are arrayed along a pretty little river that offers a pleasant spot to swim in the hot summer months. The big draw is the self-guided, 2.75-mile one-way nature walk up a sandy trail to Lower Calf Creek Falls, one of southern Utah's more famous landmarks. The waterfall tumbles several stories from a high sandstone cliff into a cool turquoise pool below. You can fish the creek for brown trout or head over to Escalante Petrified Forest State Park to try for stocked rainbow trout. Anasazi State Park, approximately 12 miles away in Boulder, offers restored Native American ruins and a museum that are well worth a visit.

Location: Near Escalante; map B2, grid g5.

Campsites, facilities: There are 14 campsites. Picnic tables, fire grills, running water, and vault toilets are available. A flush toilet is available in warm months.

Reservations, fees: Campsites are $7 and are first come, first served.

Open: Mid-Apr.–Nov.

Directions: From Escalante, drive 16 miles east on State Route 12 to the recreation area.

Contact: Bureau of Land Management, Escalante, 435/826-4291.

52 Deer Creek Recreation Area

   7

Surrounded by high sandstone walls in a narrow red-rock canyon, this campground/picnic area looks like a miniature Zion National Park. It's remote and spectacular country. From here you can head into the Escalante River backcountry for off-trail exploration of the Deer Creek and Boulder Creek drainages. Expect to do some wading if you're taking a serious day hike or backpacking trip. Be sure to visit Boulder's Anasazi State Park, which features a fascinating museum and restored Native American ruins.

Location: Near Boulder; map B2, grid g6.

Campsites, facilities: There are four sites with picnic tables and fire grills. The campground has one vault toilet. No drinking water is available.

Reservations, fees: Campsites are $4 and are first come, first served.

Open: Mid-Mar.–Nov.

Directions: From Boulder, drive on the Burr Trail six miles east to the recreation area.

Contact: Bureau of Land Management, 435/826-4291.

53 Escalante Petrified Forest State Park

    8

This park has something for everyone, and all of it's good. The campground is nestled in a small cove of Wide Hollow Reservoir at the base of a red-rock plateau. At the center of the camp is a large grassy lawn, where kids can play football or toss a Frisbee. Short, self-guided interpretive hiking trails begin at the campground and lead to large deposits of petrified wood. In the spring, Wide Hollow Reservoir offers decent fishing for stocked rainbow trout, and year-round you can enjoy swimming, rafting, boating, and water-skiing here. The best thing about the reservoir is that its shallow wetlands are the home for thousands of shorebirds. The park also makes a fine base for exploring the nearby Escalante Canyons, which are part of the newly designated, 1.7-million-acre Escalante-Grand Staircase National Monument.

Location: On Wide Hollow Reservoir; map B2, grid g5.

Campsites, facilities: There are 22 campsites for tents and RVs. A modern restroom with showers, an RV waste-disposal station, and a visitors center are available.

Reservations, fees: Reservations can be made 120 days in advance by calling 800/322-3770 Mon.–Fri. 8 A.M.–5 P.M. A $6.50 nonrefundable reservation fee is charged for each site reserved. The campsite fee is $12. Utah residents 62 years and older with a Special Fun Tag receive a $2 discount Sun.–Thurs., excluding holidays.

Open: Year-round.

Directions: Drive on State Route 12 one mile west of Escalante.

Contact: Escalante Petrified Forest State Park, 435/826-4466.

54 Triple S RV Park and Campground 5

Located between Bryce Canyon and Capitol Reef National Parks, this campground is set in a quiet, rural setting in the midst of some of the more spectacular Bureau of Land Management and U.S. Forest Service country in the state. Consider taking a short drive out to the BLM's Devil's Garden Natural Area on Hole-in-the-Rock Road; the dirt road begins five miles east of Escalante off of State Route 12. Here you'll find a small natural arch and plenty of other unusual sandstone formations. The boating, water-skiing, swimming, and fishing for planted rainbow trout are good one mile west of Escalante at Escalante Petrified Forest State Park's Wide Hollow Reservoir.

Location: In Escalante; map B2, grid h5.

Campsites, facilities: There are 21 pull-through RV sites with full hookups and 20 tent sites. The campground has restrooms, showers, picnic tables, laundry facilities, barbecue pits, a public phone, and a rock shop specializing in petrified wood and dinosaur bones. Pets are allowed.

Reservations, fees: Reservations are recommended on holiday weekends. RV sites are $12; tent sites are $8.50.

Open: Year-round.

Directions: Drive to Escalante on State Route 12. In town, State Route 12 becomes Main Street. The campground is four blocks west of the town center, at 495 South Main Street.

Contact: Triple S RV Park and Campground, P.O. Box 505, Escalante, UT 84726; 435/826-4959.

 55 Broken Bow RV Camp 8

This is another nondescript campground with access to the great hiking and four-wheeling in the area. While you're here, stop in at Wide Hollow Reservoir in Escalante Petrified Forest State Park.

Location: In Escalante; map B2, grid h5

Campsites, facilities: There are 28 RV sites with full hookups and 20 tent sites. The campground has restrooms, showers, laundry facilities, picnic tables, drinking water, a dump station, and handicapped facilities.

Reservations, fees: RV sites are $17; tent sites are $11.

Open: Year-round, 8 A.M.–10 P.M.

Directions: Follow State Route 12 into Escalante. In

town, Route 12 becomes Main Street. The campground is at 495 West Main.

Contact: Broken Bow RV Camp, 495 W. Main St., Escalante, UT; 435/826-4959.

Moqui Motel and Campground

     4

This nondescript RV park adjacent to a motel will suffice for a one-night stopover. Hikers and lovers of four-wheel-drive-vehicles can head to the Bureau of Land Management's Deer Creek and Calf Creek Falls Recreation Areas. Water recreation, including good trout fishing, is available at nearby Wide Hollow Reservoir in Escalante Petrified Forest State Park.

Location: In Escalante; map B2, grid h5.

Campsites, facilities: This small, six-site RV campground with hookups has restrooms, showers, an RV waste-disposal station, and a public phone. Pets are allowed. The park is open year-round, but water is not available in winter.

Reservations, fees: Reservations are accepted. The fee is $15.

Open: Year-round.

Directions: Follow State Route 12 into Escalante. In town, State Route 12 becomes Main Street. The campground is located at 80 West Main Street.

Contact: Moqui Motel and Campground, 435/826-4210.

Red Canyon

 10

With high spires, hoodoos, and fluorescent-red pillars, beautiful Red Canyon is like a miniature Bryce Canyon National Park. Huge ponderosa pines guard the U.S. Forest Service campground here. Trails venture into this region and surrounding canyons, offering spectacular routes for hikers, mountain bikers, and equestrians.

Location: Near Panguitch; map B2, grid g0.

Campsites, facilities: There are 37 campsites for tents and RVs. Picnic tables, drinking water, flush toilets, and fire grills are available.

Reservations, fees: For reservations, call the U.S. Forest Service National Reservation System at 800/280-2267. The fee is $10.

Open: Mid-May–Oct.

Directions: From Panguitch, drive seven miles south on Highway 89. Turn east on State Route 12 and continue approximately four miles to the campground.

Contact: Dixie National Forest, Powell Ranger District, Panguitch, 435/676-8815.

Red Canyon RV Park and Campground

   7

You'll find some shaded and grassy campsites here, but it may be a little noisy as the park is located near the junction of two busy highways. The strongest selling point is its proximity to Red Canyon in Dixie National Forest, which offers excellent hiking, horseback-riding, and mountain-biking opportunities. If fishing's your pleasure, you can head to Tropic Reservoir approximately 15 miles away. Bryce Canyon National Park lies 15 miles to the east.

Location: Near the entrance to Red Canyon; map B2, grid h1.

Campsites, facilities: There are 40 sites, 20 of which are pull-throughs. There are also eight cabins. Facilities include new restrooms, showers, a public phone, a small grocery store, and a picnic area.

Reservations, fees: Reservations are strongly recommended during the summer season. RV sites are $18; tent sites are $10 for two people. Each additional person is $1 extra. Children under 10 are free. Cabins with showers cost $39; rustic cabins are $28 for two.

Open: Apr.–Oct., depending on weather conditions.

Directions: From Panguitch, drive seven miles south on Highway 89. Turn east on State Route 12 and drive one mile to the campground.

Contact: Red Canyon RV Park and Campground, 435/676-2690.

59 Bryce Canyon Pines Country Store and Campground, RV Park & Motel

     7

The name of this quiet camp is a little deceptive: You are offered pleasant views of the towering pines that shade many of the campsites, but you won't catch a glimpse of Bryce Canyon itself. The national park and its many hiking opportunities are a short drive away. The owners offer horseback rides into the scenic, pine-shrouded country near the campground. While Bryce Canyon National Park is the big draw here, you can also drive 24 miles to beautiful Kodachrome Basin State Park or take a nature hike in Red Canyon to the west. Fish the private ponds at Ruby's Inn (see page 206), or head to Pine Lake in Dixie National Forest, approximately six miles away.

Location: Near Bryce Canyon National Park; map B2, grid h1.

Campsites, facilities: There are 45 campsites, of which 17 are pull-throughs and 25 offer full hookups. Facilities include restrooms with showers, a waste-disposal station, a public phone, laundry facilities, and a small grocery store with ice, snacks, and supplies. Sites have fire grills. A game room, a horseshoe pit, and a playground are also available.

Reservations, fees: Reservations are ac-

cepted. RV sites are $25; tent sites are $15 for two people. Each additional person over age six is $1.

Open: Apr.–Nov.

Directions: From Bryce Canyon National Park, take State Route 63 six miles north to State Route 12. Turn west and drive to the campground.

Contact: Bryce Canyon Pines Country Store & Campground, RV Park & Motel, P. O. Box 64005, Bryce, UT 84764; 435/834-5441.

60 Pink Cliffs Village

     7

An abundance of large pine trees make this a pretty spot. Currently the resort offers guided horseback rides on its 156 acres; the owners hope to guide rides into Bryce Canyon National Park itself, pending approval by the National Park Service. Hikers can explore many trails in Bryce Canyon. If you want to fish, head to nearby Tropic Reservoir or make the one-hour drive to Boulder Mountain and its many small alpine lakes in the Escalante region. Although this camp is open all year, it gets very cold during the winter months.

Location: Near Bryce Canyon National Park; map B2, grid h2.

Campsites, facilities: There are 28 RV sites with full hookups and 20 tent sites. Pink Cliffs Village offers restrooms with showers, laundry facilities, picnic tables, fire pits, an RV waste-disposal station, a grocery and gift shop, a swimming pool, a service station, and a field where you can play volleyball, badminton, and horseshoes. Pets are allowed. Telephone and cable TV hookups are available.

Reservations, fees: Reservations are recommended in the summer. RV sites are $25; tent sites are $15.

Open: Year-round.

Directions: The resort is three miles from Bryce Canyon National Park and one mile from Ruby's Inn, at the junction of State Routes 12 and 63.

Contact: Pink Cliffs Village, Box 640006, Bryce, UT 84764; 435/834-5351.

61 Ruby's Inn RV Campground

     7

Although Ruby's Inn is a large motel-and-restaurant complex, the campground here feels surprisingly separate from the development. The owners have wisely segregated the area from the rest of the inn. The tall pines shading the camp give it an air of seclusion. You can fish for trout in a small private pond on the grounds, or head to Pine Lake in nearby Dixie National Forest. This is the closest private campground to Bryce Canyon National Park, but Ruby's Inn offers a slew of recreational options in addition to what's available at the national park. In the winter it grooms cross-country ski trails and rents snowmobiles. In the summer campers can enjoy a nightly rodeo (except on Sundays), helicopter flights, mountain-biking trails, horseback riding, gold panning, wagon rides, and hoedowns. Across from the inn, Ruby's has even re-created an old-fashioned Western town full of charming little shops. Off-season campers should check in at the motel lobby.

Location: Near Bryce Canyon National Park; map B2, grid h2.

Campsites, facilities: There are 110 RV sites, 43 with full hookups and 67 with water and electric hookups. There are also 50 dispersed tent sites. Ruby's Inn has gift shops, an art gallery, a bakery, a barber and beauty shop, and two swimming pools. The campground offers a hot tub, a small grocery store, restrooms, showers, a security phone, two laundromats, and an arcade.

Reservations, fees: Reservations are strongly recommended in the summer. Full-hookup sites are $27.25, partial hookups are $23.98, and tent sites are $16.95.

Open: Apr.–Oct.

Directions: From Panguitch, drive seven miles south on Highway 89. Turn east on State Route 12 and drive 13 miles to State Route 63. The campground is on State Route 63, just south of the junction.

Contact: Ruby's Inn RV Campground, P. O. Box 22, Bryce, UT 84764; 435/834-5341.

62 North

   8

Thanks to its high elevation, Bryce Canyon is one of the best national parks in Utah to visit in the summer. Temperatures tend to be 20 degrees cooler than nearby Zion or Capitol Reef National Parks. The park's centerpiece is a beautiful natural amphitheater filled with arches, hoodoos, spires, and other strangely shaped eroded rocks in shades of buff, tan, and crimson. At sunset the rocks seem to glow an almost fluorescent red. Several excellent hiking trails lead into the area. Try the 1.25-mile (one-way) Navajo Loop Trail into the Bryce Amphitheater; it begins at Sunset Point, 1.5 miles from the campground, and descends 521 feet into the canyon. A quarter mile from the campground you'll find breathtaking views at Sunrise Point Overlook. Many campsites are shaded by pines. In the busy summer months, North campground can fill to capacity, so arrive as early in the day as possible. A shuttle system is in place to take visitors along the rim, but you can drive. Guided horseback tours of the park are available; check at the Bryce Canyon Lodge for details. Bring your own wood as the wood in the park is off-limits.

Location: In Bryce Canyon National Park; map B2, grid h2.

Campsites, facilities: There are 107 campsites for tents and RVs. Picnic tables, fire grills, drinking water, flush toilets with cold running water, and an RV waste-disposal station are available. A general store, laundry facilities, and showers are located at Sunset Point, 1.5 miles from the North campground.

Reservations, fees: All sites are first come, first served. The fee is $10; campsites are half price with a Golden Age and Golden Access pass.

Open: Apr.–Nov., though one loop of the campground is winterized and open year-round, when funding permits.

Directions: From Panguitch, drive seven miles south on Highway 89. Turn east on State Route 12 and drive 13 miles east. Drive two miles south on State Route 63 to reach the campground, which is just east of park headquarters near the entrance station.

Contact: Bryce Canyon National Park, 435/834-5322.

63 Sunset

    8

The Sunset campground is slightly closer to Bryce Amphitheater and its fascinating red-rock formations than the North campground. Sites are shaded by pine trees, and you'll see nice displays of wildflowers here in late spring and early summer. Hikes in and around Bryce Canyon can be spectacular; check with the park's visitors center for guided interpretive strolls. The Queen's Garden Trail/Navajo Loop Trail combination, a 1.8-mile loop, is among the best hikes in southern Utah. Guided horseback tours of the park are available; inquire at the Bryce Canyon Lodge. If you want to build a campfire, bring your own wood; no wood gathering is allowed in the park.

Location: In Bryce Canyon National Park; map B2, grid h1.

Campsites, facilities: There are 111 campsites for tents and RVs. Two sites are handi-capped accessible. Restrooms with cold running water, drinking water, picnic tables, and fire grills are available. A general store, laundry facilities, and showers are at Sunset Point, which is less than a mile from the campground. An RV waste-disposal station is available at the North campground.

Reservations, fees: All campsites are available on a first come, first served basis; the fee is $10. Campsites are half price with a Golden Age and Golden Access pass.

Open: Late Apr.–Nov., depending on the weather conditions in Bryce Canyon.

Directions: From Panguitch, drive seven miles south on Highway 89. Turn east on State Route 12 and drive 13 miles to State Route 63. Drive south on State Route 63 to the park. The campground is two miles south of park headquarters on the west side of the road.

Contact: Bryce Canyon National Park, 435/834-5322.

64 Pine Lake

   8

Little Pine Lake offers good angling for stocked rainbow trout. A ramp is suitable for launching small boats, or you can just paddle a raft onto the water and cast for your supper. Campsites here are shaded by pine trees near the lake. It's conveniently close to Bryce Canyon National Park and Kodachrome Basin State Park, but you're guaranteed to avoid the crowds that those places draw. Excellent hiking and horseback-riding options are available at Bryce Canyon (see the North campground, page 206, for details).

Location: Near Red Canyon; map B2, grid h3.

Campsites, facilities: There are 26 campsites. Vault toilets, picnic tables, fire grills, drinking water, and a boat ramp are available.

Reservations, fees: Call the U.S. Forest Service National Reservation System at 800/280-2267 for reservations. The fee is $8.

Open: Mid-June–mid-Sept.

Directions: Drive through Red Canyon on State Route 12. Instead of turning south into Bryce Canyon National Park, look for Forest Road 16, a dirt road heading northeast near the junction with State Route 63. Drive eight miles north on Forest Road 16, then drive four miles south on Forest Road 132 to the campground.

Contact: Dixie National Forest, Escalante Ranger District, 435/826-5400.

65 Kodachrome Basin State Park

    10

This ranks among Utah's best campgrounds. Set in a piñon-juniper forest, with campsites spaced far apart for privacy, the camp boasts impressive views of this red-rock wonderland's massive stone towers, called "chimneys." Hiking trails, appropriate for children and most less than three miles long, lead from the campground into the pink and white sandstone basin. Try the quarter-mile (one-way) trail to the Shakespeare Arch, one of the last discovered natural bridges in the area. Or follow the one-mile (one-way) Grand Parade Trail, which passes the monolithic spires that make this place unique. A horseback-riding and stagecoach concession allows disabled persons and seniors to visit the backcountry. For a side trip, drive 10 miles east of the park to Grosvenor Arch, a huge buff-colored double-arch formation.

Location: Near Cannonville; map B2, grid h3.

Campsites, facilities: There are 27 campsites for tents and RVs and a group-use area. Facilities include modern restrooms with showers, drinking water, an RV waste-disposal station, and picnic tables on concrete with fire grills. A concessionaire operates a small store inside the park.

Reservations, fees: Reservations can be made 120 days in advance by calling 800/322-3770 Mon.–Fri. 8 A.M.–5 P.M. A $6.50 nonrefundable reservation fee is charged for each reserved site. The site fee is $12. Utah residents 62 years and older with a Special Fun Tag receive a $2 discount Sun.–Thurs., excluding holidays.

Open: Year-round.

Directions: From Bryce Canyon National Park, drive two miles north on State Route 63. Head east on State Route 12 to Cannonville, then follow signs nine miles south on a paved road to the state park.

Contact: Kodachrome Basin State Park, 435/679-8562.

66 Kings Creek

    8

At an elevation of 8,000 feet, the campground sits in the midst of a pretty alpine forest beside Tropic Reservoir. It's quite popular with locals and can get crowded. Paddle a raft or launch a boat onto the small reservoir to fish for trout. It's close to Bryce Canyon National Park and its many scenic hikes (see the North campground, page 206, for suggestions). Horseback riding is fun throughout the forested area. Horse rentals and guided tours are available at Bryce Canyon Lodge and Ruby's Inn.

Location: On Tropic Reservoir; map B2, grid i1.

Campsites, facilities: The 37-site campground has flush toilets, a boat ramp, picnic tables, drinking water, and fire grills.

Reservations, fees: Campsites are $9 and are first come, first served.

Open: June–mid-Sept.

Directions: Drive through Red Canyon on State Route 12, looking for Forest Road 087, which is just east of the canyon. Drive approximately six miles south to the campground.

Contact: Dixie National Forest, Powell Ranger District, 435/676-8815.

67 Bullfrog Campground

 9

Few areas in the United States offer better boating than Lake Powell, Utah's 186-mile-long man-made reservoir. Whether you want to water-ski on open water, paddle a canoe into the narrow side canyons, cruise in a houseboat, fish for largemouth or striped bass, or take a cool dip near the shore, the lake provides an idyllic setting. Located two blocks from the lake, this campground has good views of the beautiful blue water and majestic sandstone cliffs. Campsites are shaded and some include grass, a plus during hot summer months. It's well off the highway and can be quiet during the off-season, but when the lake draws lots of visitors it can get noisy. From here it's a short walk to a sand and pebble beach along the lake.

Location: Near Lake Powell; map B2, grid i8.

Campsites, facilities: The 86-unit campground offers flush toilets, drinking water, picnic tables, fire grills, and an RV waste-disposal station. A beach and a boat ramp onto Lake Powell are situated nearby, as are showers and laundry facilities.

Reservations, fees: Campsites are $16 and are first come, first served.

Open: Year-round.

Directions: From Hanksville, drive approximately 30 miles south on State Route 95 to its junction with State Route 276. Drive approximately 25 miles south on State Route 276 to the campground.

Contact: Bullfrog Campground, 435/684-2233.

68 Bullfrog RV Park

 6

This camp is approximately a half mile from massive, man-made Lake Powell, one of Utah's premier boating destinations. It can get scorching hot here in the summer, with temperatures easily exceeding 100°F. Shade

trees guard some of the campsites. If you want to hike in the area, head to U.S. Forest Service trails in the nearby Henry Mountains. Campers who wish to continue on State Route 276 toward Hall's Crossing and the Four Corners Monument can take a 20-minute ride on the *John Atlantic Burr* ferry, which leaves from the Bullfrog Marina. You'll find a good restaurant at the Bullfrog Lodge.

Location: Near Lake Powell; map B2, grid i8.

Campsites, facilities: There are 22 RV sites with full hookups. Showers, restrooms, picnic tables, a public phone, and cable TV are available. Groceries, laundry facilities, and a full-service marina are close by.

Reservations, fees: Reservations are accepted. The fee is $25.

Open: Year-round.

Directions: From Hanksville, drive approximately 30 miles south on State Route 95 to its junction with State Route 276. Continue 24.5 miles south on State Route 276 to the campground.

Contact: Bullfrog RV Park, Box 56909, Phoenix, AZ 85079; 435/684-2233 or 800/528-6154.

69 Hall's Crossing

 8

Set a short walk from the water, this campground makes a good base for exploring Lake Powell. The man-made reservoir offers 186 miles of surface water and 1,960 miles of shoreline—more shoreline, in fact, than spans the western United States' coast from California to Washington. It's truly a boater's paradise, with powerboats speeding alongside sailboats, slow-roaming houseboats, and rafts. Anglers will find excellent fishing for crappie, striped bass, largemouth bass, smallmouth bass, bluegill, and walleye.

The camp itself is largely out in the open desert, making it vulnerable to the summer temperatures that exceed 100°F most days. Because most visitors travel by boat to the more primitive and private side canyons on the lake, the campground rarely fills up.

Location: Near Lake Powell, in Glen Canyon National Recreation Area; map B2, grid j8.

Campsites, facilities: There are 65 campsites. Picnic tables, fire pits, and restrooms with cold water and flush toilets are available. An RV waste-disposal station is nearby. Showers are available at Hall's Crossing RV Park for a small fee.

Reservations, fees: Campsites are $15 and are first come, first served.

Open: Year-round.

Directions: From Blanding, drive west on State Route 95. Turn southwest on State Route 276 and drive 29 miles to the campground.

Contact: Glen Canyon National Recreation Area, 435/684-2261.

Hall's Crossing RV Park

 8

Because of its remote location, Hall's Crossing is one of the more laid-back and quiet marinas on Lake Powell. The park is set on a small ridge with views over the water. Ample fishing and boating opportunities are available nearby at Lake Powell, the second-largest manmade reservoir in the United States (the largest reservoir is Lake Mead, in Arizona and California). Spend a day taking a 50-mile boat ride from Hall's Crossing to Rainbow Bridge National Monument. The largest natural bridge in the world, Rainbow Bridge spans 275 feet and stands 290 feet high.

Location: Near Lake Powell; map B2, grid j8.

Campsites, facilities: There are 32 RV sites with full hookups. The campground has restrooms, showers, picnic tables, laundry facilities, a grocery store, a public phone, and barbecue grills. An RV waste-disposal station is located across the street.

Reservations, fees: Reservations are accepted. The fee is $26.

Open: Year-round.

Directions: From Blanding, drive west on State Route 95. Turn southwest on State Route 276 and drive 29 miles to the RV park.

Contact: Hall's Crossing RV Park, 435/684-2261.

White House

 8

Few places can match the rugged beauty of the narrow slot canyons you'll find in Paria Canyon. The lower portion of the canyon, which stretches almost 40 miles to Lee's Ferry at the edge of the Grand Canyon, makes a terrific four-day backpacking trip. Day hikes into the area are also rewarding. Be prepared, though: Flash floods can occur and are especially dangerous in the narrow canyon. Check with the Bureau of Land Management office in Kanab for weather details, especially in late July and August, when thunderstorms can be a major problem. The small BLM campground is set in a relatively flat and open area at the edge of the wash and can be extremely hot in the summer months. One block away is the Paria River, which often dries to less than a trickle during scorching summers.

Location: Near the Paria River; map B2, grid j2.

Campsites, facilities: There are three campsites with picnic tables and vault toilets. No water is available.

Reservations, fees: Campsites are $5 and are first come, first served.

Open: Apr.–Oct.

Directions: From Kanab, drive 42 miles east on Highway 89. Look for a sign to a dirt road heading south. Continue one mile south to the campground.

Contact: Bureau of Land Management, Kanab, 435/644-2672.

WHITEWATER DORIES IN CANYONLANDS NATIONAL PARK

MAP B3

One inch equals approximately 11 miles.

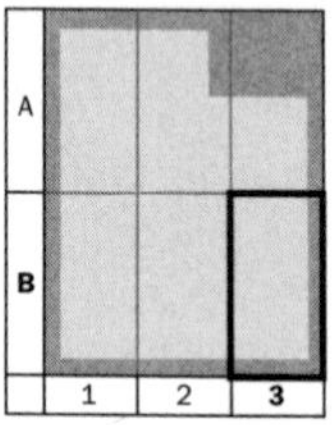

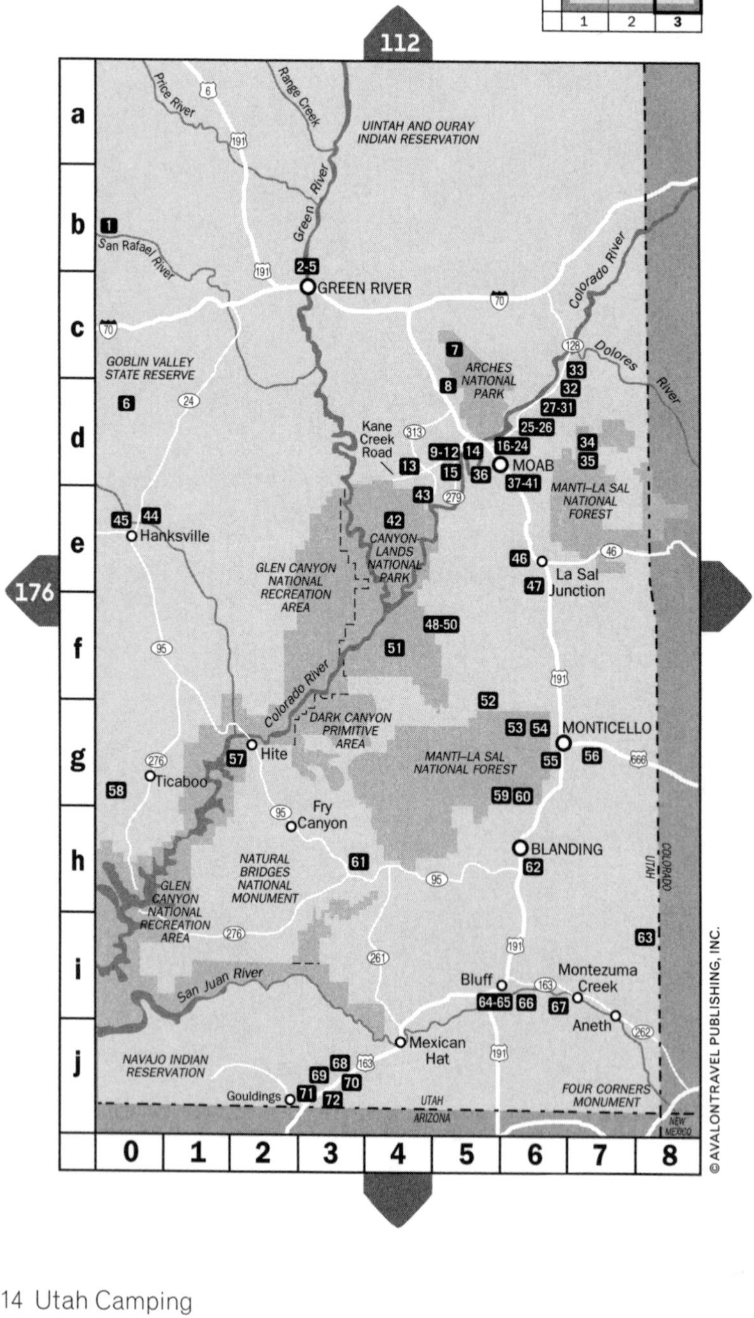

CHAPTER B3

(CONTINUED ON NEXT PAGE)

Utah's southwest corner is canyon country. The Green and Colorado Rivers and their tributaries have carved a maze of canyons into the Colorado Plateau. Rocks with names like Windgate, Navajo, and Kayenta have been crafted by precipitation and wind into fantastic shapes. The area has been home to indigenous peoples for centuries. Hundreds of cliff dwellings attest to a desert way of life that disappeared around 1200 a.d. Navajo, Ute, and Paiute Indians inhabit the area now. Rainbow Bridge, a sacred site to the Navajo, continues to spark controversy, as it is a tourist destination for the thousands who visit Lake Powell every year.

Three-Day Itinerary: Dead Horse Point State Park ⛺ Canyonlands National Park ⛺ Arches National Park ⛺ Natural Bridges National Monument (Natural Bridges Campground)

Day One
From Salt Lake City, drive south on I-80, 55 miles to the Spanish

Fork exit. Take Highway 6 54 miles to Price. From Price, go another 57 miles to Green River. Get on I-70 here and go east 20 miles to Crescent Junction. At the junction, take Highway 191 toward Moab. Your destination is the area around Moab. Camping in this area during the May through September tourist season can be problematic because it is so popular. Instead, try to make reservations at Dead Horse Point State Park (800/322-3770) or one of the private campgrounds in the Moab area.

There are good Bureau of Land Management campgrounds along the Colorado River and around the Moab Slickrock Bike Trail. Dead Horse Point has a campground and a viewpoint of the meandering Colorado River 2,000 feet below. It also includes a quarter-mile nature trail.

For an entirely different treat, check out Canyonlands National Park. The Colorado and Green Rivers separate the park into three units—The Island in the Sky, the Maze, and the Needles. The Needles and the Island in the Sky are accessible by a paved road. The relatively small but pretty campgrounds in these areas fill fast during tourist season. The Maze is four-wheel-drive country and reservations are required for camping. There is excellent hiking throughout Canyonlands. Pick up a brochure as you enter the park and choose a trail that

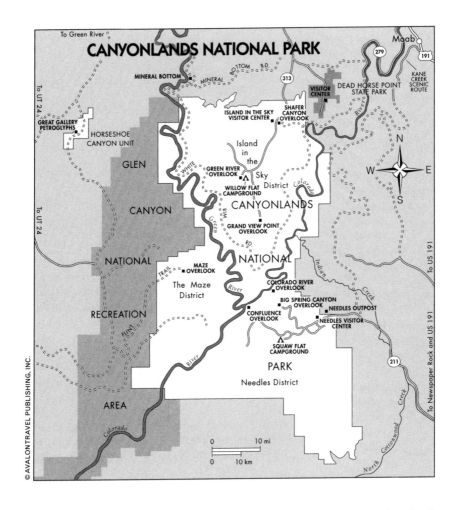

CANYONLANDS NATIONAL PARK

To Green River

Moab

279

191

MINERAL BOTTOM

MINERAL BOTTOM RD.

313

KANE CREEK SCENIC ROUTE

VISITOR CENTER

DEAD HORSE POINT STATE PARK

To UT 24

GREAT GALLERY PETROGLYPHS

HORSESHOE CANYON UNIT

ISLAND IN THE SKY VISITOR CENTER

SHAFER CANYON OVERLOOK

GLEN

Island in the Sky District

GREEN RIVER OVERLOOK

To UT 24

CANYON

WHITE RIM

WILLOW FLAT CAMPGROUND

CANYONLANDS

Colorado

GRAND VIEW POINT OVERLOOK

NATIONAL

RIM RD.

NATIONAL

MAZE OVERLOOK

TRAIL

The Maze District

COLORADO RIVER OVERLOOK

Indian Creek

To US 191

RECREATION

FLINT

BIG SPRING CANYON OVERLOOK

NEEDLES OUTPOST

CONFLUENCE OVERLOOK

NEEDLES VISITOR CENTER

To Newspaper Rock and US 191

River

SQUAW FLAT CAMPGROUND

211

PARK

Needles District

AREA

Colorado

North Cottonwood Creek

0   10 mi

0   10 km

© AVALON TRAVEL PUBLISHING, INC.

matches your capabilities. If you plan to camp at Dead Horse Point, the Island in the Sky is the closest site.

Day Two

Visit Arches National Park. The visitors center is visible from Highway 191, just before you enter Moab. Drive through the park. Take a hike. Bring lots of film. Because of publicity surrounding the 2002 Winter Olympics in Salt Lake City, the Delicate Arch has become a symbol of the state. The three-mile round-trip hike to the arch is a crowd-pleaser. Be aware that the National Park Service limits the number of people on the trail by the size of the parking lot, so plan accordingly. The campground at Arches is hard to get into in the summer. A better alternative is to camp in the same place as you did on day one of the trip. You can also choose

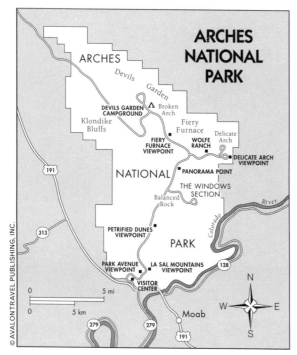

ARCHES NATIONAL PARK

ARCHES

Devils Garden

DEVILS GARDEN CAMPGROUND — Broken Arch

Klondike Bluffs

Fiery Furnace

FIERY FURNACE VIEWPOINT — WOLFE RANCH — Delicate Arch

NATIONAL — PANORAMA POINT — DELICATE ARCH VIEWPOINT

191

THE WINDOWS SECTION

Balanced Rock

River

PETRIFIED DUNES VIEWPOINT

313

PARK

Colorado

PARK AVENUE VIEWPOINT — LA SAL MOUNTAINS VIEWPOINT — 128

VISITOR CENTER

0   5 mi

0   5 km

Moab

N
W   E
S

279   279

191

© AVALON TRAVEL PUBLISHING, INC.

a new campground, either in Moab or in one of the Bureau of Land Management campgrounds dispersed along the Colorado River.

Day Three
Travel to a different kind of red rock at Natural Bridges National Monument. Go south on Highway 191 from Moab, 55 miles to Monticello and another 25 miles to Blanding. Take an hour and visit the Dinosaur Museum in Blanding. Owners Steve and Sylvia Czerkas have specialized in dinosaur skin and have a great collection of dinosaur reproductions as well as original fossils. The Edge of the Cedars State Park is also in town. Its visitors-center displays interpret the Navajo, Ute, and Anglo inhabitants of the region. Just south of Blanding, go west on State Route 275. This scenic byway takes you to Natural Bridges National Monument. Drive to the overlooks to the three natural bridges. As time and energy permit, take one or two hikes down the canyon edge to the bridges. Or stay down in the canyon and hike to all three (you'll need a car shuttle). Spend the night at the campground. It's relatively small, but it doesn't see heavy use like the national park campgrounds.

Seven-Day Itinerary: Goblin Valley State Park 🏕 Lake Powell 🏕 Natural Bridges National Monument 🏕 Hovenweep National Monument-Canyonlands National Park 🏕 Arches National Park 🏕 Dead Horse Point State Park

Day One
A visit to Goblin Valley feels like a visit to Mars. Wander among the hoodoos, especially under a full moon, and let your imagination run wild. Make reservations to stay at the campground (800/322-3770) before you arrive. To reach Goblin Valley, drive south from Salt Lake City to Green River (see directions under Three-Day Itinerary, Day One). From Green River, take I-70 west to the junction for State Route 24 to Hanksville. About 20 miles south of the I-70 or

State Route 24 Junction, take the exit to Goblin Valley. The park is about 10 miles away on a paved road.

Day Two

Lake Powell is another popular tourist destination. The Glen Canyon Dam on the Colorado River has created the second-largest man-made lake in America. To reach Lake Powell, return to State Route 24 and go south 20 miles to Hanksville. Take State Route 96 from another 45 miles or so to Hite Marina on Lake Powell. Rent a boat and find a campground on the lake, or use the campground near the marina. People flock to Lake Powell and the Glen Canyon National Recreation Area because of the water sports available here. People in houseboats, powerboats, and personal watercraft cruise its waters. Anglers come to fish for the striped and smallmouth bass that have been introduced into the lake. The contrasts between red rock, blue sky, and green water make this a scenic vacation spot.

Day Three

Leave the crowds behind and head for Natural Bridges National Monument (see Three-Day Itinerary, Day Three) Get there by continuing on State Route 95 east of Hite for about 30 miles. Take State Route 275 to the monument.

Day Four

Go farther into the Four Corners to Monument Valley. From Natural Bridges, return to State Route 95 and go east for just a couple miles to the turnoff to State Route 261. About 25 miles south, a dirt road leads to the Valley of the Gods. The road is passable only in dry conditions. It ends up on Highway 163. If time permits, go west on this road to the turnoff to the Goosenecks of the San Juan State Park. The view here is similar to that at Dead Horse Point. From the viewpoint one can see the San Juan River 1,000 feet below as it takes five river miles to cover one linear mile.

From the Goosenecks of the San Juan, go to the town of Mexican Hat. If time permits, visit Monument Valley in the Navajo Indian Reservation. The 21 miles to the Navajo Tribal Park and the driving tour through its famous monoliths are worth the time. Visit Goulding's Trading Post, originally built in the 1920s. Get a bite to eat in the restaurant. Enjoy the great view out its large windows.

Return to Highway 163 and continue 40 miles to Bluff. Take Highway 191 to the turnoff to State Route 262 and Hovenweep National Monument. This forgotten park contains a collection of unusual Anasazi cliff dwellings, round towers built into the canyon walls. Camp at the Square Tower campground.

Day Five

Take some time to see Hovenweep the next morning and then return to Highway 191. Visit the Island in the Sky section of Canyonlands National Park (see Three-Day Itinerary, Day One). Or, visit the Needles section of the park. The turnoff to the Needles is State Route 211, about 70 miles north of Bluff. Choose a hike according to your time and ability level. Squaw Flat Campground in the park is popular and hard to get into. The Needles Outpost is a private campground just outside the entrance.

Day Six
Visit Arches National Park (see Three-Day Itinerary, Day Two).

Day Seven
Stay and see more of Arches or Canyonlands or take off for Goblin Valley State Park (see Three-Day Itinerary, Day One). It's hard to go wrong in this part of the country; just try to minimize your driving and focus on the fantastic hiking.

1 San Rafael

  7

Just southeast of the geographic center of Utah, the San Rafael Swell is a wild region of sandstone cliffs and slot canyons, with few developed roads or marked trails. Roughly 65 miles long and 35 miles wide, it's a popular area for horseback riding, hiking, and four-wheel-drive exploration. Equestrians enjoy exploring the area known as "the Wedge" or "Little Grand Canyon," a deep, red-rock gorge with fascinating side canyons and rock-art sites. Beyond the small campground, the BLM allows free dispersed camping in many side canyons off the main route. Be careful to observe signs designating Wilderness Study Areas, however; vehicles are prohibited in such places. Five miles north of the campground, visit the Buckhorn Wash rock-art panel, home to prehistoric Native American pictographs and ghostlike petroglyphs. Recent preservation efforts have led to the removal of some modern graffiti that marred the site.

Location: In the San Rafael Swell; map B3, grid b0.

Campsites, facilities: There are eight sites with vault toilets, picnic tables, and fire grills. No drinking water is available.

Reservations, fees: Campsites are $6 and are first come, first served.

Open: Year-round.

Directions: In the Emery County town of Cleveland, look for a signed dirt road leading to the San Rafael Swell and the campground. Follow the marked backcountry road 25 miles southeast from Cleveland to the camp.

Contact: Bureau of Land Management, Price; 435/789-1362.

2 Green River KOA

 5

Campers get shaded sites on a pleasant green lawn in a relatively secluded spot between I-70 and Green River's business district. The Green River State Park Golf Course is across the street. The gentle-flowing Green River is ideal for canoeing and rafting; commercial outfitters in town can help you arrange a one-day trip in Desolation Canyon upstream or a four- or five-day excursion to the Mineral Canyon takeout in Canyonlands National Park. In late summer and early fall, stop at one of the nearby fruit stands and pick up locally grown cantaloupe, honeydew, or watermelons. They're some of the best eating anywhere! In early September, Green River hosts its annual Melon Days Festival, with a parade and other fun-filled activities.

Location: In Green River; map B3, grid c2.

Campsites, facilities: There are 77 RV sites with full hookups, 42 sites with water and electricity hookups, 30 tent sites, and three camping cabins. The campground has restrooms, showers, laundry facilities, a pool, barbecue grills, picnic tables, a playground, a public phone, and a grocery store. Pets are allowed.

Reservations, fees: Reservations are recommended in early September during the Melon Days celebration. Full hookup sites are $20.50, sites with water and electricity are $18.50, and tent sites are $16.50. Camping cabins are $31.50.

Open: Apr.–mid-Oct.

Directions: Follow I-70 to the town of Green River. Drivers approaching from the west should take exit 158 and follow Main Street, looking for the sign to Green River State Park on the south side of the road. Entering Green River from the east, take exit 162. The camp is a block south of the entrance to the state park, at 550 South Green River Boulevard.

Contact: Green River KOA, P. O. Box 14, Green River, UT 84525-0014; 435/564-3651.

3 Green River State Park

    8

Huge cottonwood trees shade most of the campsites in Green River State Park. A fairly large facility, the park offers grassy lawns, a day-use picnic area, a boat-launching ramp, and a recently completed nine-hole public golf course. All told, this is one of the better tent-camping areas in southeastern Utah. While the campground often fills up on holiday weekends, at other times it provides a less-crowded alternative to Moab camps flooded with visitors to Arches and Canyonlands National Parks, both approximately 45 minutes away. The Green River itself, a fine stretch of floater-friendly water, is about a half block from the camp. Local outfitters can arrange a one- or multi-day rafting trip down the Green.

Four blocks from the park, visit the John Wesley Powell River Running Museum, home of the Utah River Runner's Hall of Fame. Exhibits detail the history of river-running in the state and include replicas of early wooden boats and rafts. The museum also celebrates the life of Major John Wesley Powell, who conducted the first scientific exploration of the Green and Colorado Rivers in the mid-1800s. The friendly museum staff is knowledgeable about travel in the area, and many free brochures provide information on local attractions.

Location: In Green River; map B3, grid c2.

Campsites, facilities: There are 42 campsites. Facilities include a golf course, hot showers, a boat-launching ramp, modern restrooms, a group-use area, and an amphitheater. Restrooms are wheelchair accessible.

Reservations, fees: Reservations can be made 120 days in advance by calling 800/322-3770 Mon.–Fri. 8 A.M.–5 P.M. A $6.50 nonrefundable reservation fee is charged for each site reserved. Campsites are $11. Utah residents 62 years and older with a Special Fun Tag receive a $2 discount Sun.–Thurs., excluding holidays.

Open: Year-round.

Directions: Follow I-70 to the town of Green River. Drivers approaching from the west should take exit 158 and follow Main Street, looking for the sign to Green River State Park on the south side of the road. Entering Green River from the east, take exit 162. The park is on South Green River Boulevard, two blocks south of Main Street, beside the Green River.

Contact: Green River State Park, 435/564-3633.

4 Shady Acres

    5

Although much of the land surrounding the town of Green River is treeless and desolate, this camp is shaded by fairly large cottonwood trees. From here, it's a short, two-block stroll to the John Wesley Powell River Running Museum, with its excellent multimedia exhibits about the history of river-running in Utah. Or, you can rent a raft or canoe in town and make a little history running the river yourself.

Location: In Green River; map B3, grid c2.

Campsites, facilities: There are 104 RV sites with full hookups; some are pull-throughs, others are back-in sites. There are also 14 tent sites. The campground has restrooms, showers, laundry facilities, an RV waste-disposal station, a grocery store, barbecue grills, a public phone, a playground, and cable-TV hookups. Pets are allowed.

Reservations, fees: Reservations are accepted. Pull-through sites are $17, back-in sites are $15, and tent sites are $13.

Open: Year-round, with water available Mar.–Oct.

Directions: Follow I-70 to the town of Green River. Drivers approaching from the west should take exit 158. Entering Green River from the east, take exit 162. The park is located at 360 Main Street (its back faces the Green River State Park Golf Course).

Contact: Shady Acres Campground, 435/564-8295 or 800/537-8674.

5 United

 5

One of the larger private campgrounds in Green River, United Campground offers gravel sites and less shade cover than other area camps. The pool, however, provides a welcome respite during hot summer months. Nearby Green River State Park offers river access. Just across the way is the John Wesley Powell River Running Museum, which details the history of river-running in Utah. If campsite cooking is not to your liking, visit the Tamarisk Restaurant at the Best Western Motel for good food and views over the Green River.

Location: In Green River; map B3, grid c2.

Campsites, facilities: There are 65 sites with full hookups and 15 sites for tents. The campground has restrooms, showers, picnic tables, laundry facilities, barbecue grills, a gift shop, a public phone, a pool, a playroom, cable TV, and an RV waste-disposal station. Pets are allowed.

Reservations, fees: Reservations are accepted. Full hookups are $18.50; tent sites are $13.40.

Open: Year-round.

Directions: Take I-70 to the town of Green River. Drivers approaching from the west should take exit 158. Entering Green River from the east, take exit 162. The park is located at 910 Main Street, across from the John Wesley Powell River Running Museum. The campground is situated on the south side of the road.

Contact: United Campground, 435/564-8195.

6 Arch View

 8

Newly planted trees give shade. You'll enjoy the great views of Klondike Bluff in Arches National Park, four miles away, and the surrounding La Sal Mountains. In addition to its proximity to Arches, the camp is only 23 miles from Canyonlands National Park. Mountain bikers enjoy many routes in the vicinity, including one trail that begins in the parking area across from the camp and leads into red-rock country. Pick up a free mountain biker's guide at the campground, the Moab Information Center, or the John Wesley Powell River Running Museum in Green River. Also near the camp, off a spur road, hikers can take a short, 100-yard trek to view exposed dinosaur bones in the Bureau of Land Management's Mill Creek Canyon; obtain directions at the campground or pick up a brochure at the Moab Information Center.

Location: Near Moab; map B3, grid d4.

Campsites, facilities: There are 52 RV sites with full hookups and 33 tent sites. Restrooms, showers, laundry facilities, a game room, a grocery and gift shop, barbecue pits, and a public phone are available.

Reservations, fees: Reservations are accepted. RV sites are $18.95; tent sites are $14.50.

Open: Feb.–Oct.

Directions: From Moab, drive eight miles north on Highway 191. The camp is on the east side of the road, near the junction of Highway 191 and State Route 313.

Contact: Arch View Campground, P. O. Box 1406, Moab, UT 84532; 435/259-7854 or 800/813-6622.

7 Devil's Garden

 10

Home to the largest concentration of natural arches in the world, Arches National Park is a land of towering sandstone cliffs and fins, narrow slot canyons, and gravity-defying balanced rocks. It's spectacular terrain, so it's no surprise that Devil's Garden, the park's only campground, is one of Utah's most popular camping destinations. With spacious sites set in a juniper forest, it fills up almost every night of the year. Make certain to get here early, before 9 A.M., if you hope to camp. Right in the middle of the campground you'll find a pretty amphitheater guarded by the Skyline Arch, one of the more magical settings for an outdoor evening program in the entire National Park System. Hikers can venture three miles round-trip on the moderately difficult trail to Delicate Arch, possibly the park's best-known landmark. (It graces countless postcards, book covers, and even Utah state license plates.) Rangers also lead daily hikes into the maze-like Fiery Furnace, an easy place to lose your way among slot canyons and dead-end turnoffs; sign up for the guided trip at the park's visitors center early in the day. (Note: The park is undergoing major waterline repairs.)

Location: In Arches National Park; map B3, grid c5.

Campsites, facilities: The 54-site campground has handicapped facilities, restrooms with cold running water, drinking water, picnic tables, fire grills, group areas, and an amphitheater for evening programs. There is a seven-day stay limit, and the maximum RV length is 35 feet. Vault toilets are only available during the winter months.

Reservations, fees: All individual sites are first come, first served. Group sites can be reserved in advance. Oct.–Mar., when water is not available, fees are $10. During the warmer months, when water is available, fees are $10.

Open: Year-round, with water available Apr.–Sept.

Directions: From Moab, take Highway 191 five miles north to the park's visitors center. Drive 18 miles north to reach the campground on the park's only paved road.

Contact: Arches National Park, 435/259-8161.

8 Goblin Valley State Park
 10

This is a great camp for children! Kids' imag-

inations will get a real workout at this 3,654-acre park as they wander among the valley's wonderfully bizarre sandstone formations. They're sure to have a great time playing hide-and-go-seek with the hundreds of goblins and ghouls hidden among the rocks. The campground itself is tucked away on a paved loop off the park's main road, with some tent sites well hidden from the road. Two well-marked trails, the 1.5-mile (one-way) Carmel Canyon Trail and the three-mile (one-way) Curtis Bench Trail, wind through Goblin Valley. One mile west of the park, the San Rafael Swell offers additional hiking adventures among its numerous slot canyons. Set at an elevation of 5,200 feet, the park can be on the cold side in winter and hot in the summer.

Location: Near Hanksville; map B3, grid d0.

Campsites, facilities: There are 21 campsites. Amenities include picnic tables, fire grills, a modern restroom with showers, a dump station, and a picnic shelter. The restroom is handicapped accessible.

Reservations, fees: Reservations can be made 120 days in advance by calling 800/322-3770 Mon.–Fri. 8 A.M.–5 P.M. Campsites are $11, plus a nonrefundable $6.25 reservation fee. Utah residents 62 years and older with a Special Fun Tag receive a $2 discount Sun.–Thurs., excluding holidays.

Open: Year-round.

Directions: From Green River, drive about eight miles west on I-70. Take exit 147 and drive about 25 miles south on State Route 24. The turnoff to Goblin Valley State Park is well marked. Follow the road about 15 miles to the park.

Contact: Green River State Park, 435/564-3633.

9 Kings Bottom
 9

This tents-only campground is out of the way

on a dead-end road. Access to nearby hiking and biking trails is the draw.

Location: Near Moab, on Kane Creek: map B3, grid d6.

Campsites, facilities: There are seven sites with vault toilets but no water.

Reservations, fees: Campsites are $5 and are first come, first served.

Open: Year-round.

Directions: From Highway 191 in Moab, take the Kane Creek Road west for 2.8 miles to the Kings Bottom campground.

Contact: Bureau of Land Management, 435/259-8193.

Moonflower

 9

These walk-in tent sites are nestled off the road under fantastic slickrock.

Location: Near Moab, on Kane Creek: map B3, grid d6.

Campsites, facilities: There are eight sites with vault toilets but no water.

Reservations, fees: Campsites are $5 and are first come, first served.

Open: Year-round.

Directions: From Highway 191 in Moab, take the Kane Creek Road west for three miles to the Moonflower campground.

Contact: Bureau of Land Management, 435/259-8193.

Hunters Canyon/Spring

 9

Four of the sites are walk-in and nine can accommodate vehicles. This campground provides easy access to the Moab Rim Trail, a great path for hiking and biking. It's also close to the popular four-wheel-drive roads in Hurrah Pass, Pritchett Canyon, and Lockhart Basin.

Location: Near Moab, on Kane Creek: map B3, grid d6.

Campsites, facilities: There are 13 tent sites with vault toilets but no water.

Reservations, fees: Campsites are $5 and are first come, first served.

Open: Year-round.

Directions: From Highway 191 in Moab, take Kane Creek Road west for 7.8 miles to Hunters Canyon/Spring.

Contact: Bureau of Land Management, 435/259-8193.

Echo

 9

This campground is popular with mountain bikers.

Location: Near Moab, on Kane Creek: map B3, grid d6.

Campsites, facilities: There are nine sites with vault toilets but no water.

Reservations, fees: Campsites are $5 and are first come, first served.

Open: Year-round.

Directions: From Highway 191 in Moab, take Kane Creek Road west for eight miles to Echo Campground.

Contact: Bureau of Land Management, 435/259-8193.

Kane Springs (Tenting Site)

 9

This campground offers easy access to the area's hiking and mountain-biking trails. It's definitely primitive—the picnic tables in the creek campground are made from old cable spools, for example—but it's well worth a stay. Best suited for tents and self-contained RVs.

Location: West of Moab on Kane Creek Road: map B3, grid d6.

Campsites, facilities: Of the campground's 60 sites, eight have hookups but the majority are for tents. There are picnic tables at some sites, and water, restrooms, and showers are available.

Reservations, fees: Campsites are $14.

Open: Apr.–Oct.

Directions: On Highway 191 in Moab, go west at the McDonalds Drive-In on Kane Creek Boulevard. Keep driving up the canyon. The campground has two parts, one next to Kane Creek, which is sometimes dry, and the other up the canyon on slickrock.

Contact: Kane Springs Campground, 1705 Kane Creek Rd., Moab, UT; 435/259-8844.

14 Jaycee Park

 9

This campground is close to good rock climbing and popular mountain-biking and hiking trails. Because it's on a dead-end road, it doesn't see much traffic. The campground is on the Colorado River, so limited rafting and canoeing is possible. Check with the Bureau of Land Management for specifics.

Location: Near Moab, on the Colorado River: map B3, grid d6.

Campsites, facilities: There are seven sites with vault toilets and picnic tables but no water.

Reservations, fees: Campsites are $10 and are first come, first served.

Open: Year-round.

Directions: From Moab, drive north on Highway 191. Follow State Route 279 for 4.2 miles west along the Colorado River to Jaycee Park.

Contact: Bureau of Land Management, 435/259-8193.

15 Goldbar

 9

Most campers who stay here come to be close to the hiking and mountain-biking trails. The campground is on the Colorado River, so limited rafting and canoeing is possible. Check with the Bureau of Land Management for specifics.

Location: Near Moab, on the Colorado River; map B3, grid d6.

Campsites, facilities: There are 10 sites with vault toilets but no water.

Reservations, fees: Campsites are $5 and are first come, first served.

Open: Year-round.

Directions: From Moab, drive north on Highway 191 to State Route 279. Turn west on State Route 279 and continue 10.2 miles along the river to Goldbar Campground.

Contact: Bureau of Land Management, 435/259-8193.

16 Spanish Trail RV Park and Campground

 5

Located in the middle of Moab, near the business district, this newer park has little shade. It's convenient to restaurants, stores, and the Slickrock Bike Trail, which is three miles to the east. (For more information on other recreational options in the Moab area, see Moab Valley RV and Campark, page 228.)

Location: In Moab; map B3, grid d5.

Campsites, facilities: There are 60 RV sites with full hookups and 13 tent sites. Restrooms, showers, laundry facilities, an RV waste-disposal site, cable TV, and a public phone are available. Pets are allowed on a leash. Owners are required to clean up after their pets.

Reservations, fees: RV sites are $24; tent sites are $17 for two people. Each additional person at an RV site is $2; extra tent campers must pay $3. Reservations are accepted.

Open: Year-round.

Directions: From Moab, follow Highway 191 to the campground at 298 South.

Contact: Spanish Trail RV Park and Campground, 2980 S. Hwy. 191, Moab, UT 84532; 435/259-2411 or 800/787-2751.

17 Portal RV Park and Fishery

 6

The pretty views to the west of this campground, ideal at sunset, take in the Nature Conservancy's 800-acre Matheson Wetlands Preserve and a red-rock canyon cut by the Colorado River. The campground is on the Colorado River, so limited rafting and canoeing is possible. Check with the Bureau of Land Management for specifics. In the midday sun, however, the young trees here don't provide much shade. The mostly open terrain is well landscaped with a grassy lawn, and ponds here are stocked with rainbow trout for catch-and-release fly-fishing. The fee is $10 per hour, no state license is required, and you can rent a fishing rod at the park's convenience store. From a nearby parking area, a boardwalk leads to self-guided nature trails through the Matheson Wetlands Preserve, providing glimpses of its plentiful wildlife. Bald eagles frequent the area in winter, and a surprising variety of ducks, cranes, and songbirds live here year-round.

Location: In Moab; map B3, grid d5.

Campsites, facilities: There are 36 pull-through RV sites with full hookups and 10 shaded tent sites. There are also seven cabins. Restrooms, showers, laundry facilities, an RV waste-disposal site, and a convenience store are available. Ponds on the premises are stocked with trout.

Reservations, fees: Reservations are accepted. Full hookups with 50-amp service are $24; sites with 30-amp service are $20. Sites with water and electricity cost $14, and tent sites are $15. Cabins are $32 and $38.

Open: Year-round.

Directions: From Moab, drive three-quarters of a mile north on Highway 191. The camp is adjacent to Matheson Wetlands Preserve.

Contact: Portal RV Park and Fishery, 1261 N. Hwy. 191, Moab, UT 84532; 435/259-6108 or 800/574-2028.

18 Slickrock

 4

How close is too close? When it comes to campsites, it's when you can hear your neighbor snoring in the next tent—and that's about how close together the sites are at this park. Well, at least it's got a pool and hot tubs to keep the kids occupied after the sun goes down, and plenty of nearby recreation during the day. Arches National Park, with dozens of great hiking trails, is only three miles away. Five miles to the south, golfers can visit the 18-hole, public Spanish Valley Golf Course. The campground's staff also books four-wheel-drive, mountain-biking, river-rafting, and airplane trips out of Moab.

Location: In Moab; map B3, grid d5.

Campsites, facilities: The campground's 197 sites include 120 with full hookups, 87 tent sites, and 14 cabins. There are three sets of restrooms and showers, laundry facilities, an RV waste-disposal site, picnic tables, a grocery and gift store, barbecue grills, a pool, three hot tubs, a public phone, and cable TV. Pets are allowed.

Reservations, fees: Reservations are accepted. Full hookups are $22 for two people, plus $3 for each additional person. Tent sites are $16, plus $6 for each additional person over 18. Camping cabins are $27.

Open: Year-round.

Directions: The camp is at the north end of Moab, along Highway 191, across from the Butch Cassidy Water Park and next to Buck's Grill House.

Contact: Slickrock Campground, 1301¹/₂ N. Hwy. 191, Moab, UT 84532; 435/259-7660.

19 Moab Valley RV and Campark

 6

This grassy campground is close to Arches National

Park, making it a good alternative when the Devil's Garden campground fills up. From the camp, you get pleasant sunset views of a red-rock canyon formed by the Colorado River. Also nearby is Matheson Wetlands Preserve, an excellent spot for birding. Golfers can get in 18 holes at the public Spanish Valley Golf Course. Moab's commercial outfitters offer half- and full-day rafting excursions on the Colorado, and hiking and mountain-biking options abound on surrounding national park, BLM, and U.S. Forest Service lands. Pick up free mountain-bikers' and hikers' guides at the Moab Information Center.

Location: In Moab; map B3, grid d5.

Campsites, facilities: There are 91 RV sites and 55 tent sites. Restrooms, showers, laundry facilities, an RV waste-disposal site, barbecue pits, a public phone, and cable TV are also available.

Reservations, fees: Reservations are accepted. RV sites are $20; tent sites are $15.

Open: Mar.–Oct.

Directions: The camp is at the north end of Moab, at 1773 North Highway 191, near the Butch Cassidy Water Park and Matheson Wetlands Preserve.

Contact: Moab Valley RV and Campark, 1773 N. Hwy. 191, Moab, UT 84532; 435/259-4469.

20 Kane Springs

   9

Cottonwoods shade campsites beside the small, flowing Kane Creek, which occasionally runs dry. The camp is snuggled against a tall, red-rock cliff. Nine miles away is the BLM-managed Hurrah Pass area, and mountain bikers enjoy following the steep, winding dirt road from the campground to the pass. Along the way, they're treated to views of the Colorado River and ancient Native American rock art. The campground is on the Colorado River, so limited rafting and canoeing

is possible. Check with the Bureau of Land Management for specifics.

Location: Near Moab; map B3, grid d5.

Campsites, facilities: There are 60 campsites with nine full RV hookups, a modern restroom, and showers. Group sites accommodating up to 50 people are also available.

Reservations, fees: Reservations are accepted. Hookups are $10. Campsites are $10 in established sites and $8 in overflow and group camp area. RV sites are $12.

Open: Apr.–Oct.

Directions: From Moab, drive four miles north on Kane Springs Road along the Colorado River. The camp is located at the end of the paved road in Red Rock Canyon.

Contact: Kane Springs Campground, 435/259-7821 or 435/259-8844.

21 Riverside Oasis

   8

Riverside Oasis is located on a curve of U.S. Highway 191, so two sides face the highway—not good. It's also on a bend on the river, however, so the sites are set beneath cottonwoods and are close to the water—very nice.

Location: Located at the north end of Moab; map B3, grid d6.

Campsites, facilities: There are 39 sites, all with full hookups. Sites have grass, shade trees, grills, and picnic table. Big rigs are welcome. The campground has flush toilets, water, showers, laundry facilities, a general store, and RV supplies. Rafting, horseback riding, airplane tours, fishing, and hiking can all be arranged at the campground. There are miles of trails on Bureau of Land Management land that are popular with mountain bikers, including Moab's Slickrock Bike Trail. Jeep rentals are also available.

Reservations, fees: Campsites are $20 for two people, with $3 more for each additional person. Tent sites are $15 for two and $3 for each additional person. Reservations are recommended during the busy summer season.

Open: Mar.–Oct.

Directions: Follow North Highway 191 through town until it becomes Main Street.

Contact: Riverside Oasis, 1861 North Hwy. 191; 435/259-3424.

22 Lions Back Camp Park

    10

The facilities may be primitive, but the setting—in the slickrock and sand dunes with sweeping views—is great. The road through the campground is a challenge for low-slung vehicles.

Location: Out of Moab, near the Slickrock Bike Trail: map B3, grid D6.

Campsites, facilities: The 25 campsites include five with full hookups, many tent sites, and four cabins. Picnic tables, drinking water, vault toilets, and showers are also available.

Reservations, fees: Campsites are $7. Reservations on holiday weekends are a must.

Open: Year-round.

Directions: In Moab, go east on 400 East to Millcreek Drive. Follow Millcreek to Sand Flats Road, then follow signs to the Slickrock Bike Trail (you'll pass the country's most scenic landfill). The campground is located just before the Slickrock Bike Trail.

Contact: Lions Back Camp Park, Sandflats Rd., 800/562-0327 or 435/259-6682.

23 Moab Rim Campark

     9

This campground is far from the noise of town (and far enough off the highway so that traffic noise is minimal) and enjoys great views of the Moab Rim and the La Sal Mountains. New trees have been planted and some pic-

nic tables are covered. Mountain bike on miles of nearby Bureau of Land Management trails or raft on the Colorado River. Check local regulations first.

Location: Just out of Moab: map B3, grid d6.

Campsites, facilities: The campground's 52 sites include 10 with full hookups, 10 with water and electric, and 30 for tents. Each site has a picnic table, a fire pit, and a grill. Restrooms, drinking water, and showers are available.

Reservations, fees: Campsites with full hookups are $20; those with water and electric are $18. Tent sites are $15. A $3 charge is added for any group with more than two people.

Open: Mar.–Nov.

Directions: On Highway 191 outside of Moab.

Contact: Moab Rim Campark, 1900 S. Hwy. 191; 888/599-6622 or 435/259-5002.

24 OK R.V. Park

   9

This is a good park for horse lovers. It also has good views of the La Sal Mountains and is located at the end of the road, so traffic noise is not a problem. Access to mountain biking around Moab.

Location: At Moab's Spanish Trail Arena (for horses); map B3, grid d6.

Campsites, facilities: The 45 sites with complete hookups, plus two cabins. The campground has picnic tables, water, flush toilets, laundry facilities, showers, a gift store, and a snack bar. On weekends when there is an event (a rodeo, for example) at the arena, musical entertainment is provided in a covered area in front of the snack bar. Horses can be boarded at the arena for $10 per night.

Reservations, fees: Campsites are $20 per night. Reservations are suggested, especially during rodeos.

Open: Year-round.

Directions: On Highway 191 just outside of Moab.
Contact: OK R.V. Park, 3310 Spanish Valley Dr.; 435/259-1400.

25 Goose Island

  9

This is the first BLM-operated dispersed campground along the Colorado River after leaving Moab. The campsites are cut out of the heavy tamarisks along the river. Rafting and canoeing are available along this stretch of the Colorado River. Check with the Bureau of Land Management for specifics.
Location: Near Moab, on the Colorado River: map B3, grid d6.
Campsites, facilities: There are 18 sites with vault toilets and picnic tables but no water.
Reservations, fees: Campsites are $10 and are first come, first served.
Open: Year-round.
Directions: From Moab, drive north on Highway 191 to State Route 128. Follow 128 1.4 miles east along the Colorado River to Goose Island.
Contact: Bureau of Land Management, 435/259-8193.

26 Negro Bill Canyon

  9

For those who want to hike to Morning Glory Natural Bridge up Negro Bill Canyon, this is the closest campground. The tent-only campsites are located between the tamarisks in the sand along the river. Rafting and canoeing are available along this stretch of the Colorado River. Check with the Bureau of Land Management for specifics.
Location: Near Moab, on the Colorado River; map B3, grid d6.
Campsites, facilities: There are 17 sites with vault toilets but no water.

Reservations, fees: Campsites are $5 and are first come, first served.
Open: Year-round.
Directions: From Moab, drive north on Highway 191 to State Route 128. Follow State Route 128 three miles east along the Colorado River to Negro Bill Canyon Campground. It's on the east side of the road just past the Negro Bill Canyon Trailhead.
Contact: Bureau of Land Management, 435/259-8193.

27 Drinks Canyon

  9

This campground is more exposed than most of the other dispersed campgrounds along the Colorado River. All are in sandstone wonderland sourounding Moab. Rafting and canoeing are available along this stretch of the river. Check with the Bureau of Land Management for specifics.
Location: Near Moab, on the Colorado River; map B3, grid d6.
Campsites, facilities: There are 17 sites with vault toilets but no water.
Reservations, fees: Campsites are $5 and are first come, first served.
Open: Year-round.
Directions: From Moab, drive north on Highway 191 to State Route 128. Follow State Route 128 6.2 miles east along the Colorado River to Drinks Canyon Campground.
Contact: Bureau of Land Management, 435/259-8193.

28 Hal Canyon

    9

Oak and cottonwood trees shade this pleasant Bureau of Land Management campground near the Colorado River. Popular with mountain bikers, this is an inexpensive alternative to the private campgrounds in Moab. A few small rapids liven up this otherwise gentle-flowing stretch of the Colorado. In places the current can be strong, so be careful when swimming. Life jackets are a must for children. Rafting and canoeing are available along this stretch of the river. Check with the Bureau of Land Management for specifics. Four miles south of the camp, hikers should explore Negro Bill Canyon, where a little stream cuts through a red-rock wonderland. The well-traveled trail here ventures two miles to Morning Glory Natural Bridge. Additional hiking is available at Arches National Park, which is 10 miles from the camp.

Location: Near Moab, on the Colorado River; map B3, grid d6.

Campsites, facilities: There are 11 sites with vault toilets, picnic tables, and fire grills. There is no drinking water.

Reservations, fees: Campsites are $10 and are first come, first served.

Open: Year-round.

Directions: From Moab, drive south on Highway 191 to State Route 128. Follow State Route 128 seven miles east, then north along the Colorado River to Hal Canyon.

Contact: Bureau of Land Management, 435/259-8193.

29 Oak Grove

   9

Shaded campsites along the Colorado River are guarded on both sides by red sandstone cliffs. Like neighboring Hal Canyon, Oak Grove is a decent, inexpensive alternative to the numerous private camps in Moab. (For details on river conditions and nearby Negro Bill Canyon, see the Hal Canyon listing, page 230.) Rafting and canoeing are available along this stretch of the Colorado River. Check with the Bureau of Land Management for specifics.

Location: Near Moab, on the Colorado River; map B3, grid d6.

Campsites, facilities: There are seven sites with picnic tables, vault toilets, and fire grills. No drinking water is available.

Reservations, fees: Campsites are $10 and are first come, first served.

Open: May 20–Oct. 31.

Directions: From Moab, drive south on Highway 191. Follow State Route 128 seven miles east, then north along the Colorado River. The camp is adjacent to Hal Canyon.

Contact: Bureau of Land Management, 435/259-8193.

30 Big Bend

 9

The Bureau of Land Management opened this camp in the early 1990s while it tried to curtail undeveloped camping along the Colorado River. Some cottonwood trees provide shade. The stretch of the river along the camp is relatively gentle, with a few small rapids popular with day-trip rafters and kayakers. Four miles north of the campground on the east side of Highway 191 you'll find the Fisher Towers, which rise 1,500 feet from the desert floor. Little visited, the BLM-managed spot offers a picnic area and a short hiking trail. (For details on nearby Negro Bill Canyon, see the Hal Canyon listing, page 230.)

Location: Near Moab, on the Colorado River; map B3, grid d6.

Campsites, facilities: There are 23 sites that can accommodate RVs up to 34 feet in length. No drinking water is available, but there are picnic tables, fire grills, and vault toilets. Restrooms are wheelchair accessible, but gravel at the campsites could cause wheelchair problems.

Reservations, fees: Campsites are $10 and are first come, first served.

Open: Year-round.

Directions: From Moab, drive south on Highway 191 to State Highway 128. Follow

State Route 128 eight miles east, then north along the Colorado River to the campground.
Contact: Bureau of Land Management, 435/259-8193.

31 Upper Big Bend

  9

This campground is not as well developed as nearby Big Bend Campground. There are some shaded spots, however, so it's a good place to stay cool in the summer. Rafting and canoeing are available along this stretch of the Colorado River. Check with the Bureau of Land Management for specifics. The campground is situated in tamerisk bushes along the Colorado River just off the highway.
Location: Near Moab, on the Colorado River; map B3, grid d6.
Campsites, facilities: There are eight sites with vault toilets but no water.
Reservations, fees: Campsites are $10 and are first come, first served.
Open: Year-round.
Directions: From Moab, drive north on Highway 191 to State Route 128. Continue on State Route 128 8.1 miles east along the river to Upper Big Bend Campground.
Contact: Bureau of Land Management, 435/259-8193.

32 Hittle Bottom

    9

At this camp, another scenic spot along the Colorado River, tall cottonwood trees shade some of the sites. On a rainy summer day you may see tiny waterfalls tumble over the surrounding sandstone cliffs. The campground is especially popular with mountain bikers. Fisher Towers and Negro Bill Canyon are both approximately 10 minutes away. It can be cold here in winter.
Location: Near Moab, on the Colorado River; map B3, grid d6.

Campsites, facilities: There are 10 sites with picnic tables, vault toilets, and fire grills. No drinking water is available.
Reservations, fees: Campsites are $10 and are first come, first served.
Open: Year-round.
Directions: From Moab, head south on Highway 191 to State Route 128. On Continue on State Route 128 23 miles east, then head north along the Colorado River to the campground.
Contact: Bureau of Land Management, 435/259-8193.

33 Dewey Bridge

 8

As you travel north along the Colorado River from Moab, the terrain becomes increasingly expansive. This wide-open camp is set along the historic, one-lane Dewey Bridge. An old suspension bridge built in 1916, it's on the National Register of Historic Places and currently is only open to foot and bicycle traffic. The bridge is a popular put-in and takeout for river-rafting trips. One of the Moab area's best two- to three-day white-water adventures begins many miles upstream in Westwater Canyon, near the Colorado-Utah border; Dewey Bridge is the first place rafters can exit the water. Day trips rafting downstream from the bridge can also be enjoyable. Fans of Native American petroglyphs can take the day trip to Sego Canyon, near the town of Thompson, about 50 miles from the camp along I-70. Rock carvings here are 800–1,300 years old.
Location: Near Moab, on the Colorado River; map B3, grid c6.
Campsites, facilities: There are seven campsites. Vault toilets, picnic tables, and fire grills are available, but there is no drinking water.

Reservations, fees: Campsites are $10 and are first come, first served.
Open: Year-round.
Directions: From Moab, head south on Highway 191 to State Route 128. Continue 30 miles east on State Route 128, then head north along the Colorado River to the campground.
Contact: Bureau of Land Management, 435/259-8193.

34 Warner Lake

    10

In fall this is one of the prettiest campgrounds anywhere. Set at an elevation of 9,400 feet, lovely little Warner Lake is surrounded by quaking aspens. In summer its waters are well stocked with rainbow trout, offering anglers a decent place to cast. Campsites are quiet and shaded; some sites overlook the lake, and all are only a quick hike from the water. Other short marked hiking trails lead through forest to Oohwah Lake and Burro Pass high in the La Sal Mountains. Horses and mountain bikes are welcome on all trails.
Location: In Manti-La Sal National Forest; map B3, grid d7.
Campsites, facilities: There are 20 sites. Picnic tables, fire grills, vault toilets, and drinking water are available.
Reservations, fees: Campsites are $8 and can be reserved through the National Recreation Reservation Service at 877/444-6777.
Open: Memorial Day weekend–Oct., depending on the weather.
Directions: From Moab, drive eight miles south on Highway 191, looking for the sign to the La Sal Loop. Take the paved and then graveled road 16 miles east to the Warner Lake turnoff and continue six miles east to the campground.
Contact: Manti-La Sal National Forest, Moab Ranger District, 435/259-7155.

35 Oohwah Lake

    9

This camp should have you saying "Ooh" and "Aah," especially if you're looking to beat the desert heat in summer. Set at 8,800 feet in the La Sal Mountains, it's a pretty, cool spot amid forest near a small lake. Here you can fish for stocked rainbow trout, or follow a short, scenic hike to nearby Warner Lake. The trail is open to horses and mountain bikers alike.
Location: In Manti-La Sal National Forest; map B3, grid d7.
Campsites, facilities: There are six sites. Picnic tables, fire grills, and pit toilets are available, but there is no drinking water.
Reservations, fees: Campsites are free and are first come, first served.
Open: May 29–Oct. 1.
Directions: From Moab, drive eight miles south on Highway 191, looking for a sign for La Sal Loop. Take the paved and gravel road east to the junction with Forest Road 76. Follow the dirt Forest Road 76 approximately two miles to the campground.
Contact: Manti-La Sal National Forest, Moab Ranger District, 435/259-7155.

36 Pack Creek

     6

Whether you're up for rugged mountain biking or a relaxing round of golf, this camp, set between Moab's Spanish Valley Golf Course and the Slickrock Bike Trail, is for you. The campground is off Moab's main drag, so it tends to be quieter than other sites in the area. Tall trees shade the sites, and you can amble along Pack Creek, which runs through the property.
Location: In Moab; map B3, grid d5.
Campsites, facilities: There are 45 RV sites with full hookups and 17 tent sites. The campground has

restrooms, picnic tables, showers, laundry facilities, an RV waste-disposal site, and a playground.

Reservations, fees: Reservations are accepted. RV sites cost $16.50 and tent sites cost $10.

Open: Year-round.

Directions: Driving north on Highway 191, turn left on Spanish Trail Drive, then left again on Murphy Lane. The campground is in a quiet, residential part of town at 1520 Murphy Lane.

Contact: Pack Creek Campground, 1520 Murphy Ln. #10, Moab, UT 84532; 435/259-2982.

37 Canyonlands Campark

    4

Set in downtown Moab, this RV campground doesn't offer much of a wilderness experience, but it's close to shopping and restaurants. The pool and shaded sites make this an attractive choice during the hot summer months.

Location: In Moab; map B3, grid d5.

Campsites, facilities: The campground's 134 RV sites include 66 with full hookups and 34 with water and electricity. There are also 20 tent sites. Restrooms, showers, laundry facilities, a grocery and gift shop, a game room, barbecue grills, an RV waste-disposal site, a playground, a public phone, cable TV, and a pool are available. Pets are allowed.

Reservations, fees: Reservations are accepted. Full-hookup sites are $20, sites with water and electricity are $18, and tent sites are $15 for two people. Each additional person costs $3.

Open: Year-round.

Directions: Follow Highway 191 into Moab. The park is on the south side of Moab at 555 South Main Street.

Contact: Canyonlands Campark, 555 S. Main

St., Moab, UT 84532; 435/259-6848 or 800/522-6848.

38 Up the Creek Camp Park

   6

Here's a rarity—a park where campers can set up a tent for the night on a shaded, grassy spot without a single recreational vehicle in sight. If it's quiet you're seeking, this may be the place for you. Campsites are hike-in only and are set alongside Mill Creek. The trailhead to the Slickrock Bike Trail is about two miles away.

Location: In Moab; map B3, grid d5.

Campsites, facilities: There are 20 tent sites with picnic tables. Restrooms, showers, and a public phone are available. Dogs are welcome for a $2 fee.

Reservations, fees: Campsites are $10 and are first come, first served.

Open: March 20–Oct. 31.

Directions: Follow Highway 191 into downtown Moab, then turn east on 300 South. The campground is located at 210 East 300 South, behind City Market.

Contact: Up the Creek Camp Park, 435/259-2213.

39 Moab KOA

      7

This well-established, older campground is quiet, shaded, and one step removed from the hustle and bustle of the city. Rafting and canoeing are available along this stretch of the Colorado River. Check with the Bureau of Land Management for specifics. Nearby you'll find Moab's public, 18-hole Spanish Valley Golf Course and Ken's Lake, a popular fishing area stocked regularly with rainbow trout by the Utah Division of Wildlife Resources. For one of the most spectacular driving tours in the state, campers should take the nearby La Sal Mountain Loop.

Partially paved but negotiable by passenger car, this 65-mile road takes you from red-rock desert through piñon-forested foothills and into a cool alpine wonderland guarded by 12,000-foot-high peaks. Views of the sandstone cliffs and green Moab Valley below are truly a sight to behold.

Location: In Moab; map B3, grid d5.

Campsites, facilities: There are 50 RV sites with full hookups, and 45 tent sites. Picnic tables, camping cabins, fire grills, laundry facilities, showers, an RV waste-disposal site, a swimming pool, a game room, a family-style bathroom, a store, and a miniature golf course are also available.

Reservations, fees: Reservations are accepted. Campsites are $26.50 for two people. Additional people are $3 each. There are 22 cabins. The 18 one-room cabins are $40. The four two-room cabins are $48. Tents are $19.50.

Open: Mar.–Sept.

Directions: Follow Highway 191 to the southern outskirts of Moab. The park is located at 3225 South Highway 191.

Contact: Moab KOA, 3225 S. Hwy. 191, Moab, UT 84532; 435/259-9398 or 800/562-0372.

40 Dowd Flats RV Park

   8

Considering all the other campgrounds on public lands and in Moab, this place is a last choice. Campsites are mostly out in the open, but they enjoy good views of the La Sal Mountains. Rafting and canoeing are available along this stretch of the Colorado River. Check with the Bureau of Land Management for specifics.

Location: In Moab on Millcreek Drive; map B3, grid d6.

Campsites, facilities: There are 20 sites with water and electricity. A laundry facility, showers, and a few picnic tables are available.

Reservations, fees: Campsites are $15;

reservations are recommended in the busy season.

Open: Year-round.

Directions: From U.S. Highway 191 take Millcreek Drive east to the campground.

Contact: Dowd Flats RV Park, 1251 Millcreek Dr., Moab, UT; 435/259-3337.

41 Sand Flats

   8

This mostly open, primitive campground is next to the entrance to the Moab Slickrock Bike Trail, one of the nation's premier mountain-biking paths. The 10-mile marked loop is extremely difficult, but rewards physically fit bikers with scenic views over the Colorado River, beautiful red-rock canyons, and the surrounding La Sal Mountains. Before attempting the trail, try the two-mile practice loop to see if you're ready for the longer route. Juniper trees guard many of the sites here; others are nestled in small alcoves among the area's sandstone cliffs and petrified sand dunes.

Location: Near Moab; map B3, grid e6.

Campsites, facilities: There are 143 designated campsites with vault toilets. No drinking water is available.

Reservations, fees: All sites are first come, first served. The fee is $6 per vehicle for two people. Each additional person is $2.

Open: Year-round.

Directions: From Moab, drive three miles east on Sand Flats Road to the Sand Flats Recreation Area and the campground.

Contact: Bureau of Land Management, Moab, 435/259-6111.

42 Willow Flat

  8

With 527 square miles of rugged wilderness divided into four distinct "districts," Canyonlands National Park ranks among the more remote national parks in the Lower 48. This primitive camp is just off the pavement on the top of a plateau in the park's most accessible district, set in a piñon-juniper forest. The camp does tend to fill up, so arrive early in the day to secure a spot. Nearby you'll find panoramic views over Canyonlands' broad mesas and vertigo-inducing canyons. One of the best overlooks, Mesa Arch, is a half-mile hike from Willow Flat. The arch frames a deep canyon gorge with vistas of the often snow-capped La Sal Mountains in the distance. Other hiking trails lead to popular destinations such as Grandview Point, Whale Rock, and Upheaval Dome. Mountain bikers and four-wheel-drive enthusiasts enjoy the 100-mile White Rim Trail, which ventures into the red-rock canyon country that gives the park its name. Bring plenty of water—it's a scarce commodity in this part of Canyonlands National Park.

Location: In Island in the Sky District, Canyonlands National Park; map B3, grid e4.

Campsites, facilities: This primitive facility has 12 sites with picnic tables and vault toilets. No drinking water is available.

Reservations, fees: All campsites are $5 and are first come, first served. Backcountry camping is allowed in designated areas; a limited number of permits are issued to backpackers, mountain bikers, and four-wheel-drive enthusiasts. Reserve these sites well in advance through park headquarters.

Open: Year-round.

Directions: From Moab, drive 12 miles north on Highway 191 to State Route 313. Follow State Route 313 approximately 30 miles southwest to the campground.

Contact: Canyonlands National Park, 435/259-7164.

43 Dead Horse Point State Park

    9

Dead Horse Point State Park is relatively small, but it provides a fine jumping-off point to the hiking and mountain-biking trails in the northern part of Canyonlands National Park. Set 2,000 feet above the Colorado River on a pointed plateau surrounded by cliffs, it's a scenic spot in its own right, with overlooks providing views of the canyon below. According to park rangers, cowboys used to round up and corral wild mustangs on this jut of land; a few leapt to their deaths before they were caught (thus the area's colorful name). The quarter-mile long Dead Horse Point Nature Trail offers sweeping panoramas of the Canyonlands area and interpretive signs about the cliffrose, pygmy forest, desert varnish, stone staircases, and Mormon tea you'll encounter along the rim. Keep a close eye on children on the trail—drop-offs are steep. Since there's no water at Canyonlands National Park's Willow Flat campground, Dead Horse Point is a good alternative. Water is limited, however, so park managers ask RV owners to fill their water tanks before arriving.

Location: Near Canyonlands National Park; map B3, grid d5.

Campsites, facilities: There are 21 campsites with shaded picnic tables and tent pads. Facilities include a visitors center with a small museum, restrooms with hot and cold running water but no showers, a sewage-disposal station, a group camping area, a pavilion, and a large shelter.

Reservations, fees: Reservations can be made 120 days in advance by calling 800/322-3770 Mon.–Fri. 8 A.M.–5 P.M. A $6.50 nonrefundable reservation fee is charged for each site reserved. Campsites are $11. Utah residents 62 years and older with a Special Fun Tag receive a $2 discount Sun.–Thurs., excluding holidays.

Open: Year-round.

Directions: From Moab, drive 12 miles north on Highway 191 to State Route 313. Follow

State Route 313 approximately 22 miles southwest to the park entrance.

Contact: Dead Horse Point State Park, 435/259-2614.

Red Rock Restaurant and Campground

  3

This campground offers a little lawn and some young but fast-growing shade trees in downtown Hanksville, a remote desert town that you probably won't visit unless you're headed on the way to one of the fine outdoor attractions in the area—Goblin Valley State Park, Natural Bridges National Monument, Capitol Reef National Park, Lake Powell, Canyonlands National Park, or the Henry Mountains. The restaurant next door serves up the best food in town. You can also stop at the Bureau of Land Management's Hanksville office to take a short, self-guided tour of a restored gristmill.

Location: In Hanksville; map B3, grid e0.

Campsites, facilities: There are 65 sites with full hookups. A lawn area can accommodate 15 tents and vans. Laundry facilities, showers, restrooms, a public phone, ice, picnic tables, and a restaurant are available.

Reservations, fees: Reservations are accepted. Fees are $16 for full hookups, $12 for vans, and $10 for tent sites.

Open: Spring–fall, depending on demand.

Directions: The campground is on State Route 24, one block west of the junction of State Routes 24 and 95 in Hanksville.

Contact: Red Rock Restaurant and Campground, P. O. Box 55, Hanksville, UT 84734; 800/452-7971.

45 Jurassic Park

  3

Aside from views of the surrounding Henry Mountains, there's not much to recommend this fairly open RV park. You might stop here on the way from Capitol Reef National Park to Lake Powell and Natural Bridges National Monuments. While you're in town, visit the Bureau of Land Management's Hanksville office, which offers a short, self-guided tour of a restored gristmill.

Location: In Hanksville; map B3, grid e0.

Campsites, facilities: There are 17 RV sites and 20 tent sites. Picnic tables, fire pits, an RV waste-disposal station, restrooms, showers, and a public phone are available.

Reservations, fees: Reservations are accepted. Full-hookup sites are $15, partial hookups are $8, and tent sites are $12.

Open: Year-round.

Directions: The campground is in Hanksville, one block south of Center Street at 100 South Center.

Contact: Jurassic Park Campground, 100 S. Center, Hanksville, UT; 435/542-3433.

46 Hatch Point

  8

Although the better-developed campgrounds in this area tend to fill up fast, here you won't have to battle the crowds for a prime spot in red-rock canyon country. Nearby you'll find two beautiful overlooks onto the Needles District of Canyonlands National Park: the Needles Overlook, approximately 12 miles away, and the Anticline Overlook, approximately five miles north of the camp. You can hike to the scenic vistas or take a long drive to Moab or the entrance to Canyonlands to access four-wheel-drive roads in Lockhart Basin.

Location: Near Moab; map B3, grid e5.

Campsites, facilities: There are 10 sites. Vault toilets, drinking water, picnic tables, and fire grills are available. The maximum length for self-contained RVs is 24 feet.

Reservations, fees: Campsites are $10 and are first come, first served.

Open: Apr.–Sept.

Directions: From Moab, drive 32 miles south on Highway 191. Follow the BLM Canyon Rims Recreation Area Road 25 miles northwest to the camp.

Contact: Bureau of Land Management, Moab; 435/259-8193.

47 Windwhistle

  8

You won't encounter crowds at this mostly open Bureau of Land Management campground, a rarity for this part of popular southeastern Utah. Set on a high plateau at approximately 6,000 feet, the campground offers sweeping vistas of the surrounding country, especially the La Sal and Abajo Mountains. In winter, it snows here occasionally, and you must bring your own water. Not far from here you'll find two scenic viewpoints onto Canyonlands National Park's Needles District: Anticline and Needles Overlooks. If you want to venture to the national park to enjoy its hiking, mountain-biking, and four-wheel-drive recreation opportunities, you must drive 45 minutes each way.

Location: Near Moab; map B3, grid f5.

Campsites, facilities: There are 17 sites. Drinking water, vault toilets, picnic tables, and fire grills are available.

Reservations, fees: Campsites are $10 and are first come, first served.

Open: Year-round, with no water mid-Oct.–mid-Apr.

Directions: From Moab, drive 32 miles south on Highway 191. Look for the BLM Canyon Rims Recreation Area Road, and follow it five miles west to the campground.

Contact: Bureau of Land Management, Moab; 801/259-8193.

48 Needles Outpost

  9

A good alternative to the popular Squaw Flat campground in Canyonlands National Park's Needles District, this camp is set just outside of the park entrance. Many sites here are nestled in a juniper forest and bordered by red-rock cliffs. Although you won't get views of the national park itself, the scenic spires for which the Needles District is named are visible from most campsites.

Location: Near the Needles District of Canyonlands National Park; map B3, grid f4.

Campsites, facilities: There are 23 RV sites without hookups and 26 tent sites. Showers, restrooms, an RV waste-disposal site, a grocery and gift shop, gasoline, four-by-four rentals, and scenic airplane charters are available. A snack bar is open 9 A.M.–4 P.M in the summer.

Reservations, fees: Reservations are recommended. Campsites are $15.

Open: Mar. 19–Oct. 31.

Directions: From Moab, follow Highway 191 south 40 miles to State Route 211. Head 35 miles west on State Route 211. The campground is just outside Canyonlands National Park, near the entrance to the Needles District of the park.

Contact: Needles Outpost, P. O. Box 1349, Moab, UT 84532; 435/979-4007 or 435/259-8545.

49 Indian Creek

   8

When Indian Creek is running, this can be a fine spot to take a splash on a hot day. Some of the sites are shaded, and the camp is within walking distance of the creek and a small waterfall. It is also located at the start of a popular but rugged four-wheel-drive and mountain-biking road. Canyonlands National Park is four miles away.

Location: Near the Needles District of Canyonlands National Park; map B3, grid f4.

Campsites, facilities: There are two campsites with picnic tables and pit toilets. No drinking water is available.

Reservations, fees: Campsites are free and are first come, first served.

Open: Year-round.

Directions: From Moab, follow Highway 191 south 40 miles to State Route 211. Head approximately 33 miles west on State Route 211. Look for Lockhart Basin Road on the north (right) side of the road. Follow this dirt road approximately 2.5 miles north to the campground.

Contact: Bureau of Land Management, Monticello; 435/587-2141.

50 Hamburger Rock

 8

The sandstone Hamburger Rock is approximately four to five acres in size. Sites at this unusual little campground are cut into the rock itself, providing protection from desert winds. The setting is rugged red-rock country, and much of it is dry and desolate, but the views of nearby Abajo or Blue Mountain offer glimpses of green. The dirt road beyond the campground is a popular four-wheel-drive and mountain-biking route.

Location: Near the Needles District of Canyonlands National Park; map B3, grid f4.

Campsites, facilities: There are eight campsites. Picnic tables and vault toilets are available, but there is no drinking water.

Reservations, fees: Campsites are free and are first come, first served.

Open: Year-round.

Directions: From Moab, follow Highway 191 south 40 miles to State Route 211. Head approximately 33 miles west on State Route 211. Look for Lockhart Basin Road on the north (right) side of the road. Follow this dirt

road approximately 1.5 miles north to the campground.

Contact: Bureau of Land Management, Monticello; 435/587-2141.

51 Squaw Flat

 10

Canyonlands' Needles District is one of the more visitor-friendly sections of this remote and rugged national park. From here, short hikes lead to wonderful sights such as Pothole Point, a pocked, petrified sand dune full of potholes, some of which hold water. Another trail winds toward Cave Spring, where an old cowboy line camp can be viewed. Longer day hikes, such as the Chessler Park Trail, lead through narrow slot canyons. The camp is also close to the Elephant Hill and Salt Creek four-wheel-drive routes, among the most famous, and difficult, four-wheel-drive roads in the country. Popular with mountain bikers and four-wheelers, the Squaw Flat campground tends to fill early in the day, especially during peak season. Surrounding the camp you'll see slickrock formations—sandstone that looks as though a sand dune has been petrified in place, leaving hard, slick, rolling hills. It's textured enough for great rock scrambling, yet smooth enough for kids to play on. Campsites are spaced a good distance from one another, and many are near sandstone overhangs. In the summer park rangers lead evening campfire programs.

Location: In the Needles District of Canyonlands National Park; map B3, grid f4.

Campsites, facilities: There are 26 sites with picnic tables and fire grills. Drinking water is available at a tank next to the restrooms. Group sites are available. The maximum RV length is 20 feet.

Reservations, fees: Most campsites are $10 and are first come, first served.

Group sites, backcountry four-wheel-drive sites, and backpacking sites can be reserved by calling park headquarters.

Open: Year-round.

Directions: From Moab, follow Highway 191 south 40 miles to State Route 211. Head 37 miles west on State Route 211. Follow signs from the park entrance station to the campground.

Contact: Canyonlands National Park, 435/719-2313.

Newspaper Rock

 7

You'll find a grove of cottonwood trees along a small stream at this campground, although in periods of extreme drought the creek runs dry. The Native American rock-writing panel near this campground is one of the most impressive in the Southwest, with rock writings up to 1,500 years old. Technical rock-climbers will find challenging routes nearby. Camping is not recommended during times of heavy rains because the area sits in a flood plain.

Location: Near Monticello; map B3, grid f5.

Campsites, facilities: There are eight campsites with picnic tables and vault toilets. No drinking water is available.

Reservations, fees: Campsites are free and are first come, first served.

Open: Year-round.

Directions: From Monticello, drive about 12 miles north on Highway 191 to State Route 211. Follow State Route 211 west for 12 miles to the camp.

Contact: Bureau of Land Management, Monticello; 435/587-2141.

Dalton Springs

 8

Dalton Springs is another good summertime spot to cool off from the prickly desert heat.

Set at 8,400 feet, this mountain campground is shaded by pines and aspens. You can fish for rainbow trout at tiny Foy and Monticello Lakes, both of which are a 10-minute drive away. Canyonlands National Park is roughly a half-hour-drive away from the campground. Horseback riding trails are available in the Manti-La Sal National Forest.

Location: In Manti-La Sal National Forest; map B3, grid g6.

Campsites, facilities: There are 16 campsites for tents, trailers, and RVs. Picnic tables, fire grills, and vault toilets are available. Call the Monticello Ranger District to inquire if drinking water is available.

Reservations, fees: All sites are first come, first served. The fee is $7 per night when water is on, $5 when it's not.

Open: June–Sept.

Directions: From Monticello, drive approximately five miles west on Forest Road 105 to the campground.

Contact: Manti-La Sal National Forest, Monticello Ranger District; 435/587-2041.

Buckboard

 8

Set on a scenic loop a half hour from the Needles District of Canyonlands National Park, this high-alpine campground is a good place to escape the summer desert heat. The Abajo Mountains tower above the camp, and below it you can see beautiful red-rock country. Anglers head to little Foy and Monticello Lakes, both a 10-minute drive away, to try for rainbow trout. In surrounding Manti-La Sal National Forest, horses are welcome on trails through meadows and pine forest.

Location: In Manti-La Sal National Forest; map B3, grid g6.

Campsites, facilities: There are 13 sites for tents and RVs. Vault toilets, picnic tables, and fire grills are available. Call the Monticello Ranger District to inquire if water is available. The camp may not be suitable for large trailers.

Reservations, fees: All sites are first come, first served. Reservations can be made for two sites with the National Recreation Reservation Service at 877/444-6777. The fee is $7 per night when water is on; sites are free when the water is off.

Open: June–Sept.

Directions: From Monticello, drive approximately 6.5 miles west on Forest Road 105 to the campground.

Contact: Manti-La Sal National Forest, Monticello Ranger District; 435/587-2041.

55 Westerner RV Park

  5

You'll find shaded, grassy campsites here, and right next door is the pretty, nine-hole San Juan County Golf Course. A public swimming pool is in the neighborhood; inquire at the camp office. Monticello is a decent central location for exploring the region—Arches, Canyonlands, and Mesa Verde National Parks, as well as Hovenweep National Monument, are all within a day's drive. Also close are Natural Bridges National Monument, Monument Valley, the Goosenecks of the San Juan River, and Lake Powell.

Location: In Monticello; map B3, grid g6.

Campsites, facilities: This park has 28 sites with full hookups, laundry facilities, showers, picnic tables, and an RV waste-disposal station.

Reservations, fees: Reservations are accepted. The fee is $17, $14 if hookups are not used.

Open: Apr.–Dec.

Directions: The campground is on the south end of Monticello on Highway 191, adjacent to the public golf course.

Contact: Westerner RV Park, Box 371, Monticello, UT 84535; 435/587-2762.

56 Mountain View RV Park

 5

With Canyonlands National Park's Squaw Flat campground filling almost every night, this is a good place to beat the crowds. It's approximately a 45-minute drive from the national park. Consider driving into the nearby Blue Mountains, where you can fish for rainbow trout at little Foy and Monticello Lakes. If you want to golf nine holes, Monticello's San Juan County Golf Course is open to the public.

Location: In Monticello; map B3, grid g7.

Campsites, facilities: There are 30 RV sites; 12 are back-in sites with full hookups, the rest are pull throughs. There are also six tent sites. Restrooms, showers, an RV waste-disposal station, laundry facilities, barbecue grills for rent, cable TV, a play area with horseshoes, and a fenced pet area are available.

Reservations, fees: Reservations are recommended in summer; those with reservations must arrive by 7 P.M. to keep their places. RV sites are $17.75; tent sites are $12. A charge of $3 is added for each person in groups larger than two.

Open: Year-round.

Directions: Follow Highway 191 one mile north of its intersection with Highway 666 in Monticello.

Contact: Mountain View RV Park, P. O. Box 910, Monticello, UT 84535; 435/587-2974.

57 Hite

     9

The second-largest man-made lake in the United States, Lake Powell encompasses nearly 2,000 miles of shoreline surrounded by towering sandstone cliffs. It's a primitive, spectacular setting, and folks flock here on weekends to boat, fish, swim, water-ski, and lounge beside the deep blue water. The lake is a powerboater's paradise. Anglers cast for smallmouth, largemouth, and striped bass. The wildest whitewater trip in Utah, a three- to five-day excursion through Cataract Canyon, begins upriver in Moab and ends here. The campground offers beautiful views of the surrounding area and good access to the lake, with some leveled gravel spots and other spaces cut into the sandstone. Tenters may want to escape the crowds and set up camp at one of the side canyons within 10 minutes of the main area near the lake shore. A marina, gas station, and small store are approximately one mile away.

Location: On Lake Powell, in Glen Canyon National Recreation Area; map B3, grid g2.

Campsites, facilities: Hundreds of dispersed campsites surround the large cement boat ramp near the edge of the water with a few scattered picnic tables. There are a few level spots for RVs. A restroom with cold water and flush toilets is available near the top of the boat ramp.

Reservations, fees: Camping is $6 and sites are first come, first served.

Open: Year-round.

Directions: Hite campground on State Route 95, 45 miles southeast of Hanksville on the northern edge of Lake Powell.

Contact: Glen Canyon National Recreation Area, Page, Arizona; 602/645-8200.

Starr Springs

 8

Set in a patch of oak trees, this campground is a cooler and quieter alternative to the Hite campground, the often crowded Lake Powell destination. Starr Springs has been used as a watering hole for livestock and wildlife since pioneers first settled the area in the late 1800s. A short hiking trail offers visitors views of Mount Hillers and the surrounding

area. Equestrians can explore the open land leading to the Henry Mountains or journey down into the painted desert.

Location: On the east side of the Henry Mountains; map B3, grid g0.

Campsites, facilities: There are 12 campsites. Vault toilets, picnic tables, fire grills, and drinking water are available (be advised—the water is not approved for human use).

Reservations, fees: Campsites are $4 and are first come, first served.

Open: Jan.–Oct.

Directions: From Hanksville, drive approximately 21 miles east on State Route 95. Take the turnoff to the Bullfrog Marina at the Glen Canyon National Recreation Area and State Route 278. The well-marked turnoff to the campground is in approximately 18 miles.

Contact: Bureau of Land Management, Hanksville; 435/542-3461.

Nizhoni

 8

This scenic, forested camp serves as a trailhead for a short, fascinating trail to the ruins of an Anasazi cliff dwelling. Hikers will find other short trails in the area as well. The town of Blanding is home to Edge of the Cedars State Park, which has a self-guided, quarter-mile walk through a restored cliff dwelling. Kids especially enjoy crawling down a ladder and into a restored kiva, an ancient, circular ceremonial room used by the Anasazi. The park's excellent museum features ancient pottery, figurines, and a slide show about the culture of the Fremont, Navajo, and Ute Indians, as well as the Mormon settlers.

Location: In Manti-La Sal National Forest; map B3, grid g5.

Campsites, facilities: There are 21 campsites. Vault toilets, drinking water, picnic tables, and fire grills are available.

Reservations, fees: Campsites are $7 and are first come, first served. Reservations can be made through the National Recreation Reservation Service at 877/444-6777.

Open: May 15–Oct. 30.

Directions: From Blanding, drive approximately six miles north on Forest Road 95 to Manti-La Sal National Forest. Continue straight on Forest Road 95 four miles to a fork in the road. Bear left to the campground.

Contact: Manti-La Sal National Forest, Monticello Ranger District, 435/587-2041.

60 Devil's Canyon

    9

Perched in the cool Blue Mountains, this is one of the better public campgrounds in southeastern Utah. Pines, fir, and some juniper trees shade most of the campsites, which are spaced far apart from one another, offering privacy. The short Devil's Canyon Nature Trail features interpretive signs detailing the natural history of the area. A few miles to the south, boaters, anglers, and rafters enjoy the deep blue water of lovely Recapture Reservoir, which is set among red hills and a piñon-juniper forest.

Location: In Manti-La Sal National Forest; map B3, grid g6.

Campsites, facilities: There are 33 campsites for tents and RVs. Picnic tables, fire grills, vault toilets, drinking water, and group-camping areas are available.

Reservations, fees: Call the National Recreation Reservation Service at 877/444-6777 for reservations. The fee is $10.

Open: May–Oct.

Directions: From Blanding, drive 9.5 miles northeast on Highway 191. Look for a signed turnoff to the campground on the west (left) side of the road.

Contact: Monticello Ranger District, 435/587-2041.

61 Natural Bridges

  9

You can explore this monument in a quick one-hour drive, or spend a day or two relaxing in its spectacular red-rock setting. The nine-mile Bridge View Road loop brings you to overlooks of the park's three natural rock bridges. The largest, Sipapu Bridge, stands 220 feet high and spans 268 feet. A fun 1.2-mile round-trip hike involves climbing down stairs and ladders. Kachina Bridge, 210 feet high and 204 feet across, is a 1.5-mile round-trip trek. A short and easy stroll brings you to the smallest of the trio, 106-foot-high, 180-foot-long Owachoma Bridge. The small campground here has a quiet feel to it. Shaded by piñon trees and at 6,500 feet elevation, it's a good place to beat the summer heat. The camp tends to fill up in the late afternoon, although rangers sometimes allow self-contained RVs and trailers to park at the visitors center. A small museum features displays on Native American history, solar power, and the formation of the natural bridges.

Location: In Natural Bridges National Monument; map B3, grid h3.

Campsites, facilities: There are 13 campsites for tents and RVs. Picnic tables, fire grills, and vault toilets are available. Drinking water and restrooms with flush toilets can be found at the visitors center, a quarter mile away from the campground. The maximum RV length is 21 feet. Longer vehicles are occasionally allowed to use an overflow area; check with the visitors center for details.

Reservations, fees: Campsites are $10 and are first come, first served.

Open: Year-round.

Directions: From Blanding, drive 38 miles west on State Route 95. The campground is just north of State Route 95, a quarter mile from the monument visitors center.

Contact: Natural Bridges National Monument, 435/259-5174.

Blanding Kampark

     5

This city RV park is close to a pretty lake, Anasazi ruins, and a fascinating museum. The nearby Dinosaur Museum is more than just a roadside attraction. Its curators served as technical advisors on Steven Spielberg's *Jurassic Park*, and its exhibit on dinosaur skin is among the best you'll see anywhere. A five-minute drive north of town, beautiful Recapture Reservoir offers plenty of room for boaters, canoeists, and water-skiers. Anglers can fish here for stocked rainbow trout. (For details on the restored Anasazi cliff dwelling and museum at nearby Edge of the Cedars State Park, see the Nizhoni listing, page 242).

Location: In Blanding; map B3, grid h6.

Campsites, facilities: There are 53 RV sites with full hookups and 16 tent sites. Restrooms, showers, picnic tables, laundry facilities, an RV waste-disposal site, a grocery and gift store, barbecue pits, and two public phones are available. Leashed pets are permitted.

Reservations, fees: Reservations are accepted. Full hookups are $14; tent sites are $10 for two people. Each additional person is $3.

Open: Year-round.

Directions: The campground is at the southern end of Blanding at 861 South Main Street.

Contact: Blanding Kampark, 435/678-2770.

Square Tower

   8

The monument centers on an unusual Anasazi-ruin complex featuring square and circular towers, cliff dwellings, and ancient petroglyphs. Some of the ruins date back more than 1,000 years. After checking in at the ranger station for directions, you can drive to the dispersed sites or enjoy a two-mile, self-guided hike on the Square Tower Trail. Due to the high elevation, the camp can be cold in the winter. Before driving a long way, call ahead and make sure it is open.

Location: In Hovenweep National Monument; map B3, grid i8.

Campsites, facilities: There are 31 campsites for RVs and tents. A restroom (with running cold water but no showers), fire grills, and picnic tables are available.

Reservations, fees: Campsites are $10 and are first come, first served.

Open: Year-round. Call Mesa Verde National Park at 303/529-4461 to confirm it's open before heading out.

Directions: From the tiny town of Aneth, follow the signs 20 miles north on a paved and dirt road.

Contact: Hovenweep National Park, 970/749-0510 (cell) or 435/459-4344 (within Utah).

Sand Island

 6

Set along a gentle stretch of the San Juan River, this camp is a popular spot to start canoeing and kayaking trips. You'll encounter a few small rapids, but most of the water can be navigated by beginners. A short hike from camp leads to an Anasazi rock-art panel that dates back 1,500 years.

Location: Near Bluff, on the San Juan River; map B3, grid i6.

Campsites, facilities: This 27-site campground features vault toilets, picnic tables, and a boat launch. No drinking water is available.

Reservations, fees: Campsites are $6 and are first come, first served.

Open: Year-round.

Directions: From Bluff, drive approximately three miles west on Highway 191 to the campground on the San Juan River.

Contact: Bureau of Land Management, 435/587-2141.

Cottonwood RV Park

  7

This campground is out in the open in a hot part of the state, but it's a block off the highway, which cuts down on the noise. Bluff is a good place to start San Juan River trips.

Location: Located in Bluff, off of Highway 191: map B3, grid d6.

Campsites, facilities: There are 23 sites and 25 tent sites. The campground has restrooms, showers, water, and a dump station.

Reservations, fees: Pull-through sites with hookups are $16. Back-in sites are $14. RV sites with no hook-ups and tent sites are $10. Groups larger than two must pay $3 extra per person.

Open: March –Oct.

Directions: Main Street 3rd West. Bluff is reached by taking I-70 to Crescent Junction. Take 191 South for 131 miles.

Contact: Cottonwood RV Park, 435/672-2287.

Cadillac Ranch

 4

Bluff is a tiny, pretty town on the edge of Monument Valley. You'll find some Navajo stands where you can purchase Native American jewelry. There's not much else around here aside from a few stores and restaurants. Anglers can cast for trout, bass, catfish, and bluegill at a pond on Cadillac Ranch. No state fishing license is required, and there's no extra charge to fish.

Location: In Bluff; map B3, grid i6.

Campsites, facilities: There are 17 RV sites with full hookups and 10 tent sites. Restrooms, showers, picnic tables, an RV waste-

disposal site, and firewood and fire grills are available. Paddleboats are also available for use on the camp's pond.

Reservations, fees: Reservations are accepted. Campsites are $16.

Open: Year-round.

Directions: The campground is on Highway 191 at the east end of Bluff.

Contact: Cadillac Ranch, P. O. Box 157, Bluff, UT 84512; 435/672-2262 or 800/538-6195.

Turquoise

 6

Bluff stands on the edge of Monument Valley. It's a rugged, scenic spot, and it offers a few small shops and restaurants. Look for Native American jewelry in the area.

Location: In Bluff; map B3, grid i6.

Campsites, facilities: There are 10 RV sites with full hookups and picnic tables.

Reservations, fees: Reservations are a must. Each site is $15.

Open: Year-round.

Directions: The campground is on the corner of Highway 191 and Fifth Street West in the center of Bluff.

Contact: Turquoise, P. O. Box 66, Bluff, UT 84512; 435/672-2219.

Goosenecks State Park

  9

The big draw here is the view. Visitors look down a 1,000-foot chasm at a place where the meandering San Juan River has cut "goosenecks" in the park's red-rock terrain. As it zigs and zags through the towering canyon walls, five miles of the river cover a distance of only one linear mile. The effect is, simply put, amazing. For hiking and backpacking trips, visit the Bureau of Land Management's Grand Gulch Primitive Area, approximately 30 miles away.

Try a day hike to Junction Ruin, an Anasazi cliff dwelling; the trail begins at the Kane Gulch Ranger Station, just off State Route 261.

Location: Near Mexican Hat; map B3, grid j3.

Campsites, facilities: There are four campsites with picnic tables and vault toilets. No water is available.

Reservations, fees: Camping is free and sites are first come, first served.

Open: Year-round.

Directions: From Mexican Hat, drive approximately three miles north on State Route 163. Turn north onto State Route 261 and drive approximately one mile. Follow signs on State Route 318 to the park.

Contact: Edge of the Cedars State Park, Blanding; 435/678-2238.

69 Burches Trading Post

 6

Nestled in rugged, pretty red-rock country, this city campground adjoins a motel-restaurant complex. For $7 per person, you can take a horseback ride to view the unusually balanced rock formation that gives Mexican Hat its name, or a trip along the San Juan River. The river is approximately half a mile from the camp, and it's a good place to set off on a short rafting trip.

Location: In Mexican Hat; map B3, grid j8.

Campsites, facilities: There are six RV sites with full hookups. Restrooms, showers, picnic tables, laundry facilities, a grocery and gift shop, a public phone, and an RV waste-disposal site are also available. The Trading Post also has a restaurant and motel. Drinking water can be purchased at the store.

Reservations, fees: Reservations are accepted. Campsites are $10–15.

Open: Year-round.

Directions: The campground is in the southeastern Utah town of Mexican Hat on State Route 163.

Contact: Burches Trading Post, P. O. Box 310337, Mexican Hat, UT 84531; 435/683-2221.

70 Valles Trailer Park

 6

Mexican Hat is a scenic little town surrounded by red-rock terrain. It's the gateway to spectacular Monument Valley, where John Wayne swaggered through many classic Westerns. The campground is a bleak place in the middle of great scenery. River-rafters can float the San Juan, which runs near town. Visitors should consider side trips to Four Corners Monument and Hovenweep National Monument, which feature hiking trails among Anasazi ruins.

Location: In Mexican Hat; map B3, grid j3.

Campsites, facilities: There are 18 RV sites with full hookups and eight tent sites. Restrooms, showers, laundry facilities, picnic tables, a grocery and gift shop, barbecue grills, a public phone, and an RV waste-disposal station are available.

Reservations, fees: Reservations are recommended in the summer months. The fee is $14 for two people. Each additional adult is $5.

Open: Year-round.

Directions: The campground is at the north end of Mexican Hat on Highway 163.

Contact: Valles Trailer Park, P. O. Box 310216, Mexican Hat, UT 84531; 435/683-2226.

71 Mitten View

 10

A surreal and beautiful region, Monument Valley features high sandstone monoliths rising from the desert floor like ships stranded on an ocean of sand. Pick up a brochure for the self-guided drive through the area at the park entrance. The dirt road runs 17 miles round-trip, with 11 numbered stops at highlights such as Elephant and Camel Buttes, Totem Pole, and the Mittens Rock formations. Horseback riding concessionaires are available in the parking lot at the Tribal Park. Survey the area from John Ford Point, where the director filmed classic Westerns such as *Stagecoach* and *The Searchers*. There is a snack shop and gift shop at the visitors center. Guided tours of Monument Valley, other restricted areas, and Mystery Valley are available from vendors in the visitors-center parking lot. A three-hour Monument Valley tour costs $20 per person. It takes eight hours to see Monument Valley, Mystery Valley, and the restricted areas.

Location: In Monument Valley; map B3, grid j3.

Campsites, facilities: There are 29 RV sites with no hookups, nine pull-through sites, 38 tent sites, and nine group areas for six or more people. No water is available, but there are coin-operated showers, restrooms, picnic tables, and an RV waste-disposal station. Drinking water must be purchased at Goulding's Trading Post or in Mexican Hat.

Reservations, fees: Reservations for groups of 10 or more are required. All other sites are first come, first served. RV and tent sites are $10, group sites are $20.

Open: Year-round, except for Christmas Day, New Year's Day, and a half day on Thanksgiving.

Directions: The campground is on Highway 163, 24 miles from Kayenta and eight miles from Goulding's Trading Post. Visitors must enter the Navajo Tribal Park before they reach the campground. The fee to enter the Tribal Park is $2.50 per person ages 8–59 and $1 for those over 60.

Contact: Mitten View Campground, P. O. Box 360289, Monument Valley, UT 84536; 435/727-3353.

72 Goulding's Monument Valley Campground

 9

Set on the edge of Monument Valley, this camp is adjacent to a trading post originally built in the 1920s. It's got all the amenities, and you can't beat the proximity to world-famous Monument Valley. Here you can follow the driving tour and try to identify places where John Ford filmed his famous Westerns. The nearby trip to the Four Corners Monument—the only place where you can stand in four states at the same time—is especially fun for children. Horseback riding concessionaires are available in the parking lot at the Tribal Park.

Location: In Monument Valley; map B3, grid j3.

Campsites, facilities: There are 66 sites, 42 with full hookups and 24 pull-throughs. There are also 40 tent sites. Camping cabins, restrooms, showers, an RV waste-disposal station, laundry facilities, a public phone, groceries, ice, picnic tables, and fire grills are also available. There is a recreation room, coin games, a playground, and a hiking trail.

Reservations, fees: Reservations are recommended June–Sept. Full hookups are $23.98; tent sites are $15.26 for two people. There is a $3 charge for each additional person above the age of six.

Open: Mar. 15–Oct. 31.

Directions: Follow Highway 163 to Monument Valley. The campground is 2.25 miles west on Monument Valley Road off of Highway 163.

Contact: Goulding's Monument Valley Campground, P. O. Box 360002, Monument Valley, UT 84536; 435/727-3280.

RESOURCE GUIDE

National Forests

Utah's six national forests cover 8.2 million acres, most of which are located in high alpine regions. They provide thousands of campsites, prime fishing spots, the bulk of the state's designated wilderness, and land for the majority of Utah's downhill ski resorts.

Some, such as Wasatch-Cache and Uinta, are situated near heavily populated areas, offering thousands of urbanites a quiet retreat. Others, including the more remote Ashley, Dixie, Fishlake, and Manti-La Sal, are in primarily rural settings where campers and outdoor recreation enthusiasts share the land with ranchers and other agricultural interests.

The Wasatch-Cache National Forest, which encompasses most of the mountainous areas from Salt Lake County north to the Utah-Idaho border along the Wasatch Front, manages 1.2 million acres. Some of the state's most popular ski areas, including Alta, Snowbird, Brighton, Solitude, Snowbasin, and Beaver Mountain, are on these lands. Canyons to the east and north of urban population centers such as Salt Lake City, Ogden, and Logan provide city dwellers with a welcome break from urban life. Also within the forest boundaries are the Mount Olympus, Twin Peaks, Mount Naomi, and Wellsville Mountain Wilderness Areas, plus most of Lone Peak and half of the High Uintas. Campers and anglers especially enjoy the dozens of camping spots and fishing areas along Utah Highway 150 between Kamas and Evanston, Wyoming, known by locals as the Mirror Lake Highway.

The 947,000-acre Uinta National Forest also serves as a major urban recreation area for campers, anglers, and hikers. Located east of Utah County in Wasatch County, this forest contains two wilderness areas: Mount Nebo and Mount Timpanogos, as well as dozens of developed sites, many of which have been refurbished in recent years. The huge Strawberry Reservoir recreation complex, which includes a visitors center, several large campgrounds, boat-launching ramps, and day-use areas, is one of Utah's most important Forest Service recreation sites thanks to the reservoir's reputation as one of the nation's top trout fisheries. There are excellent horse-camping areas in Payson Canyon's Blackhawk facility and at Currant Creek Reservoir. The Alpine Loop Drive, which connects Provo and American Fork Canyons, and the Nebo Loop Drive, which connects the towns of Payson and Nephi, are among Utah's most popular fall destinations.

Covering 1.4 million acres, Ashley National Forest in northeastern Utah offers contrasting styles of recreation. The huge Flaming Gorge National Recreation Area provides every type of facility a camper could need, including marinas, boat-in campsites, highly developed campgrounds, beaches, geology tours of the Flaming Gorge Dam, a national recreation trail, and two large visitors centers. By contrast, less-developed and more primitive areas are located on the edge of Ashley's half of the High Uintas Wilderness Area, slow-paced spots like Spirit Lake, Moon Lake, White Rocks Canyon, Rock Creek Canyon, and Upper Stillwater Reservoir.

Utah's largest forest at nearly two million acres, Dixie National Forest in southern Utah provides an alpine alternative near Zion and Bryce Canyon National Parks, as well as some of the more remote country in the state. Elevations vary greatly, from as low as 2,800 feet near St. George to 11,322-foot Blue Bell Knoll on the remote Boulder Mountain north of Escalante. The Pine Valley Mountains, Ashdown Gorge, and Box Death Hollow Wilderness Areas are also found within the forest boundaries. Some of the best developed campgrounds include those in the Pine Valley area surrounding a small fishing lake; near Panguitch Lake, a popular fishing resort; in the Boulder Mountain area near some popular fishing lakes; and in the spectacular Red Canyon near the entrance to Bryce Canyon National Park. The forest also leases land to the Brian Head Ski Resort, the largest downhill resort in southern Utah. Forestlands in the area also offer excellent cross-country skiing and mountain-biking trails.

Fishlake National Forest, covering 1.5 million acres, is located in a more rural part of central Utah and features 19 campgrounds. The most developed are around Fish Lake, a popular fishing and resort area south of Salina. Anglers often fill beautiful campgrounds situated in pines and quaking aspens on busy summer weekends, enjoying both the scenery and the famous catches of trout and yellow perch. The popular Paiute ATV Trail, one of the longest developed motorized trails of its kind in the country, stretches across the Pahvant Range. The Great Western Trail near Fish Lake also offers good snowmobiling, all-terrain vehicle riding, and horseback riding.

Portions of 1.3-million-acre Manti-La Sal National Forest can be found in southeastern Utah. The La Sal Mountains, near Arches National Park, and the Blue or Abajo Mountains, near Canyonlands National Park, offer alpine camping and hiking alternatives to the blazing deserts of the slickrock parks. Dark Canyon Wilderness, west of Monticello, contains many Anasazi cliff-dwelling sites. The other major portion of this forest is on the Wasatch Plateau, which separates the towns of Manti and Ephraim on the west and Castle Dale, Ferron, and Huntington on the east. Skyline Drive, which stretches from Salina to Spanish Fork Canyon, offers one of the state's most popular four-wheel-drive adventures, especially in the fall when the leaves are changing color.

Campers wishing to use undeveloped campsites should first check with the forest supervisor's office or one of the district offices listed below to obtain a travel plan. Due to damage from overuse, Utah's national forest managers are increasingly restricting camping on undeveloped sites and encouraging use of more developed areas. Many, but not all, developed campgrounds can be reserved for a nonrefundable $8.60 reservation fee by calling the U.S. Forest Service National Reservation System at 800/280-CAMP (800/280-2267).

You are permitted to bring your dog into most national forests without paying an extra charge. The exception is Big and Little Cottonwood Canyons in Salt Lake County, where dogs are banned in order to protect Salt Lake City's water supply.

Maps of national forests are available from forest supervisor offices and district ranger offices. They can also be obtained by contacting the Wasatch National Forest Supervisor's Office in Salt Lake City at 125 South State Street, Salt Lake City, UT 84138; 801/524-3900. There is a small charge for the maps, between $6 and $7. For more detailed maps, contact the U.S. Geological Survey or one of the private map companies listed on page 257.

Stopping by a ranger district office before visiting a forest is a good idea. When addresses aren't given in the following list, it means that the town is very small and the Forest Service district office is clearly marked and easy to find.

ASHLEY NATIONAL FOREST

Headquarters:
Ashton Energy Center
355 North Vernal Ave.
Vernal, UT 84078
435/789-1181

RANGER DISTRICTS:

Duchesne Ranger District
85 West Main Street
(P. O. Box 981)
Duchesne, UT 84021
435/738-2482

Flaming Gorge Headquarters
P. O. Box 279
Manila, UT 84046
435/784-3445

Flaming Gorge Dutch John Office
P. O. Box 157
Dutch John, UT 84023
435/781-5240

Roosevelt Ranger District
244 West Highway 40
(P. O. Box 333-6)
Roosevelt, UT 84066
435/722-5018

Vernal Ranger District
Ashton Energy Center
355 North Vernal Avenue
Vernal, UT 84078
435/789-0323

DIXIE NATIONAL FOREST

Headquarters:
82 North 100 East
Cedar City, UT 84721-0580
435/865-3700

RANGER DISTRICTS:

Cedar City Ranger District
82 North 100 East
(P. O. Box 627)
Cedar City, UT 84720
435/865-3700

Escalante Ranger District
755 West Main Street
(P. O. Box 246)
Escalante, UT 84726
435/826-5400

Pine Valley Ranger District
196 East Tabernacle Street
St. George, UT 84770
435/688-3246

Powell Ranger District
225 East Center
(P. O. Box 80)
Panguitch, UT 84759
435/676-8815

Teasdale Ranger District
P. O. Box 99
Teasdale, UT 84773
435/425-3435

FISHLAKE NATIONAL FOREST

Headquarters:
115 East, 900 South
Richfield, UT 84701
435/896-9233

RANGER DISTRICTS:

Beaver Ranger District
575 South Main Street
(P. O. Box E)
Beaver, UT 84713
435/836-2436

Fillmore Ranger District
390 South Main Street
Fillmore, UT 84631
435/743-5721

Loa Ranger District
138 South Main Street
(P. O. Box 129)
Loa, UT 84747
435/836-2811

Richfield Ranger District
670 North Main Street
Richfield, UT 84701
435/896-4491

MANTI-LA SAL NATIONAL FOREST

Headquarters:
599 West Price River Drive
Price, UT 84501
435/637-2817

RANGER DISTRICTS:

Ferron Ranger District
115 West Canyon Road
(P. O. Box 310)
Ferron, UT 84523
435/384-2372

Moab Ranger District
2290 South West Resource Boulevard
(P. O. Box 386)
Moab, UT 84532
435/259-7155

Monticello Ranger District
496 East Central Street
(P. O. Box 820)
Monticello, UT 84535
435/587-2114

Price Ranger District
599 West Price Drive
Price, UT 84501
435/637-2816

Sanpete Ranger District
540 North Main Street
(P. O. Box 32-14)
Ephraim, UT 84627
435/283-4151

UINTA NATIONAL FOREST

Uinta Supervisor's Office
88 West 100 North
(P. O. Box 1428)
Provo, UT 84603
801/377-5780

RANGER DISTRICTS:

Heber Ranger District
2460 South Highway 40
(P. O. Box 190)
Heber City, UT 84032
435/654-0470

Pleasant Grove Ranger District
390 North 100 East
(P. O. Box 228)
Pleasant Grove, UT 84062
801/342-5250

Spanish Fork Ranger District
44 West 400 North
Spanish Fork, UT 84660
801/342-5260

WASATCH-CACHE NATIONAL FOREST

Wasatch-Cache Supervisor's Office
8226 Federal Building
125 South State Street
Salt Lake City, UT 84138
801/524-5030

RANGER DISTRICTS:

Evanston Ranger District
1565 Highway 150, Suite A
(P. O. Box 1880)
Evanston, WY 82930
307/789-3194 (year-round)
801/642-6662 (in summer)

Kamas Ranger District
50 East Center Street
(P. O. Box 68)
Kamas, UT 84036
435/783-4338

Logan Ranger District
1500 East Highway 89
Logan, UT 84321
801/755-3620

Mountain View Ranger District
Lone Tree Road
321 Highway 414 East
(P. O. Box 129)
Mountain View, WY 82939
307/782-6555

Salt Lake Ranger District
6944 South 3000 East
Salt Lake City, UT 84121
801/943-1794

National Parks

With five national parks, two national recreation areas, six national monuments, and one national historic area, Utah offers visitors incredible scenic and cultural diversity. From the high alpine red-rock country of Bryce Canyon National

Park to the water-oriented Flaming Gorge and Glen Canyon National Recreation Areas to the cultural resources of Hovenweep National Monument and Golden Spike National Historic Site, Utah's parks rank among the world's best.

Camping spots at the state's national parks fill quickly. This is especially true at Arches, Canyonlands, and Capitol Reef, where facilities are small. Though much larger, campgrounds do fill at Zion and Bryce as well. Since no reservations are taken for individual camping sites, those wishing to secure a spot should arrive as early in the day as possible. At Arches and Canyonlands, 9 A.M. is often not early enough.

Only Timpanogos Cave and Cedar Breaks National Monuments close in the winter, and even those offer limited access. The visitors center at Timpanogos Cave is open year-round, and cross-country skiers and snowmobilers can enjoy Cedar Breaks in the winter months. The best time to see southern Utah's national parks is often the off-season, when trails are less crowded and the scorching desert heat isn't a problem.

Pick up maps at park entrance stations or locally operated visitors centers. Or, contact the Utah Travel Council, Council Hall/Capitol Hill, Salt Lake City, UT 84114; 801/538-1030.

NATIONAL PARKS, MONUMENTS, RECREATION AREAS, AND HISTORIC AREAS

Arches National Park
P. O. Box 907
Moab, UT 84532
435/259-8161
www.nps.gov/arch

Bryce Canyon National Park
P. O. Box 170001
Bryce Canyon, UT 84717
435/834-5322
www.nps.gov/brca

Canyonlands National Park
2282 Southwest Resource Boulevard
Moab, UT 84532
435/259-7164
www.nps.gov/cany

Capitol Reef National Park
HC 70, Box 15
Torrey, UT 84775
435/425-3791
www.nps.gov/care

Cedar Breaks National Monument
2390 West Highway 56, Suite 11
Cedar City, UT 84720
435/586-9451
www.nps.gov/cebr

Dinosaur National Monument
Dinosaur, CO 81610
970/374-3000 or 435/789-2115
(Dinosaur Quarry Visitors Center)
www.nps.gov/dino

Escalante-Grand Staircase National Monument
318 North First East
Kanab, UT 84741
435/644-2672
www.blm.gov/ut

Flaming Gorge National Recreation Area
P. O. Box 279
Manila, UT 84046
435/784-3445
www.fs.fed.us/r4/ashley

Glen Canyon National Recreation Area
Box 1507
Page, AZ 86040
520/608-6404
www.nps.gov/glca

Golden Spike National Historic Site
P. O. Box 897
Brigham City, UT 84302
435/471-2209
www.nps.gov/gosp

Natural Bridges National Monument
Box 1
Lake Powell, UT 84533
435/692-1234
www.nps.gov/nabr

Rainbow Bridge National Monument, Glen Canyon National Recreation Area
P. O. Box 1507
Page, AZ 86040
520/608-6404

Timpanogos Cave National Monument
Route 3, Box 200
American Fork, UT 84003
802/756-5239 (winter)
801/756-5238 (summer)
www.nps.gov/tica

Zion National Park
P. O. Box 1099
Springdale, UT 84767
435/772-3256
www.nps.gov/zion

State Parks

Some of Utah's best camping opportunities are found in its 45 state parks, many of which are in close proximity to national parks. Facilities at some state parks include full hookups, showers, and playgrounds. Depending on the facilities, fees for overnight camping are $5–13.

Campgrounds at parks in southern Utah such as Snow Canyon, Dead Horse Point, Goblin Valley, Kodachrome Basin, Escalante, and Quail Creek tend to fill in the spring and fall and on holiday weekends. During the summer months, northern Utah's water-oriented parks, including Rockport, East Canyon, Willard Bay, Jordanelle, and Wasatch Mountain, host hordes of visitors.

The state park camping-reservation system makes planning a trip to one of these Utah parks quite simple. Reservations for individual campsites may be made 3–120 days in advance of your trip by calling 801/322-3770 or 800/322-3770, Monday–Friday 8 A.M.–5 P.M. (Mountain Standard Time).

**Utah Division of Parks and
Recreation State Office**
1594 West North Temple, Suite 116
Salt Lake City, UT 84116-3156
801/538-7220

Northeast Region Office
P. O. Box 309
Heber City, UT 84032-0309
435/645-8036

Northwest Region Office
1084 North Redwood Road
Salt Lake City, UT 84116-1555
801/533-5127

Southeast Region Office
1165 South Highway 191, Suite 7
Moab, UT 84532-3062
435/259-3750

Southwest Region Office
585 North Main Street
(P. O. Box 1079)
Cedar City, UT 84720-1079
435/586-4497

Bureau of Land Management

Though not as well known as the national parks and forests or the state parks, some of the more popular developed campgrounds run by the Bureau of Land Management (BLM) rank among the best in the state of Utah. This is especially true of the Little Sahara sand dunes near Nephi, the Calf Creek Falls Recreation Area near Escalante, the Dixie Red Cliffs facility near Saint George, and the Slickrock Bicycle Trail and Colorado River camping complex near Moab. With such remote gems as the Starr Springs and McMillan Springs sites on the Henry Mountains or Simpson Springs along the Pony Express Trail in Utah's West Desert region, campers should not pass up a stay at a BLM site.

Many spectacularly beautiful BLM lands in Utah are also open to dispersed camping. After all, the agency manages about 22 million acres—approximately 42 percent of the state of Utah. Check with the local district or resource offices listed below for rules governing the use of such lands.

BLM UTAH STATE OFFICE

Information Access Center
324 South State Street, Suite 400
Salt Lake City, UT 84111
801/539-4001

FIELD OFFICES:

Cedar City Field Office
176 East D. L. Sargent Drive
Cedar City, UT 84720
435/586-2401

Dixie Field Office
225 North Bluff Street
St. George, UT 84770
435/628-4491
Also try the Interagency Office,
345 East, Riverside Drive,
St. George, UT 84770
435/688-3200

Escalante Field Office
P. O. Box 225
Escalante, UT 84726
435/826-4291

Fillmore Field Office
35 East 500 North
Fillmore, UT 84631
435/743-6811

Kanab Field Office
318 North First East
Kanab, UT 84741
435/644-2672

Moab Field Office
82 East Dogwood, Suite M
Moab, UT 84532
435/259-6111

Price Field Office
125 South 600 West
(P. O. Box 7004)
Price, UT 84501
435/636-3600

Richfield Field Office
150 East 900 North
Richfield, UT 84701
435/896-8221

Salt Lake Field Office
2370 South 2300 West
Salt Lake City, UT 84119
801/977-4300

San Juan Field Office
435 North Main Street
(P. O. Box 7)
Monticello, UT 84535
435/587-2141

Vernal Field Office
170 South 500 East
Vernal, UT 84078
435/789-1362

National Wildlife Refuges

There are three national wildlife refuges in Utah: the Bear River Migratory Bird Refuge west of Brigham City on the edge of the Great Salt Lake; the Fish Springs National Wildlife Refuge on the Pony Express Trail in a remote part of Utah's West Desert region southwest of Tooele; and the Ouray National Wildlife Refuge southeast of Roosevelt in eastern Utah. For more information, contact the state office of the U.S. Fish and Wildlife Service at 145 East 1300 South, Suite 404, Salt Lake City, UT 84115.

RV Parks

Utah offers dozens of RV parks, which are particularly attractive to budget travelers because they provide an alternative to staying in costly hotels and motels. The RV parks range from simple gravel parking lots equipped with electricity and water hookups to elaborate facilities that include golf courses, swimming pools, hot tubs, water slides, and access to nearby theme parks. Some, like the huge campgrounds in the St. George area in southwestern Utah, provide a place for retired citizens to spend the winter months in a warm climate. There are several big parks near Salt Lake City, Ogden, and Provo that give travelers on a budget a place to spend the night near a big city, where they can enjoy sights such as Salt Lake City's Temple Square, the Great Salt Lake, or downtown shopping and tourist attractions. Some facilities, such as those in the Moab area in southeastern Utah, fill a need for camping space. Federal and state agencies in that part of the state haven't been able to keep up with the high demand for campgrounds, whereas private operators have been more than willing to make up for it by constructing some of the state's newest all-purpose RV campgrounds.

Native American Land

Native American lands are scattered throughout rural Utah, but they provide little in the way of recreation. One exception is the Navajo Reservation in southeastern Utah, which offers a campground, tours of Monument Valley, and the Tribal Park Visitors Center. The other is Four Corners, the monument where Utah, New Mexico, Arizona, and Colorado meet; it is the only site in the United States where a person can stand in four states at once. For information, write to Navajo Tribal Park, P. O. Box 360289, Monument Valley, UT 84536; or call the Parks and Recreation Department in Window Rock, Arizona, at 520/871-6647. The Utah Travel Council produces an annual listing of Native American celebrations held throughout the year.

Map Companies

Maps of individual national forests are available at U.S. Forest Service headquarters and district ranger offices. Some maps can also be obtained from the Bureau of Land Management. The Utah Travel Council offers a series of five sectional maps designed for tourists. Other sources of detailed Utah maps are:

DeLorme Mapping Company
2 DeLong Drive
P. O. Box 298
Yarmouth, ME 04096
800/642-0970

Trails Illustrated
P. O. Box 4357
Evergreen, CO 80437-4357
800/962-1643

U.S. Geological Survey
2329 West Orton Circle
West Valley City, UT 84119
801/908-5000

Utah Geological Survey
1594 West North Temple
Salt Lake City, UT 84116
801/537-3300

Other Useful Organizations

Bed and Breakfast Inns of Utah
P. O. Box 3066
Park City, UT 84060
801/645-8068

Bicycle Vacation Guide
P. O. Box 738
Park City, UT 84060
435/649-5806

Office of Museum Services
324 Suth State Street, Suite 500
Salt Lake City, UT 84114-7910
801/533-4235

Ski Utah
150 West 500 South
Salt Lake City, UT 84101
801/534-1779

Utah Campground Owners Association
1320 West North Temple
Salt Lake City, UT 84116
801/521-2682

Utah Department of Transportation
4501 South 2700 West
Salt Lake City, UT 84119
800/964-6000 (Salt Lake City only)
or 800/492-2400 (road report, nationwide)

Utah Division of Wildlife Resources
1596 West North Temple
Salt Lake City, UT 84116
801/538-4700

Utah Guides and Outfitters
153 East 7200 South
Midvale, UT 84047
801/566-2662

Utah Hotel-Motel Association
9 Exchange Place, Suite 812
Salt Lake City, UT 84116
801/359-0104

Utah Travel Council
Council Hall/Capitol Hill
Salt Lake City, UT 84114
801/538-1030 or 800/200-1160

INDEX

CAMPGROUND INDEX

ABOUT THE AUTHORS

Gayen and Tom Wharton have spent the last 25 years exploring Utah, the United States, and the world with their four children. Avid outdoor enthusiasts and campers, the couple has carved out writing careers while camping, hiking, skiing, fishing, and exploring Utah's varied backcountry.

Gayen Wharton is a former award-winning elementary school teacher and past president of the Utah Society of Environmental Education, which named her Environmental Educator of the Year in 1994. She has traded the classroom in for the open road and is currently a freelance writer. Tom Wharton is past president of the Outdoor Writer's Association of America and writes about Utah for the Salt Lake Tribune.

The Whartons are the authors of *Utah* for the Discover America Series, *It Happened in Utah* and *An Outdoor Family Guide to the Southwest's Four Corners.* Tom is also the author of *Utah! A Family Travel Guide,* published in 1987, and a contributor to seven other books, including *Wild Places,* published by Foghorn Outdoors Press in 1996.

AVALON
TRAVEL
p u b l i s h i n g

BECAUSE TRAVEL MATTERS.

AVALON TRAVEL PUBLISHING knows that travel is more than coming and going—travel is taking part in new experiences, new ideas, and a new outlook. Our goal is to bring you complete and up-to-date information to help you make informed travel decisions.

AVALON TRAVEL GUIDES feature a combination of practicality and spirit, offering a unique traveler-to-traveler perspective perfect for an afternoon hike, around-the-world journey, or anything in between.

WWW.TRAVELMATTERS.COM

Avalon Travel Publishing guides are available at your favorite book or travel store.

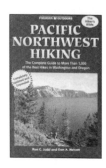

MOON HANDBOOKS

provide comprehensive coverage of a region's arts, history, land, people, and social issues in addition to detailed practical listings for accommodations, food, outdoor recreation, and entertainment. Moon Handbooks allow complete immersion in a region's culture—ideal for travelers who want to combine sightseeing with insight for an extraordinary travel experience in destinations throughout North America, Hawaii, Latin America, the Caribbean, Asia, and the Pacific.

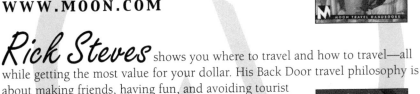

WWW.MOON.COM

Rick Steves shows you where to travel and how to travel—all while getting the most value for your dollar. His Back Door travel philosophy is about making friends, having fun, and avoiding tourist rip-offs.

Rick's been traveling to Europe for more than 25 years and is the author of 20 guidebooks, which have sold more than a million copies. He also hosts the award-winning public television series *Travels in Europe with Rick Steves*.

WWW.RICKSTEVES.COM

ROAD TRIP USA

Getting there is half the fun, and Road Trip USA guides are your ticket to driving adventure. Taking you off the interstates and onto less-traveled, two-lane highways, each guide is filled with fascinating trivia, historical information, photographs, facts about regional writers, and details on where to sleep and eat—all contributing to your exploration of the American road.

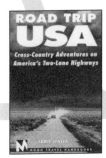

"Books so full of the pleasures of the American road, you can smell the upholstery."
~ BBC radio

WWW.ROADTRIPUSA.COM

TRAVEL ✦ SMART® guidebooks are accessible, route-based driving guides focusing on regions throughout the United States and Canada. Special interest tours provide the most practical routes for family fun, outdoor activities, or regional history for a trip of anywhere from two to 22 days. Travel Smarts take the guesswork out of planning a trip by recommending only the most interesting places to eat, stay, and visit.

"One of the few travel series that rates sightseeing attractions. That's a handy feature. It helps to have some guidance so that every minute counts."
~San Diego Union-Tribune

Foghorn Outdoors

guides are for campers, hikers, boaters, anglers, bikers, and golfers of all levels of daring and skill. Each guide focuses on a specific U.S. region and contains site descriptions and ratings, driving directions, facilities and fees information, and easy-to-read maps that leave only the task of deciding where to go.

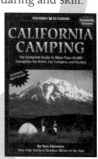

"Foghorn Outdoors has established an ecological conservation standard unmatched by any other publisher."
~Sierra Club

WWW.FOGHORN.COM

CiTY·SMaRT™ guides are written by local authors with hometown perspectives who have personally selected the best places to eat, shop, sightsee, and simply hang out. The honest, lively, and opinionated advice is perfect for business travelers looking to relax with the locals or for longtime residents looking for something new to do Saturday night.

There are City Smart guides for cities across the United States and Canada, and a portion of sales from each title benefits a non-profit literacy organization in its featured city.

www.travelmatters.com

User-friendly, informative, and fun: Because travel *matters*.

Visit our newly launched web site and explore the variety of titles and travel information available online, featuring an interactive *Road Trip USA* exhibit.

also check out:

www.ricksteves.com

The Rick Steves web site is bursting with information to boost your travel I.Q. and liven up your European adventure.

www.foghorn.com

Visit the Foghorn Outdoors web site for more information on the premier source of U.S. outdoor recreation guides.

www.moon.com

The Moon Handbooks web site offers interesting information and practical advice that ensure an extraordinary travel experience.

Will you have enough stories to tell your grandchildren?

<u>Yahoo! Travel</u>